U-BOATS IN THE MEDITERRANEAN

U-BOATS

in the

Mediterranean

1941–1944

Lawrence Paterson

Skyhorse Publishing

First Skyhorse printing 2019.
First published 2007 in the US by Naval Institute Press and in the UK by Chatham publishing.

Skyhorse Publishing books may be purchased in bulk at special discounts for sales promotion, corporate gifts, fund-raising, or educational purposes. Special editions can also be created to specifications. For details, contact the Special Sales Department, Skyhorse Publishing, 307 West 36th Street, 11th Floor, New York, NY 10018 or info@skyhorsepublishing.com.

Skyhorse® and Skyhorse Publishing® are registered trademarks of Skyhorse Publishing, Inc.®, a Delaware corporation.

Visit our website at www.skyhorsepublishing.com.

10 9 8 7 6 5 4 3 2 1

Library of Congress Cataloging-in-Publication Data is available on file.

Cover design by Rain Saukas

ISBN: 978-1-5107-3163-9
Ebook ISBN: 978-1-5107-3167-7

Printed in the United States of America

Contents

U-BOATS IN THE MEDITERRANEAN

Acknowledgements

As ALWAYS THIS BOOK could not have been written without the help, support and encouragement of many people. I would like to especially thank Sarah, Meg, James and Ernie of the Paterson Clan. Also special thanks to Audrey 'Mumbles' Paterson and Don 'Mr Mumbles', Ray and Phylly Paterson. My gratitude also goes to Graham 'Course I'm a Brummie' Jinks, Bernadette Hardaker, Tony Iommi, John Osbourne, Terry Butler, Bill Ward, Eric Singer, Tony Martin, Neil Murray, Ian Gillan, Ronald James Padavona, Michael Leventhal, Rob Gardiner and all the staff at Chatham/Greenhill, Chokehold, Graham von Pentz, Paul Robbie, Dominic Mather, Carlito Warner, Jürgen Weber and the *U-Bootkameradschaft München*, Cozy Powell (RIP), Eddie Naughton, Mike, Sheila, Mitch and Claire French, Maggie 'Oirish' Bidmead and Martin 'Tidpit the Handy' Towell.

From the ranks of the *Kriegsmarine* and Allied navies there are many veterans and their families who have helped with time and patience as I have tried to piece together this and other stories. Of the many people who have put up with my endless enquiries I would especially like to mention Jürgen and Esther Oesten, Inge and the late Ludwig Stoll, Gerhard and Traudl Buske, Georg and Frau Högel, Georg and Frau Seitz, Gesa Suhren, Hanne Suhren, Karl and Annie Waldeck, Hans-Peter and Frau Carlsen and Volkmaar König.

If there is anybody that I have not included in this list and should have, then please rest assured that it is an unintentional oversight and I hope that you will forgive me.

As a brief preface I would like to clarify for the reader that although the naval war in the Mediterranean was a complex web of interwoven services and branches of many nations' armed forces, this book is not a general study of the Mediterranean war. To do so would require many more pages and the ability to place the air, ground and naval forces into their correct contexts to a degree of completeness that space and the focus of this study will not freely allow. This is a book that deals with the deployment of what would eventually become sixty-two combat U-boats of the *Kriegsmarine*. Where applicable I have of course related it to other services of the *Wehrmacht* and their struggles on land, at sea or in the air and often it is necessary to place the U-boat men's presence into a political and strategic context. However, those men and their Type VII boats remain the core of this story. This book follows the experiences of the 23rd and 29th U-Flotillas who brought Dönitz's creed of aggressive submarine warfare into the Mediterranean, an expanse of water that has been fought over since the beginning of recorded history.

Glossary

Abwehr –	German Military Intelligence Service.
ASDIC –	Sonar used for locating submarines.
BdU –	*Befehlshaber der Unterseeboote*, U-boat High Command.
CAM –	Catapult Aircraft Merchantman; a merchant ship defensively equipped with a single fighter aircraft to be launched by catapult and ditched after a single flight.
FAA –	Fleet Air Arm.
Falke –	T4 sound homing torpedo, designed to home on the low-pitched sound of merchant ship propellers.
FAT –	*Federapparattorpedo*, German T3 pattern-running torpedo.
FdU –	*Führer der Unterseeboote*, regional German U-boat command.
FuMB –	*Funkmessbeobachtungs Gerät*, radar detection equipment.
G7a –	Standard German air-driven torpedo.
G7e –	Standard German electric torpedo (wakeless).
Heer –	German Army.
Ing. –	*Ingenieur*, Engineer (German). Inserted after rank, eg *Leutnant* (Ing.)
Kriegsmarine –	German Navy.
KTB –	*Kriegstagebuch*, German unit War Diary.
LCF –	Landing Craft Flak, an LCT (Landing Craft Tank) converted and specially equipped with anti-aircraft weaponry to act in support of amphibious assaults.
LCT –	Landing Craft Tank.
LI –	*Leitender Ingenieur*, Chief Engineer.
LST –	Landing Ship Tank.
Luftwaffe –	German Air Force.
MAA –	*Marine Artillerie Abteilung*, German naval artillery

	unit.
OKM –	*Oberkommando der Marine*, German Naval Command.
OKW –	*Oberkommando der Wehrmacht*, German Military Forces Command.
RAF –	Royal Air Force.
RAAF –	Royal Australian Air Force.
Räumboot –	(German) Small shallow-water minesweeper.
RCAF –	Royal Canadian Air Force.
Regia Marina –	Italian Navy.
RNZAF –	Royal New Zealand Air Force.
S-Boat –	*Schnellboot*, German Motor Torpedo Boat.
SKL –	*Seekriegsleitung*, Naval War Staff.
Stab –	Staff (German).
USAAF –	United States Army Air Force.
Vorpostenboot –	(German) Patrol boat, typically a converted trawler.
WO (& IWO, etc) –	(German) Watch Officer; thus IWO is First Watch Officer, IIWO is Second Watch Officer and so on.
Zaunkönig –	T5 acoustic homing torpedo, designed to target the higher pitched propeller-noise of a warship rather than merchant ships.

Comparative Rank Table

German (Abbreviation)	British/American
Grossadmiral	Admiral of the Fleet/Fleet Admiral
Admiral	Admiral
Vizeadmiral (V.A.)	Vice Admiral
Konteradmiral (K.A.)	Rear Admiral
Kapitän zur See (Kapt.z.S.)	Captain
Fregattenkapitän (F.K.)	Commander
Korvettenkapitän (K.K.)	Commander
Kapitänleutnant (Kaptlt.)	Lieutenant Commander
Oberleutnant zur See (Oblt.z.S.)	Lieutenant
Leutnant zur See (L.z.S.)	Sub-Lieutenant/Lieutenant (jg)
Oberfähnrich	Senior Midshipman
Fähnrich	Midshipman
Stabsobersteuermann	Senior Quartermaster/Warrant Quartermaster
Obermaschinist (Omasch)	Senior Machinist/Warrant Machinist
Bootsmann	Boatswain
Oberbootsmannsmaat	Boatswain's Mate
Bootsmannsmaat	Coxswain
-Maat (trade inserted as prefix)	Petty Officer
Maschinenobergefreiter	Leading Seaman Machinist
Funkobergefreiter	Leading Seaman Telegraphist
Matrosenobergefreiter	Leading Seaman
Maschinengefreiter	Able Seaman Machinist
Matrosengefreiter	Able Seaman

Introduction

'I'm glad that this call to the east has taken our attention off the Mediterranean. The South, for us, is the Crimea. To go further would be nonsense. Let us stay Nordic.'
Adolf Hitler, 17 October 1941.[1]

THE COMMITMENT OF U-BOATS to action in the Mediterranean Sea has often been described as sheer folly on the part of the *Kriegsmarine's* High Command. Indeed Karl Dönitz, *Befehlshaber der Unterseeboote* (BdU: Commander-in-Chief U-boats), tenaciously resisted the redeployment of some of his already meagre forces with which he was fighting the Battle of the Atlantic, the crux of the convoy war. Possibly a contributing factor to Dönitz's vehemence on the issue was that he knew all too well some of the difficulties submarines would face in the often clear blue Mediterranean Sea. In the First World War Dönitz had been an officer aboard *UB68*, sunk during an attack on British shipping within the region.

Nonetheless, in September 1941 the first six boats arrived for permanent service against Allied supply lines along the North African coast. Despite Dönitz's genuine misgivings, supported by Raeder in meetings with Adolf Hitler, there was some measure of logic to the ordered redeployment of the small force of U-boats. The supply routes from mainland Axis Europe to their forces in North Africa were under severe pressure from a strong British presence in the Mediterranean, the security of the Axis convoys not aided by the relative ineffectiveness of the Italian navy. *Oberkommando der Marine* (OKM) reasoned that a counter-offensive using both U-boats and *Schnellboot* coastal forces, combined with a burgeoning *Luftwaffe* presence, could alleviate this strain and allow better supply of the fledgling *Afrika Korps* that was poised on the brink of dazzling success in North Africa. German fears of an impending British offensive and the possibility of Anglo-Free French landings in French North Africa also led to a concentration of U-boats around Gibraltar where the limited sea room would inevitably, as they saw it, aid target location for the German crews. While this was perhaps true, the same effect allowed a greater concentration of British ASW forces in the same area as the U-boats and a bloody battle of attrition began – one that the Germans could not hope to win except by the total abandonment of Atlantic operations, which Dönitz steadfastly, and correctly, refused to sanction.

German and Austrian U-boats had been extremely active in the Mediterranean during the 1914–18 war, where some of their most spectacular successes had been achieved. However, during that conflict both France and Italy had been enemies and a large majority of the U-boats' victims had belonged to those nations, transporting goods from North Africa to their homelands. By 1941, when the first *Kriegsmarine* U-boats entered the Mediterranean, France had surrendered and Italy was an ally. Indeed, the background of the *Kriegsmarine*'s involvement in the region can perhaps be traced more directly to the Italian empire-building that began in 1935.

By the time that Adolf Hitler had come to power in Germany in 1933, political events in the Mediterranean were of little or no interest to the dictator. For the three major powers in the Mediterranean Sea – Italy, France and Britain – on the other hand, the subtle shifts in the balance of power within the region were crucially important. France's main points of interest in the Mediterranean, aside from the security of its southern coast, was in maintaining communications with her Syrian and North African colonies. Italy remained the dominant power, with the largest fleet-in-being based entirely within the region. As well as defending an extensive coastline, Italy also had to maintain contact with its East and North African colonies.

While France and Italy maintained an obvious geographical stake in the virtually land-locked sea, Britain relied on its ability to traverse the Mediterranean in order to ease communications with its Indian and Far Eastern empire, the Suez Canal saving thousands of miles of sailing around the Cape of Good Hope for shipping to and from India, New Zealand and Australia. It also allowed the rapid transfer of forces to Singapore should the Japanese ever pose a threat to Britain's Far Eastern possessions. Since the so-called Manchurian crisis in September 1931 when Japan attacked the rich Chinese province, triggering the start of fifteen years of war in Asia, Britain had woken to the potential threat posed by the military ambitions of Imperial Japan. In January 1932 the possibilty was brought into sharper focus with fighting around Shanghai, the centre of British investment and trading interests in China. To add to their disquiet, the resurgence of Germany and the expansion of its armed forces announced in 1935 raised the prospect of potential war in two geographically separate theatres.

However, their potentially dire predicament was alleviated somewhat by the good diplomatic relations between Britain and France and Italy, between whom control of the Mediterranean was virtually absolute. British forces within the area were better in theory than reality. Though the Royal Navy held stations at both ends of the Mediterranean – Gibraltar and Alexandria – plus the central base at Malta, the forces deployed there had been reduced to bolster the Home Fleet and the Far Eastern squadron. The same year that the *Kriegsmarine* began openly rearming and launched its first operational U-boat, the political harmony that had been established with Britain's erstwhile ally Italy was rudely shattered.

On 3 October 1935, in the face of ineffectual protests from the League of Nations, Italy invaded Abyssinia which bordered on Italian Somaliland and Eritrea. Benito Mussolini had opted to expand his East African empire, at once a sop to his own ambitions for rebuilding the forgotten glory of a Roman Empire as well as distracting Italian public attention from the economic depression with a 'colonial adventure'. On the eve of the invasion France and Italy had agreed a *de facto* alliance in the face of German strength, aimed at mutually-assured borders and the ability to keep Hitler in check. However, with Mussolini's flouting of international law by his attack on Abyssinia, the League of Nations ordered sanctions applied against Italy, to which France acquiesced, albeit reluctantly.

There was also considerable reluctance in London to abide by the League's mandate, as it was felt by many that the dubious benefits of collective security provided by the League of Nations was considerably outweighed by the loss of Italy as a Mediterranean ally. Their fears were borne out when Mussolini, all but frozen out of European politics, turned to the one major country that ignored the League's proclamations – Germany.

In Britain the First Sea Lord, Admiral of the Fleet Sir Ernle Chatfield, summed up the dire predicament that the current situation placed the Royal Navy in:

> It is a disaster that our statesmen have got us into this quarrel with Italy who ought to be our best friend because her position in the Mediterranean is a dominant one ... the miserable business of collective security has run away with all our traditional interests and policies, with the result that we now have to be prepared to fight any nation in the world at any time.[2]

Indeed there was even consideration given to withdrawing British forces from the Mediterranean proper and simply holding the Straits of Gibraltar at the western end and the Red Sea to the east, thereby allowing the transfer of forces to the Home Fleet and Far East. France alone would be left to hold Italy in check, though this option was soon dismissed. Amongst the fiercest critics of this possibility was a man soon to return to the post of First Lord of the Admiralty, Winston Churchill.

> The British domination of the Mediterranean would inflict injuries upon an enemy Italy which might be fatal to her power of continuing the war. All her troops in Libya and in Abyssinia would be cut flowers in a vase. The French and our own people in Egypt could be reinforced to any extent desired, while theirs would be overweighted, if not starved. Not to hold the Central Mediterranean would be to expose Egypt and the Canal, as well as the French possessions, to invasion by Italian troops with German leadership.[3]

Nonetheless, predictions of a strengthening of relations between Europe's two fascist states were soon proved correct. Hitler remained one of Mussolini's few remaining trading partners, increasing Italian dependence on the Nazi state. Whether Italy triumphed or failed, Hitler stood to gain from the invasion of Abyssinia. If Italy should succeed then a wedge would have been successfully driven between her and France and Britain opening the way for an Italian-German concorde. If Mussolini failed or caved into international pressure and withdrew, then Italian attentions would be distracted from Austria which Hitler meant to occupy as soon as was practicable. Indeed it was largely as a bulwark against such an occupation that Italy and France had so readily come to agreement during the previous year. Now that relationship was in tatters and the two fascist states were ever more closely aligned.

As it transpired, Italy's brutal invasion of Abyssinia was successfully concluded in May 1936, though the conquerors would face years of guerilla skirmishes before eventually being forced from the country by British forces in 1941. In June 1936 Italy combined its colonies of Italian Somaliland, Eritrea and Abyssinia into one administrative area known as Italian East Africa, divided into six regions. The following month the League of Nations abandoned its sanctions.

Tensions remained high in the Mediterranean, particularly among British naval leaders who recognised the perilously weak forces they maintained in the region. This heightened sense of alarm was soon exacerbated by the next crisis to strike the Mediterranean region in 1936, one in which Germany would be actively involved.

Chapter 1

The Spanish Civil War

BY 1936 SPANISH POLITICS HAD CLEARLY polarised into bitter opposition between left- and right-wing parties, each alternating as the government with every new election. The left-wing parties had merged to form a Popular Front, which was narrowly voted into power during February. As the ensuing street violence and turmoil reached crisis point in mainland Spain, General Francisco Franco Bahamonde, commander of Spanish troops in the North African colony of Spanish Morocco, declared his opposition to Spain's ruling government on 17 July, sparking civil war within his country. Later, on 1 October he was named Commander-in-Chief of the Nationalist Army and Chief of the Spanish State by the Nationalist rebels.

The Spanish Naval Attaché in Paris – *Capitán de Corbeta* (Lieutenant Commander) Arturo Génova – resigned his post and joined Franco's Nationalist cause as naval adviser. With him he took a long and trusting relationship with Admiral Wilhelm Canaris, head of the *Wehrmacht's Abwehr* intelligence service since 1935. Canaris, an ardent opponent of Communism, lobbied on behalf of Génova to his superiors in Berlin for armed assistance to be given to the Nationalists, who possessed no submarine force, while their Republican opponents had a flotilla of twelve boats. Génova believed that one of the most urgent matters facing Franco was the breaking of the stranglehold that Republican naval patrols off Gibraltar had on Nationalist troops trapped in Spanish Morocco and unable to return to Spain.

Coupled with this, the left-wing opposition was receiving a steadily increasing amount of arms from France and the Soviet Union in convoys that were free from Nationalist interference. However, Canaris was refused his request by the head of OKM, *Konteradmiral* Günther Grusse. Hitler, allowing the use of Lufthansa and *Luftwaffe* Junkers Ju 52 aircraft to ferry 13,900 waiting Nationalist troops and their equipment of the so-called 'Army of Africa' back to Spain, had dealt with the initial problem of troop transport, but he still shied away from direct military intervention, meanwhile assuring the British and French governments that no war material would be sent to Franco from Germany.

While Germany privately vacillated over whether to commit itself to more open support for the Nationalist rebellion, Italy displayed no such qualms and pledged immediate military aid, transferring two submarines and their crews to Spanish waters during October 1936. On 24 October the Italian Foreign Minister Count Ciano met with Hitler to sign the declaration that formed the Rome-Berlin Axis – 'in the interests of peace and reconstruction' – and also to announce to the German dictator Italy's new Spanish naval commitment.

This was perhaps the spark that Germany had been waiting for and the *Luftwaffe*'s 'Condor Legion' moved to Spain. While it is true that most of the Condor Legion was from the *Luftwaffe*, there were also major components from both the Army (*Heer*) and Navy (*Kriegsmarine*). The *Heer*'s main battlegroup was named 'Imker' ('Beekeeper'), commanded by *Oberst* Wilhelm Ritter von Thoma. Von Thoma's unit comprised volunteers from Panzer Regiment 6 of the 3rd Panzer Division. Their primary task was to train Franco's ground troops in modern armoured warfare tactics. The primary weapon of 'Imker's' Panzer troops was the Panzer I, handed over to the Nationalist rebels at the end of the training period. Indeed although assigned the task of training, von Thoma's men did go into action during the war, von Thoma famously remarking that the experience gained and ability to practise his own tactics made Spain a 'European Aldershot'. The main *Kriegsmarine* contingent comprised a group of instructors, codenamed 'Nordsee'. They arrived in Spain during November 1936 to provide training in gunnery (both ship and coastal), mine warfare, communications and torpedo boat warfare. The *Kriegsmarine* also dealt with logistical supply of the Condor Legion.

Shortly after Hitler's establishment of the German military presence in Spain, OKM also decided to detach two of their new Type VII U-boats from the 'Saltzwedel' Flotilla to the Nationalist cause. These two boats – *U-33* and *U-34* – would operate covertly and independently of further operational orders. Under the codename 'Training Exercise Ursula' (named after Karl Dönitz's only daughter) both submarines slipped quietly from Wilhelmshaven on 20 November 1936, two days after Germany and Italy formally recognised the Franco regime as Spain's legitimate government.

The two young regular commanders were replaced for this delicate undertaking by more experienced men, *U-33*'s Ottoheinrich Junker replaced by Kurt Freiwald, while aboard *U-34* Ernst Sobe handed over command to the veteran Harald Grosse. The latter had navigated in Spanish waters in 1931 during the trials of *E1*, a U-boat constructed in Spain and thus allowing the Germans to develop submarine designs overseas, such work being strictly forbidden under the terms of the Treaty of Versailles. Both temporary commanders brought with them their familiar watch officers for the duration of 'Ursula'. The man delegated in Berlin to closely supervise the operation and provide a link between the boats and OKM was *Konteradmiral* Hermann Boehme, Admiral Commanding the Fleet (*Flottenchef*). As the boats prepared for their secret 'war' their crews were sworn to lifelong total silence regarding their forth-coming experience 'on pain of death' in an 'Exercise Order' (*Ubungsbefehl*) issued by OKM on 6 November 1936.

Once they were at sea, the two U-boats painted out any identification markings before separately passing quietly through the English Channel *en route* for Biscay. Both silently penetrated the Mediterranean during the night of 27 November, easing past patrolling Republican warships while remaining surfaced on a still and moonless night. Their briefing stated that should they be challenged they were to declare themselves British and hoist the Royal Navy ensign. Fortunately, they were never compelled to attempt such a subterfuge. Once through the Straits of Gibraltar, both U-boats waited for Italian submarine operations to cease in order to prevent any 'friendly fire' incidents.

On 30 November German patrolling began, the two U-boats separated by an imaginary line drawn along the 0° 44' west longitude line, *U-34* to operate west of this line around Cartagena, *U-33* to the east. In the case of an emergency that required one of the German boats to enter port, they were instructed to use the Italian naval base at La Maddelena, flying an Italian ensign as they put in. Clandestine patrolling caused anxiety in the naval high command. Eight days before the two German submarines began their respective missions, Italian submarine *Torricelli* claimed the first victim of the undersea battle. After German surface ships engaged on an ostensible international 'peace-keeping' mission had seen and reported heavy units of the Republican fleet anchored outside of Cartagena, *Torricelli* crept cautiously towards the Republicans, the large warships sheltering from possible air attack, safe in the knowledge that their Nationalist enemy possessed no submarines. Minutes after *Torricelli* reached a suitable submerged firing position, two torpedoes ploughed into the machinery spaces of the cruiser *Miguel de Cervantes*, disabling the ship for the rest of the Civil War. The Republicans immediately blamed 'foreign submarines', their allegation proved by the recovery of fragments of warheads of Italian manufacture. Italian security regarding their submarine activity was in any case virtually non-existent, their active involvement in Spain's conflict an open secret within their own country.

But German military leaders had a very different attitude, fearing immediate and far-reaching political complications if their level of involvement in Spain became known. Initially it also appeared as if their beneficiary General Franco was not going to win the war, Republican forces more than holding their own in combat, albeit with Soviet material assistance. Worse still, both *U-33* and *U-34* were operating in a state of some confusion. Slow laborious communications with OKM, often worded in extremely ambiguous language to foil any attempt at enemy code-breaking, conspired to sow uncertainty amid the men actually at sea.

Konteradmiral Hermann Boehme, in charge of the realities of 'Ursula', felt further hamstrung as time passed, the two U-boats being under strict orders from his superiors to only engage Republican warships. When OKM learned that Boehme had requested Nationalist naval authorities not to sail warships within the German operational zone, they forbade any further communication of this kind, fearing a possible security breach. Questions of which targets were legitimate passed from Freiwald and Grosse to Boehme, transmitted at night as the two U-boats lay 20 miles from the coast to recharge batteries and use their radios. Boehme in turn passed the query to Berlin, which inevitably denied them the freedom to act against any but the most clearly identified target, ever more restrictions placed on what was considered as legitimate prey.

During the evening of 1 December 1936 L.z.S. Grosse engaged a Republican destroyer near Cartagena, but missed, his single torpedo impacting on nearby rocks. On 5 December, and again three days later, he tried further attacks against similar targets, also missing with his single shots. Perplexed by consistent failure, torpedo malfunction appeared to Grosse and his officers as the most likely explanation for their lack of success. Fortunately no betraying fragments from the stray torpedoes were searched for or found by the Republicans. Likewise L.z.S. Freiwald in *U-33* was having no success. Several attempts at closing merchant and military shipping had been frustrated, either by an absence of firm target identification – as was the case on the night of 5 December when the Republican cruiser *Méndez Núñez* passed before his tubes with darkened destroyer escorts – or defensive manoeuvring by the target vessels. OKM issued a strict edict to Boehme for transmission to his commanders that: 'The lack of visible success must not lead to such determined action that camouflage and preventing compromising Germany are not considered the highest priority.'

Finally German willpower gave out and the War Minister *Feldmarschall* Werner von Blomberg issued orders that clandestine U-boat operations were to be discontinued as of 10 December. Plans to send further 'Saltzwedel' boats on a war footing to the Mediterranean theatre were scrapped and the two submarines were scheduled to begin their voyage home the following night. Italy had willingly taken over the task of naval operations in support of the Nationalists, and Hitler was satisfied that the attention drawn by Italy would remove the spotlight from German expansionist rumblings in central Europe. Ironically it was at this point that *U-34* scored Operation 'Ursula's' sole success.

On 12 December, while passing Málaga *en route* for the Straits of Gibraltar, lookouts aboard Grosse's boat sighted the low silhouette of Republican submarine *C3*, patrolling 4 miles from the sun-baked coast and Málaga's main lighthouse. *C3* was part of the troubled Republican Spanish Navy, riven by internal upheavals that mirrored the nation as a whole. Officers were frequently redistributed throughout various naval postings as a result of the mixed loyalties peculiar to civil war. The submarine service had suffered less than their surface counterparts, but still remained below its peak efficiency as men rotated through the crew ranks. The Spanish submarine's commander, *Alférez de Navío* Antonio Arbona Pastor, had been IWO (First Watch Officer) aboard the submarine *B5* at the time of the outbreak of the war. However, after receiving the order for the flotilla to sail to the Straits of Gibraltar to hamper the passage of troops from Africa to Spain, there was a quick and violent redistribution of flotilla officers. Arbona was put in command of *C3*, replacing its Nationalist captain Javier Salas Pintó. The crew of *C3* pledged support to Arbona and he was confirmed by the Chief of the Flotilla and for the Minister of the Navy on the following day. *C3* then sailed for Gibraltar.

The Spanish submarine had initially been allocated the area around the Straits of Gibraltar in an effort to inhibit the transfer of Franco's men from Africa to the Spanish mainland. Shortly afterward she was transferred to the Cantabric Sea. However, various mechanical difficulties forced more than one return to Cartagena for repairs, the latest fault resulting in the loss of one diesel engine. Unable to effect proper repairs the submarine departed Cartagena on 10 December bound for Málaga, stopping briefly in Almería to disembark some faulty machinery. It was a little past 14.00 and the Spanish crew had just finished their midday meal. Nearby *U-34* swiftly submerged and approached her unwitting quarry. Grosse ordered a single torpedo fired, worried that the trail of bubbles left by the G7a torpedo might give warning to his target and identify from where the attack was launched. He had no cause for concern. The 'eel' struck *C3* broadside 8 metres from its bow at 14.19, tearing the bow from the rest of the hull and sending it straight to the bottom in 70 metres of water.

Of forty-seven men aboard only three survived; seamen Isidoro de la Orden Ibáñez and Asensio Lidón Jiménez, flung clear by the blast while they were throwing food scraps overboard, while the third was Merchant Marine Captain (*Capitán de la Marina Mercante*) Agustín García Viñas, seconded to the submarine as navigation officer and talking to the commander in the conning tower when the torpedo struck. One of the nearby fishing boats rescued the three shocked survivors, later transferring them to the hospital ship *Artabro*.

Fortunately for Germany the Republican disaster was eventually attributed to an internal explosion, despite initial fears of foreign submarine attack. Eyewitnesses from the nearby anchovy fishing boats *Joven Antonio* and *Joven Amalia* reported either little or no explosion but instead a huge cloud of 'white steam or smoke', pointing at the possibility that the German warhead did not detonate on impact but sheared through the submarine's outer hull, seawater flooding rapidly onboard to cause an explosion within the battery compartment. It was the fourth German torpedo to be launched in Spanish waters, and the only one to have hit its target. By the end of December both U-boats were back in Wilhelmshaven, their transit from the Mediterranean again made by running surfaced at night, and returned to the control of their original commanders. The first intervention in the Mediterranean by *Kriegsmarine* U-boats and Germany's covert naval war in Spain was over.

While the Germans' involvement in naval combat operations had ended, Hitler had been correct in his judgement that Italian submarine patrols would attract the world's attention. Urged by Franco during 1937 to reinforce the Nationalist blockade of Republican ports and thus strangle the supply of arms from other 'neutral' countries, Mussolini increased his submarine commitment. Unbeknown to the Italian navy, British codebreakers had long ago penetrated their ciphers – thanks in large part to the Italian habit of enciphering and transmitting articles from the newspaper *Il Popolo d'Italia* – and were well aware of their involvement. France, also well aware of the identity of the 'unknown' submarine forces responsible for increased sinking of French and British merchant ships, called an international conference in Nyon, Switzerland where they hoped to counter such aggression. In fact they succeeded, Italy withdrawing its submarines before the conference had met. The so-called 'Nyon Agreement' of 1937 thus established clearly the rules and responsibilities of non-Spanish nations in evacuating nationals of foreign countries trapped in Spain. It also defined the rules for the protection of neutral shipping when passing through the war-torn coastal waters, and navies from several nations became a permanent fixture in Spanish waters, obeying the letter of the law if not the spirit. Even Italy, vilified privately as the submarine 'pirates' of the war, were given an area to patrol openly as an air of compromise and conciliation dominated the meeting.

German U-boats were seen in Spanish waters and ports again as they joined the 'peace-keeping' forces, supervising the supposed blockade of Spain by non-interventionist forces and monitoring French and British warships that had been allowed to patrol in an ASW role under the Nyon rules. Between July 1936 and April 1939 fifteen separate U-boats mounted forty-seven patrols around Spain. There they honed their future combat skills with games of cat and mouse against their future enemies.

Though the U-boats experienced no further combat, the *Kriegsmarine's* pocket battleship *Deutschland* was bombed by a Republican aircraft off

Ibiza on 29 May 1937, killing twenty-three sailors and injuring over seventy. In retaliation Hitler furiously ordered her sister-ship the *Admiral Scheer* to bombard the Spanish town of Almería. An hour of bombardment killed twenty-one civilians and injured fifty-three but no further attacks on German ships occurred. German national prestige was restored.

Chapter 2

U-boats into the Mediterranean

On 3 September 1939 when war between Germany and the existing western Allies was declared, Karl Dönitz was woefully short of the 300 U-boats he had wanted before hostilities began. With only fifty-seven U-boats at his disposal – thirty of which were small Type II coastal boats capable of little more than operations in the North Sea – the ability to blockade Great Britain into submission was clearly beyond his capabilities. Equally, locating enemy convoy traffic in the expanse of the Atlantic Ocean was difficult at best, a forlorn hope at worst. Therefore, areas identified as natural convoy 'choke points' were targeted, including the Straits of Gibraltar.

The Straits possessed some unique characteristics that could both aid and hinder U-boat operations, characteristics that had first been discovered in the seventeenth century and expanded two centuries later into a recognisable scientific fact. The only natural entrance from the Atlantic Ocean to the Mediterranean Sea, water flowing both into and out of the Mediterranean must pass its constricted channel, at its narrowest point only a little over 8 miles wide. These two directional flows formed two different currents. A strong surface current brings water in from the North Atlantic, while Mediterranean water, saltier and thus denser because of a high evaporation rate (up to one metre per year), sinks beneath the surface current and flows out into the North Atlantic. This lower current is known as a thermohalene and faces an obstacle during its outward passage. Near the western end of the Strait there lies a ridge running from North Africa to the Spanish peninsula which forces the outward flow up where it collides with inflow from the Atlantic. This collision generates a series of internal waves that travel along the boundary between the two currents back into the Mediterranean. Therefore entering the Mediterranean was best achieved using the surface inflow – which for U-boats meant running on the surface past one of the narrowest and most heavily defended waterways in Europe.

As early as 2 October 1939 the first OG (Outward to Gibraltar) convoy

17

formed at sea off Land's End bound for Gibraltar, the Iberian Peninsula and onward into the Mediterranean and ports beyond Suez. OG1 consisted of thirty-seven ships, forming under the protection of Royal Navy warships, which were due to hand their charge over to a French escort group south of Ouessant. In turn the HG (Homeward from Gibraltar) convoys carried material from the Far East via Port Said as part of the 'Green' convoy system. From Gibraltar they were designated with the prefix HG; HG1 leaving for Liverpool on 26 September 1939.

On 9 October, Dönitz decided to attempt to use three of his longer-range boats against this confined channel where they were surely to find targets.

> I intend to use the large boats in the Mediterranean, approximately between Gibraltar and Oran. There are so many reports of convoys there that it should be worthwhile to send them in spite of the long approach route and the consequent short period in the operations area. I think there will be very little opportunity for warfare according to Prize Law, but the chances of attacking without warning should be many. Also the long narrow sea areas makes a certain amount of cooperation possible between boats, even with so few. There is also the point that it is policy, especially now with so few boats available, to worry the enemy in as many and as remote places as possible. He is then forced to provide for anti-submarine action everywhere and to maintain patrols. This means a weakening of local defences. The more forces the enemy is able to use in anti-submarine operations the more necessary it becomes for us to change the operations areas frequently and thus avoid the expected concentrated attack.[1]

The three boats selected were *U-25* and *U-26*, the only two Type I boats constructed, soon shown to possess so many deficiencies in operational use that they were rapidly discarded, and a Type VIIB, *U-53*. *U-25*, captained by the experienced skipper Kaptlt. Viktor Schütze, was the first to depart Wilhelmshaven on 18 October followed shortly thereafter by *U-53* and *U-26*, commanded by *Kapitänleutnants* Ernst-Günther Heinicke and Klaus Ewerth respectively. The three boats were ordered to gather southwest of Ireland before sailing southeast and rendezvousing off Gibraltar, where-upon *U-26* would lay a minefield across the mouth of the British harbour, after which the three boats would slip through the Straits and into the western Mediterranean to plunder the expected mass of shipping. Ewerth's boats had been stripped of all but the most essential code and cipher material as part of Standing War Order Number 17 that covered the risk of losing a boat in shallow water where such books might be recovered. Consequently, Ewerth's ability to communicate with BdU and other boats within his vicinity was somewhat reduced, though Dönitz considered that the restricted area of operations and clear orders would make this less of a problem.

However, the operation was almost doomed from the outset. While Schütze waited southwest of Ireland for his rendezvous with the other boats he was directed towards a convoy northwest of Lisbon. After failing to make contact BdU again redirected him, this time against unescorted French Convoy 20K that Schütze found north of Cape Ortegal and attacked on 31 October. Firing four contact-fused torpedoes at the steamer ss *Baoulé*, Schütze was exasperated to see no detonation despite a textbook approach in calm sea conditions. Determined to not let his faulty weaponry defeat him, Schütze surfaced *U-25* and attacked the steamer with gunfire, eventually sinking the ship. There his luck completely deserted him. During the firing of the 10.5cm gun, the concussion had cracked the supporting crosspiece of the forward torpedo-loading hatch which promptly leaked a significant amount of water at all but the shallowest depths. Unable to go deep and extremely vulnerable to depth charges with such a structural weakness, a furious Schütze broke off his patrol and headed home.[2]

Meanwhile *U-53* had remained southwest of Ireland awaiting the arrival of *U-26*. Eventually Heinicke was directed instead to head toward Gibraltar and make the final rendezvous there. While in Biscay, Heinicke sighted a northbound convoy off Lisbon which he proceeded to shadow, sending beacon signals to attract other boats to the target. After three days the operation was called off with no successful attack. *U-53* was forced to return to Kiel due to lack of fuel where Heinicke was judged to have acted too cautiously when he could have attacked the convoy, and was promptly relieved of his command and temporarily posted to the auxiliary cruiser *Widder*.

Thus only *U-26* remained on course. *Kapitänleutnant* Ewerth arrived as planned off Gibraltar, but attempts to lay his minefield across the harbour mouth were thwarted by combined bad weather, bright searchlights and roving anti-submarine patrols. Reloading with torpedoes he opted to sail through the Straits and entered the Mediterranean while remaining surfaced. There the boat sailed fruitlessly, though Ewerth claimed a single ship torpedoed and sunk, a claim given little credence in post-war analysis. Dispirited, Ewerth sailed back through the Straits of Gibraltar and headed home – the only U-boat to enter and successfully leave the Mediterranean during the Second World War. On 5 December 1939 *U-26* entered Wilhelmshaven harbour, as recorded in the BdU War Diary:

> *U-26* entered port. She did not carry out her minelaying operation off Gibraltar as the weather there was too bad. She was afterwards in the Mediterranean, as ordered, but apparently struck a poor time for traffic.

The result of her patrol is one steamer sunk. Very little for 44 days. The stormy weather is mainly to blame. The C.O. cannot be blamed for not carrying out the minelaying operation because he did not consider it possible in view of local conditions.

These things can only be judged at the time. But he did not take long enough to make his observations; he should have at least made one more attempt in different weather conditions.

It was a mistake to send *U-25*, *U-26* and *U-53* into the Mediterranean. *U-25* had to return before she ever got there, *U-53* did not get through and *U-26* hardly encountered any shipping worth mentioning. This patrol shows all the disadvantages of a long outward passage. The boat can only operate for a few days and the operation is without success if she does not come upon any traffic in those few days.[3]

Dönitz's initial enthusiasm for an attack against Gibraltar and its Mediterranean convoy traffic had completely faded and he would not consider the idea until forced to by his Commander-in-Chief two years later. The Atlantic remained his *Schwerpunkt*, his focus of effort, and Gibraltar convoy traffic was felt to be more vulnerable in Biscay as opposed to the narrow and easily defended waterway that led to the Mediterranean. By June 1940 this view was amply reinforced when the fall of France gave the U-boats bases on the Atlantic coast.

As Germany swept to victory over Holland, Belgium and France, Mussolini vacillated on whether or not to enter the spreading European conflagration in 1940. On Monday 18 March 1940 Hitler met the Italian leader at the Brenner Pass that lay on the border with Italy and the Greater German Reich. There, aboard Mussolini's special train, the Italian dictator was virtually lectured on Germany's future plans by his counter-part.[4] Hitler and his Foreign Minister Joachim von Ribbentrop spouted facts and figures at Mussolini and his Foreign Minister Ciano that defined German military strength, seeking ultimately to persuade the Italians to enter the war. Twelve weeks later, on 10 June, Italy did just that, throwing its meagre weight into an unsuccessful incursion into the south of an already defeated France, which officially surrendered to Germany on 22 June, though an armistice was not signed with Italy until two days later, a mark of the contempt with which the French viewed Mussolini.

As German troops occupied northern and western France, the independent state of Vichy France was established, taking its name from the government's capital in Vichy, southeast of Paris near Clermont-Ferrand. While officially neutral, Vichy largely collaborated with Germany, operating as a puppet state headed by the First World War hero Marshal Henri Philippe Pétain. It controlled an unoccupied zone in Southern France, large swathes of North Africa and scattered French colonies. Central to Vichy naval operations was another veteran of the First World War, Admiral Jean-François Darlan, who had been given command of the entire French Navy during 1939. With the fall of France, Darlan supported Pétain and was subsequently rewarded by being retained in his post as Minister of the Navy, ordering the majority of the fleet to French North Africa.

Once more the British gave serious consideration to withdrawing from the Mediterranean and concentrating an already immensely overstretched Royal Navy on the war against Germany that raged across the Atlantic and in home waters. The First Sea Lord and Chief of the Naval Staff, Admiral of the Fleet Sir Dudley Pound, strongly recommended such an action, withdrawing the eastern Mediterranean fleet at Alexandria to Gibraltar. However, the British Joint Planners' Report that Pound's memorandum had instigated concluded that although there was strategic sense in a withdrawal, it would also be seen as a sign of virtual surrender by the Middle Eastern Muslim countries, losing Britain its position there, which included oil pipeline terminals at Haifa and in Syria, as well as jeopardising its hold on India and within the Far East. Moreover it would politically 'discourage' the people of South Africa, New Zealand, Australia and India. Ultimately Churchill would not even entertain the idea of a withdrawal. On 23 June, in his capacity as Minister of Defence, Churchill formally vetoed Pound's proposal and committed Britain to holding the Middle East, especially Iraq, Palestine, Aden, Egypt and Sudan, effectively taking the war to Italy rather than committing the forces to tackling Germany.

The northern Mediterranean coastline was now a fresh theatre of war. The British blockade of Axis countries was now extended to include the whole of France. Facing the possibility of the large Vichy fleet joining the Axis, the Royal Navy neutralised the Vichy fleet at Oran on 3 July, only the battlecruiser *Strasbourg* escaping the accurate bombardment. This attack at Oran caused 1,147 French casualties and fury within Vichy France, particularly stoking the fires of Anglophobia that burned within Admiral Darlan. The Royal Navy then finally clashed inconclusively with Italy's fleet on 9 July off Punta Stilo, chasing the rattled Italians back to their port without loss.

Upon Italy's declaration of war, Mussolini possessed one of the largest submarine fleets in the world. With 115 boats at his disposal it was surpassed in numerical strength only by the Soviet Union, which at that stage was still on the conflict's sidelines. However, a qualitative strength did not match this quantitative one. The Italian boats were largely slow and ponderous vessels, slow to dive and thus unsuited to the harsh demands of what was soon to be a largely aircraft-dominated Mediterranean. They possessed no effective fire control and were generally made from poor quality material home-produced in Italy. Furthermore, Italian submarine tactics before the outbreak of hostilities had been predominantly static, relying on an enemy to approach the submerged boat in order for a successful torpedo attack to be made. This contrasted strikingly with German doctrine which preached attack, preferably while remaining surfaced and able to use the boats' higher surface speed and small silhouette to its full advantage. Nonetheless, Italian submarines prepared to take the war to the British Mediterranean forces, a small number also transferring with great skill through the Straits of Gibraltar to serve under German command in the Battle of the Atlantic. Italian land forces launched an invasion of British Somaliland on 4 August, occupying the capital Berbera fifteen days later. On Friday 13 September 1940, Italian troops crossed the border between Libya and Egypt. Within three days they had captured Sidi Barrani, 60 miles from their starting point, with spearheads still aimed east.

For Germany, the Axis cause within Italy's prescribed territory – the Mediterranean – appeared to be safely under control. The Tripartite Pact was signed between Japan, Italy and Germany on 27 September and *Grossadmiral* Erich Raeder moved to secure permission for naval operations in the Mediterranean during that month. He sent two memoranda to Hitler advocating attacking and eliminating British strength in the Mediterranean Sea and the Near East. His proposal involved conquering Gibraltar (with Spanish assistance, codenamed Operation 'Felix'), seizing the Suez Canal and then pushing through Palestine and Syria to the Turkish border. Raeder's plan envisioned German air bases in Vichy North Africa that could ultimately aid the Battle of the Atlantic, as well as severing the British communication links with their Near and Far Eastern units, providing support for the Italian invasion of East Africa. Subsequent domination of the Indian Ocean would therefore become a real possibility while pressure from German-held or dominated countries in the Middle East would virtually negate the necessity of Hitler's long-held ambition – the invasion of the Soviet Union.

However, Spain's General Franco was less than effusive about joining the Axis when Hitler finally met with the Spanish leader on 23 October. The two leaders failed to reach any agreement over terms by which Spain would enter the war and provide support for the Gibraltar invasion during what were long and difficult discussions. Hitler had in fact lost faith in Spain as a truly fascist country as long ago as the Civil War. He considered Franco a leader who lacked a mass political movement backing him and never truly felt that Franco would become a fully-fledged partner of the Axis. Likewise, a meeting between Hitler and Pétain provided no firm commitment by Vichy France to actively assist Germany beyond mere passive collaboration, and Hitler returned to Germany dispirited and once more fixated on the invasion of Russia the following year. The Mediterranean again slipped from Hitler's strategic view, relegated to only an Italian problem. But it would shortly prove to be anything but.

On Monday 28 October 1940 Italy attacked Greece in what was to prove a badly timed and calamitous invasion. Irritated by German troops moving into Romania without consulting him, Mussolini had decided on his own fresh adventure within what he considered his sphere of influence. Turkey immediately declared itself neutral in the Graeco-Italian conflict and by early November the Italians were reeling and Greek troops on the offensive, swiftly taking 5,000 prisoners from the Italian 3rd Alpine Division and receiving reinforcement from British and Commonwealth troops. Hitler was furious at his ally, the madness of an invasion over mountainous territory in the face of an oncoming Greek winter immediately apparent to the German leader. However, he presented an even-tempered front to the crestfallen Italian dictator when the two finally met once more at the Brenner Pass.

Catastrophe mounted on catastrophe for Mussolini's forces as the Greeks continued their advance in Northern Greece and Albania where the Italians had attempted another offensive on 8 November. That same night a supply convoy designated 51st Transport Squadron comprised of ten ships with six destroyer escorts and the nearby presence of two Italian cruisers and four more destroyers, was intercepted and destroyed by British Force K – the cruisers HMS *Aurora* and *Penelope* and the destroyers HMS *Lance* and *Lively* based at Malta. The action was the first major success for the British hunting group, though its pattern was to be repeated over and over again to the detriment of Axis supply to North Africa. The Italians were obliterated at virtually no cost to their attackers. The sole British casualties were six canaries that died of heart failure aboard HMS *Penelope* when the guns fired, though an anonymous crew member recorded in the ship's log that '. . . it is interesting to note that the [remainder of the] ship's canaries seemed to toughen up after this, and later on a number of them would sing on deck during the most violent actions.'[5] Italian propaganda attempted to claim success against the Royal Navy, though their effort was openly mocked by Vice Admiral (Malta) W T R Ford: 'It is with great regret that I see in the Italian broadcast that one of the cruisers received two hits and a destroyer one hit during torpedo bombing. I can only think that in view of the lack of damage I saw today the dockyard is more efficient than I thought or your camouflage excellent.'[6]

On 11 November 1940, Fairey Swordfish torpedo bombers of the Fleet Air Arm from HMS *Illustrious* also took the initiative at sea, attacking the Italian fleet at Taranto claiming three battleships, two cruisers and two auxiliaries damaged in what was the prototype aerial attack on an enemy harbour.[7] That same day Italian aircraft based in France made their first and last attack on mainland Britain when they raided the Thames estuary with little success. It was to prove a symptomatic example of Italy's fortunes at war. Italian troops had been driven back across the Kalamas River by the middle of November, Greek troops pushing forward in Albania throughout the month that followed. On Friday 6 December the Italian Supreme Commander Marshal Badoglio voluntarily resigned, the Naval Chief following on the following Sunday.

On Monday 9 December Wavell's 'Thirty Thousand' opened their first desert offensive – Operation 'Compass' – and Italian troops in North Africa were captured in their thousands as their fragile morale shattered. With German eyes now on rescuing their ineffective ally in the eastern Mediterranean, and with no progress made in obtaining Franco's guarantee of assistance, Operation 'Felix', the proposed invasion of Gibraltar was formally cancelled by *Feldmarschall* Keitel two days later. With an almost unbroken chain of reverses on every front including Eritrea, now under pressure from a fresh British attack, Mussolini appealed directly to Hitler for military assistance. On Wednesday 12 February 1941, Lieutenant General Erwin Rommel arrived in Tripoli at the head of the first German troops to land in North Africa. Ten days later he attacked El Agheila.

In Greece British and Commonwealth troops had begun landing as part of Operation 'Lustre', to reinforce the Greeks in the event of a German attack. This was to prove disastrous for the British desert campaign as their best troops and armour were abruptly diverted to the Balkans, an area that had long fixated Churchill. The German alliance with Romania and Bulgaria had opened a very real threat of attack by *Luftwaffe* units on British naval forces in the Aegean. The dreams of a Balkan alliance that Churchill had harboured since his last great disastrous adventure in the region in 1915 evaporated as Turkey steadfastly remained neutral and Bulgaria joined the enemy camp. On 25 March Yugoslavia signed the Tripartite Pact, further imperilling the Greek nation, though a *coup d'état* deposed the pro-German government, providing a brief illusion of Allied solidarity.

While the Italian forces in Abyssinia continued to reel backward under British pressure, Rommel's 5th Light Division – soon to bear the title of the *Afrika Korps* when combined with the 15th and 21st Panzer Divisions – hammered Allied positions in North Africa. In Iraq, Rashid Ali el-Gillani mounted a pro-Axis coup and six *Luftwaffe* He 111 bombers (from squadron KG4) and three Messerschmitt Me 110 heavy fighters (ZG26 and ZG76) aircraft of *Oberst* Junck's eponymous air *Gruppe* arrived in Mossul to support the Iraqis. Shortly thereafter they were joined by an Italian group of Cr 42 fighters. Finally on 6 April, German forces invaded Yugoslavia and Greece. The Axis retreat was over. By the end of the month Yugoslavia had capitulated, the Greek Army had surrendered, British troops had virtually evacuated mainland Greece and Rommel had crossed the Egyptian border headed east. A single ray of hope for the Allies was the surrender of both the Iraqi rebel forces by the end of May and Italian troops in East Africa.[8] Syria too was soon wrested from Vichy control, the country having been used as a staging post for the *Luftwaffe* units in Iraq and thus seen as a threat to British interests. British and Australian forces had therefore invaded Syria and Lebanon, capturing Damascus on 17 June as elements of the Royal Navy and Royal New Zealand Navy blockaded Beirut, engaging the Vichy destroyer *Guépard* during the operation. However, despite these military successes the internal security of British possessions in the Middle East relied on the dominance of Imperial forces to prevent insurrection.

While the initial deployment of German troops in North Africa had been unimpeded by the British due to their ill-fated intervention in mainland Greece and on Crete, this state of affairs changed to the detriment of Rommel's forces after the successful German invasion of Crete and ending of a brief Palestinian insurrection. By April 1941 British forces had been forced to limp away from mainland Greece by German invaders, with 12,000 killed, wounded and missing along with 209 aircraft, 8,000 trucks and numerous tanks and artillery pieces lost despite the best efforts of another brilliantly handled Royal Navy evacuation, Operation 'Demon'. In less than a month the same débâcle was to be repeated from Crete, which was captured in an audacious German airborne assault. Despite successfully lifting 16,500 men to safety from the island garrison, the Royal Navy had two battleships and an aircraft carrier badly damaged, three cruisers sunk, five more heavily damaged, six destroyers sunk and another seven damaged. *Luftwaffe* attack had proved murderous to the Royal Navy's Mediterranean presence, effectively halving it at one stroke.

Further to the east Vichy-held Syria was quickly overrun by British, Australian and Free French troops and, although the Balkans were lost, the eastern Mediterranean countries appeared secure, on land at least. But the threat remained to the Suez Canal and its vital link between Atlantic and Indian Oceans. By 28 April Rommel had reached the Egyptian border after battering through inexperienced British and Commonwealth desert forces that had been denuded by Churchill's despatch of men to Greece. The Germans had even managed to capture the British commander General Neame himself, as well as Lieutenant General Richard O'Connor – commander of the British Western Desert Force – with whom Neame had been conferring when their unescorted car was intercepted by a German spearhead unit. Behind the German front lay the single besieged Allied stronghold of Tobruk, while at sea there was the small island of Malta. The key to stopping Rommel lay in his supply routes that trailed across the Mediterranean to North Africa, Tripoli being his main supply port and Malta remained an unwelcome thorn in the Germans' side.

During the summer of 1941 Axis supply convoys bound for Rommel's *Afrika Korps* were hammered by Allied submarines and aircraft, mostly based on Malta. German shipping reserves were already extremely low in the Mediterranean. By late August there were eleven freighters used for ore transport which could not be spared for supply convoys to the *Afrika Korps*. A further seven were already in use within the Aegean and Black Seas which again could not be spared for use elsewhere. Raeder recommended the use of French merchant shipping, or non-French shipping found within French ports and able to be commandeered. Furthermore he acknowledged to Hitler on 26 August that Italy possessed an estimated 299 ships totalling 1,119,954 tons that they were unwilling to use for supply convoy work – husbanding them instead for use after the end of the war when historically merchant reserves were low due to losses.[9]

However, in the light of the Allied onslaught on Italian convoy routes, it is perhaps easy to understand Mussolini's reticence to use his merchant fleet. Ships trailing from the Italian peninsula towards North Africa were decimated, Italian air and naval power being unable to prevent the mauling. Despite possessing the largest fleet in the Mediterranean, the *Regia Marina* appeared to lack the will and energy required to safeguard their precious charges. On the eve of Mussolini's declaration of war, the *Regia Marina* stood at six battleships, two of them of modern 35,000-ton *Littorio* class, seven heavy cruisers, twelve light cruisers, twelve flotilla-leaders, twenty-eight modern destroyers, nineteen old destroyers, sixty-nine torpedo boats and 117 submarines of varied type and tonnage. Nonetheless, Italy comprehensively failed to hold the Royal Navy in check – its air force similarly unable to dominate or even match the RAF and Fleet Air Arm. Eventually Rommel himself pleaded with OKW to provide some kind of support for the essential supplies that he needed to prosecute war in the desert. Egypt lay distant, the Suez Canal the glittering prize that could have massive impact on strategic planning should the Germans manage to take and hold control of it. The road to Palestine then beckoned, followed by the Arabian lands with their copious oil reserves and then on into southern Russia and the Caucasian oilfields.

However, this in itself was not enough to justify the commitment of U-boats to the Mediterranean Sea, as Raeder explained to Hitler on 25 July 1941, echoing Dönitz's opinion on the matter:

Situation in the Mediterranean – Transport of supplies is the main problem ... Preparations are being made to transfer a *Schnellboot* and *Räumboot* flotilla at the end of the eastern campaign. In answer to a question by the *Führer*, the C-in-C Navy replies that it is not possible to send submarines into the Mediterranean as this would handicap operations in the Atlantic. Moreover, British submarines and aircraft are the forces used in the Mediterranean to attack transports, and these cannot be combatted with submarines. Italian anti-submarine defence must be properly organised for this purpose.[10]

Hitler steadfastly refused to accept the logic of Raeder's argument. He felt that British forces were sure to launch an attack against Sollum and towards its surrounded garrison at Tobruk and that Italian forces would inevitably crumble. Rommel's still assembling *Afrika Korps* remained the sole hope for Axis control of North Africa and Hitler was determined that he should be supported by every means available. He decided on the transfer of three pairs of U-boats to the region, primarily to interfere with the British seaborne supply route from Alexandria and Port Said to the area around Benghazi and Tobruk. After raising the subject repeatedly at situation meetings held at his *Wolfsschanze* headquarters at Rastenburg in East Prussia, he finally issued a direct order on 17 September for the six U-boats to enter the Mediterranean, two of them already at sea and ordered to divert towards the perilous passage through the Straits of Gibraltar.

> In accordance with orders from Naval War Staff, preparations are to be made immediately to send German submarines into the Mediterranean. Six boats are envisaged for a start, they are to operate from the base at Salamis against enemy supply lines, especially those to the coast of North Africa. Operational control is to be in the hands of Naval Group Command South.[11]

Thus the first U-boats – *U-75, U-79, U-97, U-331, U-371* and *U-559* – were directed to transit the Straits of Gibraltar and enter the Mediterranean, heading for operations against British supply traffic running from Alexandria to Tobruk in the eastern Mediterranean. Arguably this represented the most direct use of German U-boats in support of a land campaign, the nearest parallel possibly being the invasion of Norway, though in that operation the U-boats were concerned with the protection of naval units and interception of the enemy. Named the 'Goeben Group' the first of them, *U-371*, passed the British picket ships at Gibraltar on the night of Sunday 21 September 1941, transmitting a prearranged signal to BdU denoting successful entrance into the Mediterranean. Within a week both *U-559* and *U-97* had followed, the last of the group finally entering their new area of operations on the morning of 5 October.

Dönitz, aware that he had lost the battle to keep his submarines in the Atlantic, was also certain that it would be no brief assignment for his men. He steadfastly refused to accept the validity of Mediterranean operations when his already meagre forces were achieving little in the Atlantic. Recent attempts at intercepting Allied convoy traffic from Freetown had resulted in abject failure with only intermittent and brief contact reports from U-boats and reconnaissance aircraft. Where once U-boats had ravaged the area during the previous spring, British convoys were now successfully evading the hunters. Dönitz was irritated and despondent, recording his frustration in the BdU War Diary on 10 October 1941:

The [convoy] traffic situation must have completely changed. A convoy is believed to be leaving Freetown between the 12th and 14th October. If the attempt to pick it up also brings no results, then consideration will be given to the breaking off of operations in the south. The boats which are being used there are badly needed in the north, all the more so because boats have also been taken away from there for other theatres of operation. At the beginning of October the actual situation was as follows:
    There were:
    4 boats in the area of operations in the North Atlantic
    9 boats in the area of operations in the South Atlantic
        As opposed to that there were:
    9 boats returning to base
    4 boats approaching the area
    3 boats on convoy tasks
    6 boats in the Mediterranean
    3 boats in the North Sea
    This splitting up of forces has made it obvious that it is scarcely possible to find targets with only a few boats in the North Atlantic.
    There are no possibilities of counter-balancing this by operations in the Mediterranean and the North Sea. In both these areas the traffic is made up of the smallest types of craft, which are difficult to attack and to hit. Success is accordingly slight. It must be emphasised repeatedly that the enemy today can no longer be found and successfully attacked by small numbers of boats. In September, on the contrary, there was a weakening instead of a strengthening of forces in the main operational area: The effect of sending five new boats to the front was nullified by the fact that three were lost and two small boats were given over for training purposes. The transfer of boats to the Mediterranean and the North Sea therefore only took place at the expense of operations in the Atlantic. *U-371* reported that it had been hit in a gunnery action, and had sustained losses and damage. It set out on return to base. A German boat entered Salamis for the first time.

This last sentence announced the inauguration of Salamis as an operational U-boat station. *U-331* eased into harbour after a difficult and largely disappointing patrol. *Oberleutnant zur See* Freiherr Hans-Dietrich von Tiesenhausen had completed his second war patrol since commissioning his boat on 31 March 1941. His first venture had been into the Atlantic, unsuccessfully attempting to attack northbound Convoy HG69 while lying in wait with other boats between Gibraltar and the Azores. Indeed Dönitz went so far as to record that his lack of success had resulted from 'several mistakes' made while operating against the convoy, though he expressed the hope that they could be put down to his inexperience and would not be repeated as the commander matured into his role with greater familiarity with his command.

Von Tiesenhausen had been ordered, like the five other 'Goeben' boats, to intercept British supply shipping between Alexandria and Tobruk. *U-331* had slipped through the Straits of Gibraltar on the night of 29 September, finally seeing action 11 days later. Sighting three British barges under tow by a tug near the coastline in the Gulf of Sollum, von Tiesenhausen had surfaced and engaged them at 04.30 in a gun action, the barges' shallow draught making them virtually impossible to attack with torpedoes. In the fierce battle that followed the 372-ton Landing Craft Tank *LCT18* was damaged after catching fire, but return fire also slashed across *U-331*, killing *Bootsmann* Hans Gerstenich as he manned the U-boat's 8.8cm deck gun and wounding another of his crew. Von Tiesenhausen broke off the encounter and retreated beneath the waves, later surfacing and carrying out a burial at sea. It was an inauspicious start to the U-boat campaign in the Mediterranean and one largely mirrored by the remaining 'Goeben' boats. *Kapitänleutnant* Heinrich Driver's *U-371* had plucked forty-two survivors of the Italian torpedo boat *Albatros* from the sea after the ship had been sunk off Sicily by the submarine HMS *Upright*. Failed attacks on 20 October saw the boat shelled, chased below and depth-charged, suffering sufficient damage to force Driver to break off his patrol and head for Salamis where he docked on 24 October, two weeks after von Tiesenhausen's *U-331* and one day after Kaptlt. Wolfgang Kaufmann's *U-79*.

Kaufmann believed that he had experienced fractionally more success than his comrades. A little before midnight on 18 October he had attacked a small convoy comprising British tugboat *No307*, and the landing craft *LCT13*, *LCT17* and *LCT18*. Kaufmann fired a full bow salvo of four torpedoes at the crowded transports and observed a violent explosion that led him to claim success, though British records disagree. At 03.34 on the morning of 21 October he again attacked a small British unit that was stationed as fire support for the Tobruk garrison, hitting the 625-ton gunboat HMS *Gnat* off Bardia and blowing off 20 feet of her bow. Although claimed as a monitor named '*Terror*' and confirmed sunk, the *Gnat* was actually towed to Alexandria by HMS *Griffin* where thought was given to marrying the 'Insect' class gunboat's aft section to the forward section of HMS *Cricket*, the stern of which had been severely damaged by dive bombers near Tobruk in June 1941, though her damage was soon deemed so severe that the ship was stricken and converted into an immobile anti-aircraft platform. She was later broken up in 1945.

The arrival in port of *U-331* also marked the first arrival for the newly formed 23rd U-boat Flotilla commanded by the U-boat ace and Knight's Cross holder Kaptlt. Fritz Frauenheim, formerly the captain of *U-101*.[12] Frauenheim's new command had been officially raised in September 1941 as soon as Hitler's decision to send boats to the Mediterranean had become final. Correspondingly a completely new organisational and administrative structure was imposed for the inbound U-boats, directly overseen by one of Dönitz's most trusted subordinates, K.K.Victor Oehrn. From September all operations in the western Mediterranean as far as the Straits of Messina had come under BdU control. Eastwards of that area, the commander of the 23rd U-Flotilla had exercised regional control under the direction of the Admiral Aegean, V.A. Erich Förste. In November a new regional *Führer der Unterseeboote* office was formed, originally named FdU Italian (after briefly designated FdU Mediterranean) and immediately subordinate to Förste, his office in turn a subsidiary of *Marinekommando Süd*.[13] Dönitz later recorded the ensuing structural changes in the BdU War Diary on 11 November 1941:

A review of the organisation of Operational Control in the Mediterranean resulted in the following decisions:

1. Submarine Operational Control must be carried out from Rome, as this is the only way of ensuring sufficiently close cooperation with the other operational H.Q.s.
2. Submarine Operational Control in Rome must also take over control of the submarines in the eastern Mediterranean if large scale operations render this imperative.
3. The difficulty of the task demands not only a personality with special qualifications but also that he must be given a sufficiently responsible position.
4. A fully equipped base with a flotilla organisation must be created for the boats operating in the western Mediterranean.

In accordance with these views, Naval War Staff has been requested:

a. To create 'FdU Mediterranean on the staff of German Admiral Rome', military subordinate to BdU and operationally subordinate to the German Admiral.
b. The following are to come under the command of 'FdU Mediterranean': 23rd U-Flotilla, Salamis, which will retain tactical control in the eastern Mediterranean so long as the task remains a local one in the Tobruk – Alexandria area.

29th U-Flotilla, Spezia (to be newly formed).

The 23rd U-Flotilla was the first to be officially formed at Salamis, erstwhile base of the Hellenic Navy on a small island off Athens within the Saronic Gulf. Salamis is perhaps most famous for the naval battle fought in September 480 BC between the Persians and the Greek City-States. The subsequent Persian defeat stopped the absorption of Greece into their empire and thus arguably facilitated the eventual rise of what would become modern western culture.

The port lay in a bay on the island's eastern coast, directly opposite the town of Salamis to the west across the island's narrow waist. The port faced the Greek mainland and its town of Perama, separated by a narrow strait that led northward into the broad expanse of Eleusis Bay. The military port itself was sheltered below arid hills, the solid rock of which would soon house air raid shelters that in time would become essential. The Germans inherited a port that had already suffered at the hands of the *Luftwaffe*, still bearing some of the scars of the invasion. The semi-submerged hulks of two pre-dreadnought battleships *Kylkis* and *Lemnos* (the ex-USS *Mississippi* and *Idaho* handed over to the Greeks in 1916) lay alongside the quayside, sunk by Ju 87 Stuka attacks in April 1941.

Along with Salamis the *Kriegsmarine* were able to make use of other nearby shipyard facilities, albeit ones of a rudimentary nature compared to those available in Germany. Northeast of the island was Skaramangas Bay, part of an almost land-locked lagoon, that boasted a new shipyard. The shipyard had been established by the Greek Navy in 1939 and named the Royal Hellenic Naval Shipyard for the express purpose of building two torpedo boats. However, despite heavy initial government investment, the outbreak of war found the small complex still non-operational though equipped with some of the necessary facilities. Though it is fair to say that the German invaders were never completely welcome in Greece, relations with the civilian population in Salamis were cordial if not overly friendly, as Otto Wagner of the Salamis base remembered: 'We had a good relationship with the Greeks, and had developed a good mutual understanding'.[14]

One month after Salamis' designation as a U-boat base, the 29th U-Flotilla based on the Italian mainland at La Spezia came into being, with a subsidiary centre within the Adriatic at Pola, site of the U-boats' station during the First World War. Pola is a harbour town on the southwest tip of Istria. The islands of St Catherine, St Andrew and Uljanik divide the harbour into three port basins, the military harbour and Croatian Pomorski Arsenal situated in Vergorola Bay, overlooked by a fourteenth-century castle atop the hillside. Naturally well protected, the base at Pola offered two passages to the sea, one directly from the Aegean to the west and the other through the Fazana Strait. Taking command of the newly raised administrative unit was K.K. Franz Becker, previously a staff officer in Brittany's French U-boat regional command. The new flotilla took as its emblem a symbol that recalled the time spent by men at Salamis. A kicking donkey soon adorned U-boat conning towers, referring to the large number of wild donkeys that lived on the arid Greek island.

By 2 November 1941, the last of the 'Goeben' boats had tied up in Salamis' harbour. *Kapitänleutnant* Hans-Otto Heidtmann's *U-559* had arrived on 20 October, claiming a successful attack with a four-torpedo spread two days previously on an unknown destroyer escorting three troop barges. It is probable that this was the same small convoy comprising Tug *No307* and the LCTs *LCT13*, *LCT17* and *LCT18* that *U-79* attacked two hours later. If so, the 'destroyer' remained unharmed. Heidtmann had already launched unsuccessful attacks against enemy steamers on the nights of 4 and 10 October, before finally claiming victory.

Kapitänleutnant Udo Heilmann's *U-97* put in on 28 October, two victory pennants flying from the boat's raised periscope after sinking the 1,208-ton Greek steamer SS *Samos* and half-an-hour later the 758-ton British tanker SS *Pass of Balmaha* in the early morning of 17 October as they sailed from Alexandria to Tobruk escorted by the corvette HMS *Cocker*. Heilmann spotted the small convoy at 00.55 on 17 October, 1941, firing a spread of three torpedoes at 02.17 that missed. A second spread of two torpedoes hit the *Samos*, which turned over in minutes taking all but three of her thirty-four crewmen down with her. Another two-torpedo spread was fired and one hit the *Pass of Balmaha*, which promptly exploded, a cloud of smoke and flames seen rising about 300 metres into the air marking the end of the ship's entire complement – her master, fifteen crew members and two gunners.

However, Heilmann's luck did not last and a week later the boat's IIWO, Victor-Wilhelm Nonn, was badly injured in an accident onboard, forcing the boat to head for Salamis. On 2 November, *U-75* finally reached its new home, Kaptlt. Helmuth Ringelmann having sunk two tank landing craft, *LCT2* and *LCT7*, by torpedo and gunfire in the first hours of morning on 12 October off the Libyan coast east of Tobruk. Ringelmann rescued some survivors from the water to be landed as prisoners of war before retreating from the scene. On 25 October he missed a destroyer with an attempted torpedo attack before heading to Salamis.

The initial foray into action by the six 'Goeben' boats had netted an estimated 4,091 tons of enemy shipping plus Heidtmann's unidentified destroyer, for an outlay of weeks at sea and expenditure of nearly all torpedoes aboard. It was not a result that augured well for Dönitz's men. The BdU recorded his initial observations on the new theatre of operations on 21 October after von Tiesenhausen and Heidtmann had been debriefed.

U-79 reported from the Mediterranean that it was on its way back as it had expended all torpedoes. Apparently (the W/T message was picked up slightly corrupt) it torpedoed the monitor *Terror* [in fact the gunboat HMS *Gnat*] in square CP6797, besides that it sank another vessel. It reported: otherwise all shots missed.

According to this report and the short reports which have been submitted by *U-331* and *U-559* the situation in the Mediterranean seems to be somewhat as follows: The supplies to Tobruk were carried out by vessels with a very shallow draught (lighters, barges, etc.), which were escorted by torpedo boats and escort vessels. It is not possible to torpedo vessels like these with the torpedoes which are available (except when shooting with surface runners).

It seems questionable whether the aim of the operation, namely stopping supply traffic to Tobruk, will be accomplished in this manner, and whether it would not be more efficacious to operate in the eastern Mediterranean off Alexandria, Beirut, etc. with all boats (at present there are two boats off Alexandria.

Almost as if to emphasise the displeasure with which Dönitz viewed the new deployment, three days later the BdU War Diary also recorded the official handover of responsibility for Mediterranean operations to *Marinekommando Italian.*

A special W/T organisation came into force from 08.00 on the 25th October for Mediterranean boats. At the same time the boats were to change over to the operational command of the 23rd U-boat Flotilla, which directs the operations in the Mediterranean under the directions of Group Command South. The events in the Mediterranean will no longer be dealt with in the War Diary of the C-in-C U-boats.

Chapter 3

Success!

NOVEMBER 1941 SAW A DISTINCT EASING OF German pressure on the Atlantic convoy routes. The Mediterranean theatre now presented a new problem for Dönitz as skilled workers were transferred from German and French dockyards to Greece in order to work on the boats that now lay immobile in Salamis. The resultant delays in turn-around for Atlantic boats decreased the numbers on active patrol which meant that only twenty-four Allied ships were sunk in the Atlantic and North Sea throughout November and December, compared to twenty-five in October alone and fifty-four the previous month. Obviously the redirection of manpower was not the only cause for such lack of success for Dönitz's boats, but it continued to irritate their commander.

Salamis was found to be inadequately manned and equipped to cope with the U-boats already arriving for overhaul, let alone allowing expansion of operations in the eastern Mediterranean. La Spezia was being rushed into service for U-boats planned to operate in the western Mediterranean while subsidiary harbours at Palermo and Maddalena were to be made ready as emergency operational bases.

La Spezia, in the Ligurian region of northwest Italy, was the principal Italian naval dockyard, the two other major centres being Taranto and Venice. The military dockyard was constructed between 1860 and 1865, superceding Genoa as the regional naval dockyard. The Military Arsenal used by Mussolini's navy was built in 1869, which had immediately boosted the port's strategic importance at that time. The port then received substantial improvement and expansion during the early years of Italy's fascist regime. The size of the dry dock was increased from 151 to 201 metres and a submarine repair facility added to the arsenal. A dedicated fuel depot was built, alongside a jetty equipped for the delivery of fuel oil, water and electricity to boats in harbour. Geographically La Spezia also lay within a relatively short distance from Italy's industrial heartland, including the major centres of Genoa, Turin and Milan. It was also a naturally protected area though the disadvantage of that was that the mountainous terrain provided limited, though easily defended, road access. With Italian air and naval units failing to interdict British supply to North Africa and failing to protect Axis convoys that were regularly savaged *en route* to Rommel's embattled troops, Hitler despatched *Luftwaffe* formations to the area under the command of *Feldmarschall* Albert Kesselring. He also proposed to send a total of fifty U-boats to the Mediterranean in support of the North African campaign. Indeed Rommel had complained to OKW on 9 November 1941 that of 60,000 troops promised as reinforcements, only 8,093 had actually arrived. His fuel supplies were negligible and yet he clearly faced an imminent attack by the rebuilding British forces facing him. On 12 December Hitler held a conference in Berlin at which the naval strategic situation was discussed with K.z.S. von Puttkamer, the permanent naval representative at Hitler's headquarters. The OKM records show that at that time thirty-six boats were in or *en route* to the Mediterranean, leaving thirty-six other operational boats, three of which were in Norway and five in the South Atlantic. A total of twenty-five U-boats carried the weight of the war in the Atlantic and only six would be available for Operation '*Paukenschlag*' – the attack on shipping off the coast of the United States.

During November the post of FdU Italian was formally established in Rome and Dönitz sent one of his most able and trusted officers to take the position. *Korvettenkapitän* Victor Oehrn departed immediately for Italy and threw himself into his new post with his customary vigour. However, the posting of Oehrn to this office caused some ire at OKM where Raeder considered that a man of at least K.z.S. rank and former flotilla command experience should have been used instead. Raeder insisted that Oehrn be demoted to the role of deputy for a new FdU Italian and the disappointed Oehrn waited in Rome for his replacement to arrive.

Special tasks in the Mediterranean:
On account of the order to increase commitments in the Mediterranean, *U-205*, *U-433*, *U-81*, *U-565* (all outward bound into the North Atlantic) have been recalled if their charts were not adequate, or if their equipment was sufficient they have been sent direct to the Mediterranean.[1]

During November this second group of U-boats, Group 'Arnauld' – named in honour of the *Pour le Mérite* winner Arnauld de la Perière of the First World War who had made the Mediterranean his most successful hunting ground aboard *U-35* – headed for the Gibraltar Strait. They were scheduled to be followed by Group 'Bennecke' (*U-96*, *U-332*, *U-402* and *U-552*) during December.

Kapitänleutnant Fritz Guggenberger's *U-81* was the first of the 'Arnauld' Group to pass Gibraltar, and he did so in bold style. He crept carefully to

Cape Tarifa, Europe's southernmost point, evading the attention of Spanish fishing vessels and using the bright neutral navigation beacons to aid his voyage. By 02.35 *U-81* was nosing slowly past Gibraltar itself, surprised and heartened to find an absence of British patrol craft though forced to continually avoid Spanish trawlers with lighted nets fishing for sardines. By sunrise he was through, receiving orders from BdU to take up position east of Gibraltar with *U-205*, who had crept through earlier during the same night, and maintain radio silence unless enemy action threatened the other boat.

Once out of sight of Gibraltar's formidable mass, *U-81* received further radio intelligence that indicated a British task force was sailing in their direction. Italian reconnaissance aircraft had indeed spotted the most powerful group of British ships in the Mediterranean. Gibraltar's Force H comprised the aircraft carriers HMS *Ark Royal* and *Argus*, the battleship HMS *Malaya*, the light cruiser HMS *Hermione* and seven destroyers. The British ships, formed into this strike unit on Churchill's urging, had recently savaged Italian convoy traffic and were returning from delivering thirty-seven Hurricanes and seven Blenheim aircraft to the hard pressed island of Malta as part of Operation 'Perpetual'. Not long after the initial report, *U-205* sighted Force H, steering west at 16 knots. *Kapitänleutnant* Franz-Georg Reschke attempted an attack with a three-torpedo spread. Although detonations were heard aboard the boat as it raced away submerged to escape possible retaliation, there were no hits, at least one torpedo exploding in the wake of HMS *Legion*.

Guggenberger was faced with a dilemma. *U-81* had eased through the Straits of Gibraltar and managed to get clear of the dangers of the heavily patrolled sea-lane. Now, in order to maximise his chance of spotting the fast-moving British ships he felt compelled to retrace his course into the confined waters leading to Gibraltar. It was a risky strategy. While true that the enemy would be compelled to steer a predictable course, *U-81* would in turn be left with little room to manoeuvre if discovered. Nonetheless, adhering to Dönitz's principles of constant attack and aggression, Guggenberger ordered course set for Gibraltar, taking *U-81* on a deep test dive to ensure all systems functioned perfectly. During the voyage to the planned intercept point a minor fault was discovered in one of the diesel engines, though it was not felt to be serious enough to warrant deviating from his new plan.

U-81 was forced under at several points due to distant sightings of aircraft and a destroyer, until in the afternoon Force H was first detected on the horizon. At 15.30, half an hour later than Guggenberger had estimated, the foremast of a battleship was sighted and *U-81* was taken to periscope depth. The enemy were steaming almost directly for his position and *U-81* was brought to battle stations. Force H steamed echeloned to port with HMS *Malaya* leading and HMS *Ark Royal* and *Argus* following. A protective screen of destroyers raced at the flanks of the formation, one seeming to bear directly for *U-81*, though it passed harmlessly astern as Guggenberger held his nerve. At 16.36, with the target ships at a range of almost 4,000 metres, the first of a full bow salvo of four torpedoes was fired, each aimed 150 metres apart from the last and the first shot targeted on *Malaya*. *U-81* reared upward at the bow with the sudden loss of weight and men were rapidly ordered to run forward so that their weight would prevent the submarine breaching the surface. With torpedoes running and the boat's trim restored, Guggenberger took *U-81* down to await the results of his attack.

Six minutes and six seconds later the unmistakable sound of a torpedo detonation echoed through the water. A second explosion was heard 90 seconds later. Guggenberger believed that his first torpedo had struck HMS *Malaya*, the second detonation possibly a destroyer or even aircraft carrier past the battleship. However, there was little time to speculate as destroyers almost immediately located the echo of *U-81* with ASDIC and rapidly began the hunt. For the next five hours the British hunters dropped over 160 depth charges – counted aboard the U-boat by the *Obersteuermann* who spat a prune stone into a tin for every explosion, though his methodical chewing was finally exhausted long before the last charge had been dropped. *U-81* frequently altered its depth and heading to try and shake the pursuit and Guggenberger's skilful evasion resulted in no real damage, the destroyers finally giving up their chase shortly before midnight. *U-81* eventually surfaced and began the process of recharging batteries, air and crew as it departed from the area. Behind it, the drama aboard HMS *Ark Royal* was reaching a climax.

Captain L E H Maund had been on the flight deck of his ship HMS *Ark Royal* when he felt the ship violently shudder and saw smoke billowing from the bomb lift doors. Racing to his bridge he initially thought that they had suffered an internal explosion, so his first course of action was to reduce the ship's speed. However, communication lines had been severed and the ship's telegraphs jammed in position and several minutes passed before verbal orders were relayed to the engine room to take the way off the carrier. *Ark Royal* had already begun to list seriously to starboard and it was soon apparent they had been torpedoed. Below decks, where most of the crew had been, there had been no doubt as to what had occurred. The torpedo had struck abreast of the bridge, the decks whipping violently with the concussion, visibly lifting several fully-loaded torpedo bombers into the air before they crashed back down on splayed undercarriages. Lights went out in several compartments and smoke billowed into some of the ventilators nearest the explosion. Below the waterline four men were on duty in the lower steering position, main switchboard and telephone exchange. There the blast was extremely severe, the compartments plunging into darkness and a heavy mixture of fuel oil and seawater gushing through ruptured bulkheads. Three of the four men clambered to safety, while Able Seaman E Mitchell was never seen again – miraculously the only casualty of the attack.

The *Ark Royal* had been hit in what was arguably the worst possible position. An initial hole 130 feet long by 30 feet wide was rapidly being increased by the water drag during the time taken to bring the ship to a dead stop, hull plating peeled off by the friction. The starboard boiler room, air spaces and oil tanks flooded, as did the main switchboard and the lower steering position. The starboard power train was also knocked out. Being dead amidships the list would be most severe and flooding was taking place in an area that meant four main compartments, plus over 106 feet of the ship's starboard bilge, were immediately flooded. The water level rose inexorably as flooding took hold of the stricken aircraft carrier. Maund had decided to evacuate all surplus men, fearing heavy losses if the carrier capsized as HMS *Courageous* had done in 1939. The destroyer HMS *Legion* nosed alongside and the transfer of 1,487 men was completed within half an hour. This decision itself was to cost the ship dearly. All personnel had been initially withdrawn from the machinery spaces and assembled topside in order to determine who should leave the ship and who should remain on board. As a result of this, damage-control measures were only initiated forty-nine minutes after the hit, the flooding having been uncontrolled for this period in which the centreline boiler room started to flood from below. During the evacuation of the machinery spaces several covers and armoured hatches were left open, allowing the flooding to spread further than otherwise would be expected. Those that left the ship included the entire staff of shipwrights and key members of the electrical staff, depriving the damage-control crews of much-needed expertise. There were still further delays before the repair crews returned to the machinery spaces and attempts at counter-flooding started.

The desperate battle to save the ship began in earnest. Counter-flooding and pumping had temporarily arrested the starboard list, but with many systems failing, ventilation amongst others, the temperature in the engine rooms was rocketing. The tug *Thames* had in the meantime arrived from Gibraltar and eventually the stricken carrier was taken in tow, two dynamos restored by 22.00 and some lights and pumps restored. Hopes had begun to edge upward with flooding brought largely under control and even reduced in the starboard engine room.

However, below decks the situation was deteriorating. Weakened joints had begun to burst and water flooded fresh areas of the ship. Though the list had been halted, the *Ark Royal* had begun to settle lower in the water and soon a cracked boiler casing sent the temperature in the engine room soaring. Escaping funnel gases were soon prevented from being vented by water that flowed into the elbow of the port boiler room funnel and the working spaces became an inferno with numerous fires breaking out. Steam pressure began to drop and with it the lighting and pumps and gradually the list increased once again despite extra current supplied by destroyer HMS *Laforey*. At 04.30, with the ship's list at 35°, Maund ordered her abandoned, all the men either transferred by ropes or plucked from the sea where they had jumped. One hour and 19 minutes after the initial explosion all power failed aboard the ship.

At 06.13 HMS *Ark Royal* finally disappeared forever. Amazingly all but one of the ship's company had survived – including the two ship's cats. One of the feline complement had already had a similar experience. Plucked from the sea off a small piece of wreckage after the carrier had gone down, 'Oskar' had been rescued in very similar circumstances by the Royal Navy once before. His original home had been aboard a battleship that the *Ark Royal* had famously tangled with – the *Bismarck*.[2] In Brest, where *U-81* had recently been stationed as part of the 1st U-Flotilla, Guggenberger's former flotilla commander Hans Cohausz succinctly summed up German opinion in his flotilla war diary after news of the sinking was confirmed: '*Ja die Deutschen sind im Mittelmeer!* (Yes, the Germans are in the Mediterranean!)' For Guggenberger and the men of *U-81* it was an almost surprise victory when they too learnt of their successful sinking of the *Ark Royal*. It also quickly resulted in the award of a Knight's Cross to the young commander, the first awarded to a U-boat captain in the new theatre of operations.

On land, five days after the carrier's sinking, the newly formed British Eighth Army launched Operation 'Crusader' against Rommel's now-predominantly German lines. By 1 November 1941 the area under command of General Sir Claude Auchinleck, as C-in-C of Britain's Middle East forces, included Syria, Cyprus, Palestine and Trans-Jordan, Egypt, the Sudan, part of Eritrea, and Aden with spheres of influence that included Turkey and the Balkans, Crete, Libya, part of French Equatorial Africa, and Arabia. Iraq and Persia were then transferred to Auchinleck's command early in January 1942, the remainder of Eritrea in February, and Malta in March. It was a vast area and he decided it would be prudent to remain on the defensive on his northern front and take the war to the enemy in North Africa. Though the spectre of German pressure from the Caucasus loomed, it was felt that a swift defeat of the Axis forces in the west would be possible before having to turn attention to the north.

As the British tried to break through to Tobruk, the Royal Navy continued to supply the trapped garrison, as well as concentrating once more on the interdiction of Axis supply convoys. In turn, the German transfer of U-boats to the Mediterranean was increased as well. To keep the pressure on the western end of the Straits of Gibraltar, *U-453* and *U-375* were ordered to proceed at cruising speed to grid square CG89. In the Atlantic *U-552*, *U-85*, *U-133*, *U-571* and *U-577* were ordered to return to western France for refitting in preparation for attempted breakthrough past Gibraltar, though this was later cancelled. Furthermore, *U-96*, *U-98*, *U-201* and *U-332*, all already having been at sea on lengthy patrols, were ordered to operate in the Mediterranean after refuelling covertly from German tankers code-named 'Gata' and 'Bernardo', which were posing as interned merchant ships in the Spanish harbours of Cadiz and Vigo respectively.[3] However, when both *U-98* and *U-201* reported that a return passage to western France was not feasible should their attempted refuelling at the neutral ports fail, they were reassigned to mid-Atlantic patrol areas until their fuel was exhausted. *Kapitänleutnant* Wilhelm Dommes' *U-431* was already *en route* for the Straits, due to proceed through on the night of 24 November. Dommes was further instructed to continue his passage immediately to the east, as was *U-205* which had engaged Force H, which was instructed to refuel in Messina if absolutely necessary before heading for Alexandria.

In the Allied camp there had been some brief but sharp exchanges between Churchill and Admiral Sir Andrew Cunningham, C-in-C of the Mediterranean Fleet, as to the best way to proceed with naval operations in support of 'Crusader', the British Admiral being exasperated by the latest example of interference from Churchill and his deskbound Admiralty. In the early hours of 24 November, the day following the final failure of British troops to break through to Tobruk, suffering grievous tank losses in the process, Cunningham was informed of intelligence indicating that two Italian convoys were at sea and headed for Benghazi. He himself took command of the battle fleet (HMS *Queen Elizabeth*, *Barham* and *Valiant*) while he ordered cruisers of Forces K and B to intercept.

Meanwhile the focus of the western Mediterranean U-boats remained squarely on the sea-lanes that straggled from Alexandria to Tobruk, which was soon to come under fresh Axis assault.

> The Naval Liaison Staff in Rome has informed me that preparations for the attack on Tobruk on 26 November are being concluded. It was apparently not yet known that this attack was being prepared when I was in Berlin consulting with the Naval War Staff on 8 November, otherwise this would have come out in discussions regarding operations in the Mediterranean.
>
> This attack will occasion considerable movements by the British Alexandria forces, but no more than two boats of the 23rd U-Flotilla could be in position on 26 November off Alexandria-Tobruk.
>
> I have, therefore, proposed to the Naval War Staff that three boats be sent at once from the western Mediterranean, thereby taking into account that the number of boats in the western Mediterranean will be temporarily reduced.[4]

Four days later Dönitz increased the number of U-boats deployed against that particular supply route.

U-81 and *U-433* have also been ordered to proceed immediately into the operational area off Tobruk (in accordance with Order for special operations in the Mediterranean) ... The reason for this is that in North Africa the British have started an offensive on the whole front.[5]

On 25 November 1941 *U-331*, one of Dönitz's first three redirected boats, sighted Cunningham's battle squadron in square CO6858 east of Raz Assaz and attacked with four torpedoes. It had already been an eventful patrol for von Tiesenhausen. He had had a seven-man commando team aboard, and was ordered to land them on the coast where they would head inland to lay explosives on the coastal railway running from Alexandria that ferried supplies to the British troops facing Rommel. The seven raiders were successfully offloaded on the night of 17 November, a crewman rowing them ashore in the boat's inflatable west of El Alamein. The U-boat crewman and one of the soldiers remained with the dinghy while the demolition party headed into the darkness. Two British soldiers discovered the two men on the beach, the German commando killing both with a knife. Upon the return of the six others, dawn was already breaking and the group hid in a nearby cave awaiting darkness on the 18th. *U-331* returned to retrieve the group but the inflatable overturned in surf as they attempted to row back. The eight men returned to the beach where they were found again and immediately captured. Following interrogation, the charges were found and defused as *U-331* retreated to sea.

Von Tiesenhausen had been lying submerged by day and surfacing by night as he waited for traffic running the gauntlet to Tobruk when the hydrophones detected faint propeller noise. After cautiously sweeping the clear sunny skies von Tiesenhausen ordered his boat surfaced, crash-diving almost immediately as an unspotted aircraft swept overhead. No attack followed, but the shaken commander opted to remain submerged for the following few hours. *U-331* edged slowly toward the hydrophone trace until at 14.30 von Tiesenhausen sighted destroyer masts through his periscope. Gradually the hull shapes appeared over the horizon, larger shapes becoming visible in the background. The enemy convoy abruptly zigzagged away from *U-331* and von Tiesenhausen ordered the boat surfaced and hurried east to a fresh intercept point. As the enemy altered course once more it approached *U-331* on a reciprocal course, the U-boat promptly crash-diving and plotting an attack course. With the sun behind him, obscuring his periscope, von Tiesenhausen watched as the unmistakable shape of three battleships with four destroyers steaming line abreast ahead of them became clear.

As the leading huge hull filled his vision von Tiesenhausen swung his boat sharply and prepared to fire at point-blank range. Four torpedoes arced away from *U-331* as the boat was ordered down as quickly as possible. However, with little speed and the sudden loss of weight, the LI (Chief Engineer) momentarily lost control, the conning tower inexorably rising until it broke surface and stayed above the water for over half a minute as crew struggled to bring it under, fearing at any moment the crunch of a ramming destroyer. At last the depth gauge began to descend, the boat plunging into the depths before finally arresting its dive at over 250 metres – well beyond its maximum rated test depth. Above them chaos had erupted.

The broaching U-boat had been seen aboard HMS *Valiant*, which was at the end of the line of three battleships. As the formation had begun a turn to echelon to port a mighty explosion was seen against *Barham*, the middle ship. Almost immediately *U-331* was spotted only 130 yards away off the starboard bow. Course was altered to attempt to ram, but the U-boat disappeared before the battleship was able to reach her. The target was so close that even the ship's pom-poms were unable to depress sufficiently to open fire at the target. Meanwhile, the *Barham* had been badly hit.

A great tower of water had leaped up amidships on the *Barham*, so that only her bows and stern were in sight. I yelled to the captain, who was just below in his sea cabin, and we swung around and increased speed to try and find the attacker by tell-tale torpedo tracks ... I had only seen one plume of water, so I thought she would be fairly safe, as battleships can stand more than one torpedo and reach port with ease. I could not watch her myself, for I was searching for tracks to starboard as we raced toward her. Then, to my amazement, I heard someone say 'God, she's going!' I took a quick look at her and she was listing heavily ...

It was an agony not to watch her every second, but I still kept my eyes glued to starboard ... Suddenly she started heeling over quickly, but before she had gone far she was rent by a colossal explosion, and completely disappeared in a vast puff of smoke, which reared its head a thousand feet into the air like a cobra ready to strike.[6]

HMS *Barham* had been struck a fatal blow and capsized, within minutes the hull exploding, an event captured on film and which has become one of the iconic images of the war at sea. Although Vice Admiral Pridham-Wippell and 450 others had been rescued, some fifty-five officers, including Captain G C Cooke, and 806 men perished.

The impact of the U-boats in the Mediterranean was heavy. The *Ark Royal* was gone. A fortnight later the *Barham* was struck by three torpedoes and capsized in as many minutes with the loss of over 500 men ... On the night of December

18 an Italian submarine approached Alexandria and launched three 'human torpedoes' ... They fixed time bombs, which detonated early on the morning of the 19th under the battleships *Queen Elizabeth* and *Valiant* [and the destroyer HMS *Jervis*]. Both ships were heavily damaged and became a useless burden for months. Thus in the course of a few weeks the whole of our eastern battle fleet was eliminated as a fighting force.[7]

Nor was that to be the end of the Royal Navy's disastrous few months. The day after *Barham* had been sunk, the Australian sloop HMAS *Parramatta* was escorting the heavily-laden ammunition ship *Hanne* to Tobruk, accompanied by the escort destroyer HMS *Avon Vale*. At about midnight the three ships were about 25 miles north of Bardia off the Libyan coast. It was pitch dark and raining with a heavy surging sea running, the steamer *Hanne*'s master confused as to her route into Tobruk. Lieutenant Commander Jefferson H Walker closed to hail from the *Parramatta* by megaphone. Within half an hour the two ships were steaming slowly at about three knots, running parellel to each other. All the while the three ships were being followed by *U-559* whose watch had sighted them silhouetted to the north east of their pitching conning tower in a flash of lightning. Heidtmann slowly followed and at 00.12 fired three torpedoes at a range of 2,200 metres, his target noted in the boat's War Diary as a 'merchant ship behind which a small vessel was visible.' All three torpedoes missed.

Disappointed, Heidtmann ordered tubes reloaded and closed the target as it neared Tobruk. Finally at 00.46 he fired his last loaded torpedo at a range of 1,500 metres, hitting HMAS *Parramatta* squarely amidships. There were two almost simultaneous explosions, the second probably in the magazine and the sloop was torn open, all lighting failing. Walker immediately ordered her abandoned as she rolled almost straight away to starboard and sank. Only twenty-one survivors were rescued by HMS *Avon Vale*, a further three managing to swim to the Libyan coast where they were rescued by advancing British troops. One hundred and thirty-eight men, including all the officers, were killed.

Further Royal Navy casualties were the 515-ton patrol yacht HMS *Rosabelle*, torpedoed and sunk by Oblt.z.S. Unno von Fischel's *U-374* in the same attack in which he destroyed the anti-submarine trawler HMT *Lady Shirley* south of Gibraltar immediately after passing through the narrows into the Mediterranean from Brest. On 14 December the cruiser HMS *Galatea* was torpedoed and sank almost immediately off Alexandria after being hit by *U-557*, the Italian submarine *Dagabur* having missed her the previous day.

Captain E W B Sim's HMS *Galatea* was operating as part of the 15th Cruiser Squadron, Force B, returning to Alexandria from an unsuccessful search for Italian convoys bound for Benghazi. On the night of its destruction the cruiser had already undergone seven hours of dive-bomber attacks when *U-557* hit her on the port side with three torpedoes in quick succession. The cruiser turned over and sank in three minutes, Captain Sim, twenty-two officers and 447 ratings were killed in the attack, the destroyers HMS *Griffin* and *Hotspur* rescuing only 100 survivors. Aboard the *Galatea* that night were two war correspondents, one of whom, Larry Allen, survived the attack and filed an eyewitness account that was published in the newspaper the *News of the World*.

It was at midnight, after having beaten off dive-bombing attacks for more than seven hours while patrolling with a squadron of cruisers and destroyers off Cyrenaica that *Galatea's* loudspeaker ordered gunners to stand-by. A young Marine roused me from sleep in the captain's cabin. I ran to the commander's cabin and informed Reuter's correspondent Mr. Alexander Massy Anderson. Adjusting lifebelts, we raced towards the bridge.

We had hardly started to run when the first torpedo clanged into the ship with a burst of flame, rocking the cruiser. Torpedoes seemed to chase us along the deck. A second projectile crashed through amidships. A third struck forward just under a six-inch gun turret. The cruiser listed quickly, and the whole ship shuddered. I knew it was too late to reach the bridge, so dashed behind a six-inch gun turret forward over the starboard side quarter-deck as the entire ship dipped deeply into the sea on the port side.

I caught hold of the starboard deck rail as the cruiser rapidly turned on her port side, unscrewed the nozzle of the lifebelt hung around my neck, and blew into it with all the breath I could summon.

The cruiser flopped completely over to port, sending me sliding down into the sea. Hundreds of officers and ratings poured into the water. I heard Anderson at the rails shout something to a ship's officer. I never saw him again.

Knowing I could not swim, and fearful lest the old lifebelt I retrieved after the bombing of HMS *Illustrious* on January 10 would collapse, my body slipped deep under the water with scores of others as the cruiser, with a tremendous suction, disappeared in a huge lake of oil. I feared, too, that the torpedoes' fire might have reached *Galatea's* magazine, and that the explosion would blow us all to bits, but there was only a muffled blast as she took the death plunge.

I felt I must have swallowed gallons of oily scum and water before I bobbed to the surface and tried to float, holding my lifebelt high close to my chest. Around me there were hundreds of bobbing heads ... A sailor helped me clamber aboard the boat, but a score of others had the same idea. Her rear section rapidly filled with water and was pushed down by the weight of a dozen more bodies. I struggled forward to the starboard side. Several sailors followed me. The boat dipped and suddenly turned over.

Again I went under, then, groping blindly, grasped the wheel of a motor launch and pulled myself into the front cockpit. Then the launch sank. A lone sailor and myself hung on the tip-most point of the bow until she slipped beneath the waves.

Desperately I tried and succeeded in getting hold of a small floating spar. I tucked it under my left arm and joined scores of others in cries for help in the pitch darkness, hoping to attract the attention of the destroyers. But no one had a torch. At that moment I saw a huge black silhouette of a destroyer about 75 yards ahead. 'Help, I am drowning', I heard a sailor in the water near me cry. 'Keep going' I gasped. 'Look, there's a destroyer ahead.' That seemed to give him a new burst of energy. He swam towards it. I tried hard, but could not get an inch closer.

A big wave swamped me again with a mouthful of oil. Then, almost miraculously, there was a wave from behind that carried me almost directly under the propeller of the destroyer *Griffin*. I shouted for help until I felt all the glands of my throat burn. Suddenly a long oily rope was flung over the destroyer's side. I grasped it, but there was no strength left in my hands.

'Hang on' a ship's officer shouted. 'We will pull you up.' 'I can't', I answered, as the rope slipped through my fingers ... Then a young British sailor ... saved my life. He passed a heavy rope under my armpits, tied it around my neck, and flung the end to the quarter-deck of the destroyer. Three others slowly pulled me out of the oily mess and flopped me aboard like a wet fish.[8]

U-557 withdrew and Kaptlt. Paulshen radioed his success to Rome before beginning his return journey to Salamis. Ironically, it was to be a short-lived victory and an accident accounted for *U-557*, the result of what would now be termed 'friendly fire'. On the night of 16 December, two days after the successfully sinking of HMS *Galatea*, the U-boat was sighted by the Italian torpedo boat *Orione* south of Crete while escorting a fuel transport from Suda Bay to North Africa. The *Orione* immediately turned to ram the misidentified submarine and destroyed *U-557* along with her entire crew.

In the Far East Japanese forces would soon sink two unescorted capital ships – the battleship HMS *Prince of Wales* and the battlecruiser HMS *Repulse* – while in December almost simultaneously with the Alexandria debacle the cruiser HMS *Neptune* of the Malta-based Force K and the destroyer HMS *Kandahar* were sunk and the cruisers HMS *Aurora* and *Penelope* damaged by the same minefield after unsuccessfully trying to intercept an Italian convoy headed from Naples to Tripoli with supplies for Rommel's *Afrika Korps*.

During the final month of 1941 the newly deployed U-boats could at least count these major victories against the Royal Navy to their credit, despite the comparative lack of success against merchant traffic. Indeed, while by the end of 1941 U-boats had only accounted for a confirmed twelve merchant ships totalling 40,684 tons, the Royal Navy's Mediterranean force had been emasculated. In Alexandria Cunningham was left with three light cruisers and a few destroyers still functional, while in Gibraltar Force H had been reduced by damage, loss and withdrawals to other regions so that only an old battleship, one obsolete carrier and a cruiser remained. On land Rommel had been forced to retreat, but the Eighth Army had exhausted itself as well as their German opponent and halted at the beginning of 1942 on the line between Cyrenaica and Tripolitania where it had been a year previously. War with Japan had added further strain to a stretched Royal Navy. Conversely, on 11 December Germany and Italy declared war on the United States, unleashing the strongest industrial might of the western Allies against them. Three days before Hitler's blustering declaration of war against the United States, at 12.00 on 8 December, K.A. Weichold's Rome-based *Marinekommando Italian* assumed command of U-boat operations in the Mediterranean, Victor Oehrn began keeping the FdU Italian War Diary.

At sea during those same turbulent days *U-568* was preparing to slip through the Straits of Gibraltar. As Kaptlt. Joachim Preuss sailed *U-568* toward the Straits on 7 December he was informed by radio while west of Lisbon that from midday the following day his boat would pass into the hands of FdU Italian, a radio message also informing him of the Japanese attack on Pearl Harbor. However, it was not until the early hours of 9 December that *U-568* was on its actual approach to the perilous narrow passage into the Mediterranean.

9.12.41. 08.44: Submerged. Intention: to run underwater by day during the eastward transit, and surface at twilight so that by moonrise Gibraltar would have been passed, within 24 hours.

10.51. Surfaced to ventilate boat. To the west a watcher [*Bewacher* – guard ship] sighted, estimated 8,000 metre range. Dived again. We can hear two watchers searching the area, they stop temporarily and listen. Can't see anything in the periscope.

19.54. CG9493. Surfaced. Dived again, the watcher approaching from the east and lights of a boat visible to the west.

20.18. Surfaced.

24.00. CG9593. In the Straits of Gibraltar, two watchers sighted near Tarifa travelling under the lee of the coastline so our boat travels between the guards and very bright searchlights. Conditions especially unfavourable by Tarifa, so we must get past.

10.12.41. 00.18. Between Tarifa and Europa Point. Dived as a watcher was approaching at high speed from the east. Passed the boat closely to starboard, stopped temporarily nearby.

00.30. Surfaced. The watcher turned by Tarifa sailed back along the Spanish coast to the east. Therfore adjust our course toward the southeast more over to the African side. In line with the central Europe Point six to eight regular bright lights can be seen ... I'm not sure if they are fishing boats so I dive.

01.14. Creeping towards the east. Three vessels above, each of them we can get a fix on, make listening searches, temporarily stop and start, and throw 'firecrackers' [? depth charges] about. Boat running well between 30 metres and a maximum of 50 metres depth, the water layers reflecting the sonar well, sometimes breaking the waves entirely (especially when the motor is stopped).

04.12. CG9649. Surfaced. Alarmed by a motorboat (minesweeper silhouette) at 3000 metres running at very high speed. On the eastern horizon the moonlight is very bright, so I dived quickly and carried on underwater.

05.48. Surfaced.

08.00. CG9667 ... Sea state 1, clear. Nothing in sight.

10.40. Aircraft to port. Alarm. Flew to the east.

12.04. Alarm from two-motor land-based aircraft. Believed to be Bristol Blenheim. Dived.

Preuss and his weary crew had successfully passed into the Mediterranean.

While the ordeal of such men continued at sea, Victor Oehrn noted the dispositions of what were now twenty U-boats under his responsibility.

Eastern Mediterranean: *U-431*, *U-565*, *U-562* and *U-557*.

Western Mediterranean: *U-372*, and *U-453*.

Proceeding to the eastern Mediterranean: *U-208*, *U-568*, *U-374*, *U-573* and *U-652*.

Proceeding to western Mediterranean: *U-375*.

Returning to Spezia: *U-81* and *U-205*.

Attached for special operations to Admiral Aegean (interception of Soviet tankers): *U-371*.

In Salamis: *U-75*, *U-79*, *U-97*, *U-331* and *U-559*.

None in Spezia.

Expected from Atlantic in near future: *U-74*, *U-77*, *U-432* and *U-569*.[9]

Three boats had been lost – *U-95*, *U-208* and *U-451* – and several damaged trying to pass Gibraltar and forced to abort (*U-202*, *U-71* and *U-563*), leaving twenty listed as active in the Mediterranean, as opposed to only five active in the Atlantic on 15 December. Those boats that were operating within the eastern Mediterranean were to remain under the tactical control of the 23rd U-flotilla as the communications that would allow direct command of the U-boats from Rome were not yet in place. The western Mediterranean boats on the other hand were to be tactically controlled from Rome, assisted by use of the large radio transmitters that BdU had established in western France. In turn, new regulations were introduced so that all *Luftwaffe* reconnaissance reports transmitted on various wavelengths were to be repeated by a central station on a single wavelength, monitored by the FdU in Rome.

Of immediate concern to Dönitz were the dangers posed by the Gibraltar passage and the dearth of U-boats in the Atlantic.

> In considering the present U-boat situation in the Mediterranean and the intended further increase in numbers of U-boats there, it must be clearly seen that most of the experienced U-boat Commanders and crews of German U-boats are in the Mediterranean, or must proceed thence. Regarding passage through the Straits of Gibraltar the following are my views:
>
> 1) Passage through the Straits of Gibraltar has become more difficult following the sinking of the *Ark Royal* owing to increased patrol lines and particularly to air patrol, which extends far to the east and west and also goes out at night. In view of the latter, surface passage is made more difficult owing to the distance to be covered; when there is a full moon, passage submerged and on the surface has become impossible.
>
> 19 boats have passed Gibraltar, 11 of these after the sinking of the *Ark Royal*. Three boats were lost in passage, three were damaged by aircraft bombs and had to return to western France.
>
> 2) Passage through the Straits of Gibraltar to the west is considerably more difficult since it is against the current. When, after completion of operations in the Mediterranean, most of the U-boats will return into the Atlantic, considerably stronger patrols off Gibraltar are probable. Extensive losses will probably result.
>
> 3) Operations by U-boats in the Mediterranean are at the moment absolutely necessary. However, there is danger that the U-boats may become trapped there one day and excluded from the battle of the Atlantic. A solution of this question must, however, be held up pending further developments.[10]

It was not only Dönitz who regretted the loss of such veteran boats to the Mediterranean when they were sorely needed in the Atlantic. *Korvetten-kapitän* Hans Cohausz, commander of Brest's U-boat flotilla, noted in his War Diary after the departure of *U-79*, *U-81*, *U-331*, *U-372*, *U-374*, *U-557* and *U-559* – and the aborted attempt by *U-202* after damage *en route* – from his control to La Spezia: 'Eight veteran boats out of nine are now in the Mediterranean flotilla.'[11]

Of more immediate concern to Oehrn in Rome was the lack of space in the designated Mediterranean ports for what he expected would be the number of U-boats that would soon be operational in the region. Allowing for one boat being at sea for every one in port, there was space for between sixteen and twenty boats. Salamis could handle four boats in its dockyard simultaneously, La Spezia between four and six. On 29 November

OKM/SKL had issued a directive that permanent occupation of attack areas in and around the Mediterranean would comprise ten boats in the eastern half of the sea, and fifteen boats to east and west of Gibraltar in a ratio of eight to seven. Thus there would be eighteen U-boats on permanent station in the Mediterranean. Using Oehrn's shipyard-versus-operational ratio this entailed a total deployment of thirty-six U-boats, with a shortfall of places for eight already present. The decision was taken to reinforce the 23rd U-Flotilla with *U-206*, *U-71* and *U-562* while the *Steuben* Group would join the already deployed five boats west of Gibraltar, increasing the pressure in the western Mediterranean by the 29th U-Flotilla.

The *Kriegsmarine* desired that rather than drastically increasing the number of bases available, they should have fewer that were run more efficiently. One in the Adriatic was also strongly desired, possibly at Monfalcone or Trieste. Initial plans to utilise Brindisi and Naples were to be investigated but these were dismissed relatively quickly as being too vulnerable to enemy air attack.

Nonetheless, *Admiral* Ernst Kratzenberg, of SKL's *Amtsgruppe Ubootswesen Bauabteilung* (U-boat Construction Office) (SKL U II) headed a German commission despatched by SKL to inspect the possibilities of new bases in all the ports named above. Brindisi was found to be capable of dealing with one or two boats at its current condition, though repair facilities were 'slight'. Naples on the other hand could deal with four boats. Docking conditions were, however, described by Kratzenberg as 'difficult' whenever the number of boats to be accommodated numbered more than two. There would also be no facilities for the storage of electric torpedoes for at least another four to five weeks. He suggested that Naples be considered solely as a last resort.

By 18 December FdU Italian had accepted Kratzenberg's findings. Brindisi was agreed as being out of the question, along with Naples, which had become the main port for Italian submarines. La Spezia had facilities for five boats, expanded to six if 110 Italian specialist workers could be supplied to the *Kriegsmarine*. In addition the OTO (Italian dockyard) Muggiano had been found to have immediate facility for dealing with a single boat, though diesel repairs were suspected to be beyond the yard's capabilities. Three more boats could be handled there if a further 350 Italian workers could be provided. In the Adriatic, the *Scolio Olivio* dockyard at Pola had immediate capacity for two boats. After the installation of machine tools that had been requested from Germany and the conscription of 100 specialised workers, it was felt that six boats could be handled at once, providing that help could be given by the *Cantiero Riuniti dell Adriatico* dockyard at Monfalcone. The existing submarine barracks at Pola would need to be emptied in order to house the *Kriegsmarine* personnel.

Amidst this period of expansion, relations between the *Regia Marina* and the *Kriegsmarine* were at a high point. The Italians had requested that responsibility and immediate command of dockyard work within its ports remain completely under their own control, with the exceptions of torpedo, fire control and gunnery workshops. The German construction commissions were to remain purely advisory and a technical liaison staff with skilled translators was appointed to deal with matters between U-Flotillas and the Italians. The Germans readily agreed and work at expanding the capabilities of Italian-controlled yards was immediately underway and soon progressed faster than the *Kriegsmarine* had expected.

At sea agreement was also easily reached. The areas designated for German U-boat operations were 23° 30' E to 31° E south of 33° in the eastern Mediterranean and west of 3° E for the western Mediterranean. However, Italian plans to bring back several of their boats stationed in Bordeaux were strongly opposed by the *Kriegsmarine* as they considered the overcrowded dockyards already insufficient and rightly feared that Italian priorities would be focussed away from the *Kriegsmarine* boats. As events transpired, the Italian boats stayed out of the Mediterranean.

In Rome on 11 December, FdU Italian had prepared to protect two large Italian convoys from Italy to Tripoli and Benghazi by once more targeting the main British naval threat. They had sailed on 13 December and were protected by the main force of the Italian fleet. As the supply ships put to sea U-boats were ordered to congregate off Alexandria to attack the enemy 'from [grid-reference] CP7522'. With FdU in tactical command the U-boat operation was code-named '*Afrika*', the captains being briefed to attack the enemy as they entered or left Alexandria, only being permitted to attack warships of cruiser size and above – with the exception of large destroyers if the firing conditions were extremely favourable – or merchant ships of 4,000 tons or over, unless seen to be especially valuable targets. *U-75*, *U-77*, *U-79*, *U-133*, *U-371*, *U-374* and *U-568* were all ordered into position to hunt for targets.

Tension with Spain had briefly flared during December after Kaptlt. Egon Reiner von Schlippenbach sank the Spanish motor tanker MT *Badalona* off Motril in Southern Spain. After passing through the Straits of Gibraltar on the night of 8 December, *U-453* had lingered south of the Spanish mainland in search of targets. During early evening on 13 December von Schlippenbach's watch had sighted the 4,202-ton tanker, which they signalled to stop and prepare to show papers. The Spaniard attempted to flee, radio signals being picked up from the panicking merchant. A warning shot across the bow brought the ship to a halt after which a small German search party boarded the vessel. Despite the ship proving itself neutral, von Schlippenbach opted to sink the ship by torpedo due to its failure to stop and its repeated signals to what was assumed to be the British forces at Gibraltar. Upon reaching La Spezia, the young commander was berated by Oehrn for his decision to sink a ship from a country that was both friendly to Germany and provided covert in-harbour refuelling for U-boats, though no disciplinary action resulted.

At the end of 1941 Dönitz was preparing to order six more boats into the Mediterranean as ordered by OKM. After the next full-moon period, *U-83, U-451, U-202, U-573, U-133* and *U-577* were all to pass the Straits of Gibraltar, followed by a planned further five boats at the full-moon period in the middle of January and four more the following month. But Dönitz continued to oppose the redeployment of his men and was able to use current statistics to help his case, as he recorded within his War Diary on 30 December:

My views regarding further operations in the Mediterranean and the distribution of boats which become available, have been forwarded to Naval Staff as follows:

1) In Naval War Staff letter, Secret 2024, orders were given for operations simultaneously by ten U-boats in the eastern Mediterranean and 15 west and east of the Straits of Gibraltar, divided approximately into half. This entails sending about 34 boats into the Mediterranean.

2) At present there are 23 U-boats in the Mediterranean. Therefore, 11 more must be sent into the Mediterranean. This number is higher than that given in letter BdU Ref. No. 2047 Group Command, Secret, to make good any losses sustained.

3) Up to now passage through the Straits of Gibraltar, after sinking of the *Ark Royal* has cost 33% losses. From 24 U-boats which were sent into the Mediterranean after the sinking of the *Ark Royal,* four were lost in the Straits of Gibraltar, four (*U-71, U-96, U-558* and *U-563*) turned back owing to bomb damage and only 16 got through into the Mediterranean. The transfer of 11 further boats into the Mediterranean, therefore, entails sending 17 U-boats for this purpose, since five or six U-boats must be expected to be lost or damaged in the passage through the Straits.

4) The simultaneous operation, as ordered, by seven U-boats west of the Straits of Gibraltar also entails about ten U-boats being available for this purpose since even in the new moon period loss must be expected in this very heavily patrolled area.

5) It should, therefore, be investigated whether the value of operations in the Mediterranean and off Gibraltar and prospects of successes by U-boats outweigh those high losses.

   a) Operations by U-boats in the eastern Mediterranean have up to now had an adverse effect on the African campaign. If we succeed in putting out of action in that area a large ship our own transport facilities to Africa will be considerably improved. Up to now anti-U-boat activity has been very weak in this area but, on the other hand, enemy traffic has been heavy. Therefore, U-boat operations in the eastern Mediterranean are justified. There are chances of success and losses up to now have been slight.

b) In the area west and east of Gibraltar there are strong defence forces. Aircraft, even by night, at full moon. Enemy traffic to the east up to now slight. During the passage of the military transports or targets suspected by the Naval War Staff, for the attacks on which boats have been disposed in the Gibraltar area, particularly heavy escorts are certain. Prospects of success, therefore, are slight and very difficult. Attacks can only be made with heavy losses.

6) BdU is, therefore, of opinion that operations simultaneously by as large a number as 15 boats, as ordered, in the Gibraltar area are not economical. BdU considers ... disposition of about two to three boats east and west of the Straits of Gibraltar for patrol, with sweeps to the Straits if necessary, to be justified.

7) He proposes, therefore:

a) Sending of two to three further U-boats into the Mediterranean. Therefore, sending of U-boats into the Mediterranean temporarily concluded. BdU does not reckon on return of these boats into the Atlantic in the near future

b) Disposition simultaneously of only three boats west of Gibraltar.

8) The proposal under 7) will also have a good effect on the resumption of the conduct of the war in the Atlantic. For this reason also BdU considers that forces should not be kept in the Gibraltar area if this is not economical and larger numbers should not be sent into the Mediterranean than absolutely necessary, since this means that the best U-boat Commanders and crews are no longer to be reckoned with for the Battle of the Atlantic.[12]

In fact only three boats had actually been lost before or during attempts to enter the Mediterranean. *U-204* was depth-charged by the sloop HMS *Rochester* and the corvette HMS *Mallow* within the Straits and sunk with all hands on 19 October. The U-boat had taken successful part in the 'Breslau' group lying in wait for convoy HG75 from Gibraltar, scheduled to attempt the passage of the Straits of Gibraltar soon after the operations ceased. After the sinking the British tanker MV *Inverlee* on 19 October, the two Royal Navy ships hunted and found their quarry. Another member of this trio was *U-208*, located and sunk by the destroyers HMS *Harvester* and *Hesperus* off Gibraltar on 7 December, a day after received radioed instructions from Dönitz to proceed through the Straits and onward to the eastern Mediterranean. Finally, on 21 December, Kaptlt. Eberhard Hoffman's *U-451* was attacked and sunk by depth charges from a Swordfish of 812 Squadron FAA south-southwest of Cape Spartel while approaching Gibraltar. SubLt. P Wilkinson's Swordfish 'A' was based aboard the old carrier HMS *Audacity*, operating to the west of Gibraltar. A single survivor, IWO Oblt.z.S. Walter Kohler, was later rescued and taken prisoner.

Coupled with these losses, a further five boats had been sunk in the Mediterranean. The first was *U-433*, depth charged near Málaga, brought to the surface and sunk with gunfire from the corvette HMS *Marigold*, leaving thirty-eight survivors including the commander Oblt.z.S. Hans Ey to be taken prisoner on 16 November, one day after successfully passing through the Straits. *U-95* was also sunk not long after successfully entering the Mediterranean. Sailing off Cabo Sacratif, Spain, at a little past midnight on 28 November, the U-boat was spotted on the surface by the Dutch submarine *O21* and sunk by torpedo. Jan Biesemaat, a rating aboard *O21*, recalled the attack:

On the afternoon of 27 November we were ahead of our sailing schedule and, in order to stay within the territory, we needed to dive at around 3 o'clock. We surfaced again after dark and continued our course, zigzagging at a speed of 15 knots.

The watch was changed at midnight ... I was on the forward watch. This means that you search a sector of 180 degrees together with the officer from the watch who is also responsible for the two look-outs who keep an eye on the aft side ... There were a few wisps of clouds here and there; it looked as if the water were blending with the night air. Mr Kroeze, the Second Officer, had eagle eyes. He always saw everything; it was incredible.

Mr Kroeze suddenly says to me, 'Bies, three rings ...!' So I ring the bell in the tower hatch three times, which means alarm and that the commander must report to the bridge and the head of the engine room to the engine room. The captain comes rushing in and asks Kroeze what's going on. 'I see a silhouette directly ahead', he says. We look but no one can see what it was. You could only see a bow wave. I couldn't look because I was on the forward watch. We were close to the Spanish coast and lights were twinkling everywhere. It was possible that there were more enemy ships in the area. You never knew.

And then the commander says, 'Both engines slow'. We were moving quickly at the time. And naturally the bow wave was approaching quickly. 'I think it's a submarine', says Kroeze. Suddenly a blue light flickers behind us. Someone was signalling with a covered light. The light flickers again as our English signalman/telegraphist Rees climbs the stairs. Rees doesn't recognise the code. We then know for sure that we're dealing with a German submarine. The commander ordered full speed ahead, because you shouldn't let such a boat get too close or it will fire. We had used up almost all our torpedoes during the patrol. We didn't have a single torpedo left at forward and not one shell left for the deck gun. Only two torpedoes left in the aft tubes, no more. The commander gives the order to 'reverse' and then 'stop the engines'. The submarine approaches us at high speed. Now it is simply a matter of which one of us is going to be the first to fire; after all, we're lined up opposite one another. The commander is on the bridge casing because he doesn't have any more direction indicators, not a damn thing.

The commander aims with his thumb over the bridge casing. 'Fire! he cries. The torpedo is launched in the direction of the submarine. By the way, I only know this by word of mouth because naturally I had to keep an eye on the situation ahead.

Because the weather was good and there was a full moon, the U-boat must have seen the torpedo coming because it turned to port. This probably deflected the torpedo, which didn't explode. As the U-boat turns away, we turn with it. The commander is still on the casing of the bridge and the chief officer, while looking over his thumb across the stern, cries, 'Fire!' Our second torpedo hits the U-boat precisely behind the tower. In its death throes the U-boat sticks straight up into the air. And then disappears into the depths ... You could instantly smell cordite.

We were nearby when we heard cries for help in three or four different languages. The commander had already fished 22 Italians out of the water, so he says, 'We should get them out'. We see the Germans swimming and holding onto each other. One of them is unconscious and is being held above water by the others. He's the helmsman who was blown off the bridge. Because I'm small, I'm able to sit on the braces of the protective cover of the hydroplanes. You're then sitting a little bit above the water. In that way I was able to grab a guy by the wrist and pull him up, after which he was handed over to someone sitting on the hydroplanes. Our engines were stopped at this time. Fuel oil was floating on the water everywhere and there was this awful cordite smell. A truly disgusting stench! So we pull up the Germans ... The German survivors of the U-boat were locked up in the aft torpedo room of the *O21* after being given dry overalls. Twelve Germans were fished out of the water by the *O21*, among them the submarine ace Gerd Schreiber as well as a war correspondent who was present on the bridge in order to record the glorious moment of the annihilation of an Allied ship on film. It's all in the game![13]

It transpired that Schreiber was beaten to the launch of his torpedo by seconds, the large number of survivors being due to the watch still being on the conning tower and the gun crew standing by in case of torpedo failure.

While *U-557* was destroyed by the mistaken attack of the Italian torpedo boat *Orione* on 16 December, the last two losses were suffered during the attacks against convoy traffic running the gauntlet between Alexandria and Tobruk. Both *U-75* and *U-79* had been among the '*Afrika*' group. *Kapitänleutnant* Helmuth Ringelmann's *U-75* was one of the few to report some success after attacking three ships east-northeast of Sidi

Barrani on 28 December. Two of the three ships were estimated at 4,000 tons and 5,000 tons respectively, the third unknown. In fact Ringelmann hit and sank the British steamer SS *Volo*, a 1,587-ton merchant. The remaining two claimed victories remain unconfirmed. Shortly after this attack, destroyer HMS *Kipling* located and depth-charged *U-75* to the surface, thirty of the crew managing to escape and be captured while the remaining fourteen, including Ringelmann, were lost with their boat.

U-79 was found while attempting to attack Convoy AT5 in conjunction with *U-559* and *U-562* on 23 December. Two destroyers of the escort group, HMS *Hasty* and *Hotspur* subjected the boat to a sustained ASDIC hunt and depth charge attacks before Kaptlt. Wolfgang Kaufmann brought his battered boat to the surface and ordered it scuttled. Their attackers rescued all forty-four men aboard, though it was not until March 1942 that BdU was able to release the names of the first thirty POWs from this boat that it had obtained through the International Red Cross. The same day that Kaufmann and his crew were taken prisoner, Oblt.z.S. Eitel-Friedrich Kentrat brought *U-74* into Messina for repairs to the boat's muffler valve. *U-74* had passed through the Straits of Gibraltar on the night of 16 December and headed to the eastern Mediterranean. A fruitless period spent off the coasts of Egypt and Cyrenaica was followed by two days off Malta, before the need for repairs forced Kentrat to break off his patrol.[14]

Kapitänleutnant Heinrich Schonder had also brought a fresh boat, *U-77*, through the Strait on the night of 15/16 December. Unlike Kentrat, however, Schonder claimed one kill for his patrol, the British steamer SS *Empire Barracuda* sunk west of Asilah, Morocco immediately before passing Gibraltar. Once inside the Mediterranean, Schonder found no targets and reached Messina on 19 December. Within two days the boat was at sea once more, Schonder reporting no enemy shipping in Benghazi harbour on Christmas Day.

Kapitänleutnant Heinrich Heinsohn's *U-573* passed through the Gibraltar Strait and into the 29th U-Flotilla on the night of 20 December, the following day announcing his arrival with the torpedoing of the 5,289-ton Norwegian freighter SS *Hellen* near Cape Negro, Morocco. The Norwegian ship had left Gibraltar under escort from the armed trawler HMT *Maida* in ballast during the evening to sail to Melilla and there embark a cargo of iron ore. Approximately four nautical miles from Cape Negro – technically neutral territory – she was hit on the port side by two torpedoes, the ship's Third Mate having seen the tracks of the G7a steam-driven torpedoes, but was unable to react in time. One torpedo exploded between holds number one and two, the second squarely in number two hold. With bulkheads ruptured the freighter began to sink almost immediately by the head, listing to starboard as she went down. As the survivors were taken aboard the trawler, Heinsohn departed, arriving at

Messina on 27 December and transferring on to Pola three days later. It was to be the sole success of his U-boat captaincy.

The last 23rd U-Flotilla boat to dock in 1941 was Kaptlt. Hans-Werner Kraus' *U-83*, which had also entered the Mediterranean during December. After fruitless patrolling off Egypt, Kraus docked at Messina on 23 December. Two days later the boat was at sea once more, but this time was forced to return after suffering heavy damage from depth charge attack after attempting to close a convoy in Grid Square CO5676. The boat arrived at Salamis harbour on 30 December and would not leave for two months as the available dockyard workers struggled to make repairs.

Chapter 4

From West to East

By THE BEGINNING OF 1942, twenty-one U-boats were stationed in the Mediterranean. In total five had been lost thus far. On 1 January 1942 *U-652* put into La Spezia, home of the 29th U-Flotilla. *Oberleutnant zur See* Georg-Werner Fraatz's boat had been on attachment to the Admiral Aegean for the interception of Soviet merchant traffic headed through the Dardenelles. Fraatz and his men had already completed one patrol in the Mediterranean after passing Gibraltar on 28 November 1941, having refuelled from the tanker 'Gata' at Cadiz. A single French steamer, the ss *St Denis*, had been torpedoed and sunk south of Balearen before the boat had docked at Messina on 12 December. Two days later *U-652* had been attached to the Aegean command. At the narrow entrance to the Dardenelles, off the Gallipoli Peninsula, Frattz had torpedoed and sunk the 6,557-ton Soviet tanker MV *Varlaam Avanesov* on 19 December. It was their sole success of the patrol, the boat being relieved by *U-97* that same day and beginning its homeward trek.

Kapitänleutnant Udo Heilmann's *U-97* would likewise not last long at its appointed post. On 8 January Heilmann was ordered by the Admiral Aegean to break off his patrol and head for Salamis due to a crewman falling ill aboard his boat. *U-97* entered Salamis at 10.15 the following day. The boat sailed once more on 12 January in order to regain its station at the entrance to the Black Sea, but the deployment of U-boats off the Dardenelles was finally cancelled by SKL on 29 January and Heilmann once more headed south to his Greek base.

Oehrn's earlier expectation that thirty-six boats would soon be available for service in the Mediterranean was proved false in the first few days of 1942. Dönitz confirmed the final number of boats to be committed to the area as an absolute maximum of twenty-five. The BdU had finally managed to successfully persuade OKM that his already slender strength was needed more in the Atlantic rather than acting in support of the *Afrika Korps*.

In connection with further operations in the Mediterranean, High Command ordered the following on 29 December along the lines of my request (secret order 2220):

1) To send only two to three more boats to the Mediterranean. Therewith further commitments in the Mediterranean are finished.

2) Prime area of the Mediterranean is the east. Only two to three boats are to operate in the west.

3) Three boats are committed to the area west of Gibraltar. Commitment of boats around Azores still in effect.

With this decree the end of further commitments in the Mediterranean and corresponding increase of Atlantic activity gives evidence that the situation has become more practical.

The renewal of the U-boat war in the Atlantic will have to be considered on the following points:

a. The number of combat boats, which are to carry the load, is smaller than before the Atlantic battle. Before the beginning of the Mediterranean campaign the number of combat boats was 73. Today, without the 25 boats in the Mediterranean and perhaps 2 more, the figure today is 65, of which three are in the rich area west of Gibraltar.[1]

The first days of January 1942 found the *Afrika Korps* once more struggling against the Allied advance in 'Crusader'. Rommel had been forced to retreat from Gazala in Libya, British forces relieving the trapped garrison at Tobruk on 10 December and recapturing Benghazi on Christmas Eve 1941. The last day of 1941 found the battered *Afrika Korps* at El Agheila, the point from where Rommel first launched his attack. On 2 January British and Commonwealth troops took Bardia on the Gulf of Sollum, capturing 8,000 German and Italian prisoners, so U-boats and *Luftwaffe* units were ordered not to attack any ships under 6,000 tons on an easterly course east of Bardia in case they were carrying Axis POWs.

The deployment of the 'Afrika' group off Alexandria ended at midnight on 5 January, Oehrn recording no success at all and continuing to plot the presumed positions of *U-75* and *U-79*, which were causing concern due to their failure to answer signals. The five surviving 'Afrika' boats – plus the two that had been sunk – were ordered to redeploy to the west, lying in a rough diagonal line stretching to the northeast from Sidi Barrani. *U-331* was ordered to the sea area off Ras Aamer to hunt supply convoys bound for the port of Benghazi.

On 15 January *Luftwaffe* recconnaissance reports reached FdU Italian of a large Allied convoy moving west from Alexandria. To augment the boats already ranged against it *U-205*, *U-133* and *U-577* were ordered to form a patrol line parallel to the North African coast, each boat to be stationed approximately 60 miles from the other. Unbeknown to the Mediterranean

U-boat command, *U-577* had already been destroyed by this time. *Kapitän-leutnant* Herbert Schauenburg's boat, which had passed the into the Mediterranean on the night of 22 December 1941, had been attacked by Sunderland 'X' of 230 Squadron RAF northwest of Mersa Matruh and sunk with all hands.

Only hours after the redeployment order was received by the two remaining boats concerned, a little before midnight, Reschke's lookouts sighted the convoy and he attacked, joined by Kaptlt. Hermann Hesse's *U-133*. Both boats claimed success, *U-205* reporting two hits two seconds apart on an unknown steamer, *U-133* claiming a probable hit on a destroyer as well as two premature detonations from a full four-torpedo bow salvo. Allied records fail to confirm these claims. However, there was no dispute over an attack made by *U-133* against Convoy MF3 early on the morning of 17 January. Southeast of his previous attack, Hesse sighted and torpedoed the destroyer HMS *Gurkha*. It was the second British destroyer lost to U-boats in January – HMS *Kimberley* had been hit and sunk by Schonder's 'Afrika' boat *U-77* five days previously, reported to FdU as the sinking of a *Jervis* class destroyer, her 'stern torn off' by the attack. Schonder had almost immediately come under attack by two Allied aircraft patrolling off Tobruk, though *U-77* escaped unscathed.

But it was not only the Royal Navy that suffered in the early days of 1942. A second U-boat was also lost in January 1942. *Oberleutnant zur See* Unno von Fischel's *U-374* was sighted on 12 January by lookouts on the Malta-based submarine HMS *Unbeaten* east of Catania, Sicily. A pair of bow torpedoes hit the U-boat and destroyed her, a single survivor being rescued by the British submarine as it nosed through the scattered wreckage and oil slick.

The remainder of January yielded little for the U-boats. On the evening of 29 January Dommes aboard *U-431* hit an unidentified British patrol yacht, estimated at 1,000 tons, with a single torpedo. It was in fact the 331-ton minesweeping trawler HMT *Sotra*. Dommes himself was on the receiving end of an attack by HMS *Thunderbolt* southwest of Crete on 6 February. The British submarine missed with both torpedoes and gunfire, before Dommes managed to escape. Two nights after the sinking of HMT *Sotra* Könenkamp's *U-375* hit another unidentified warship, this time a destroyer, though the hit reverberated through the water as only a dull thud – the torpedo failing to explode.

During January, the confirmation of the reduced number of boats to be deployed in the Mediterranean forced a rethink about the required shipyard capacities that had plagued Oehrn through his tenure thus far. Work in the Italian and Greek harbours was sluggish in comparison to elsewhere, later rated officially as '10 to 15% slower' than German shipyards. However, the actual enlargement of the La Spezia and Salamis

U-boat installations had taken place at a far greater pace than expected due to superlative work by the Italian labourers and excellent cooperation between the *Regia Marina* and the *Kriegsmarine*. With the number of boats now set at twenty-five, there was considered to be sufficient dockyard space already and a third base was no longer necessary. However, FdU Italian proposed moving the Salamis base to Pola in the Adriatic. Though Salamis provided shorter sailing times to operational areas within the eastern Mediterranean, Pola was felt to be safer from possible air attack, offer better facilities for personnel and supply traffic as well as allowing closer contact between the flotilla commander and U-boat commanders and crew. Eventually, however, the problems involved in transferring the base were thought to outweigh the potential benefits and the scheme was scrapped.

On 27 January 1942 K.z.S. Leo Karl Kreisch, a former cruiser captain who had commanded both the *Nürnberg* and the *Lützow*, officially took command as FdU Italian, Oehrn being relegated to the role of his senior staff officer. Amongst his first tasks was the co-ordination with the *Luftwaffe's* X *Fliegerkorps* of a twelve-day experiment in combined operations. Three aircraft based in Crete were to fly daily late-afternoon reconnaissance missions solely in support of U-boat operations. All sightings were still routed to the *Fliegerkorps* headquarters in Rome, then onwards to Kreisch and thence to the nearest U-boats at sea. However in the words of a post-war interrogation of von Tiesenhausen: 'He did not think ... that squadrons reporting direct to the Navy would be an improvement as [*sic*] recce information is so contradictory that it must be vetted to get positive results.'[2] The *Luftwaffe* in the Mediterranean was not equipped with contact marker buoys as they were in the Atlantic and so all reports were transmitted using reference to U-boat chart grid squares, but the aircrew navigators were often barely trained or equipped for the precise fixing of coordinates over a vast expanse of water with no visible landmarks.

All available U-boats (except *U-331*) were ordered into the waters off Alexandria and the Suez in an attempt to engage British warships and supply vessels as Dönitz ordered the effort intensified. Thus von Tiesenhausen's *U-331* remained the only boat deployed in the western Mediterranean during this period. On 16 February he rescued the five-man crew of a downed Italian aircraft from the waters off Tobruk, the following evening running aground in soft mud in poor visibility while running at low speed. The U-boat spent nearly nine hours during the night stranded and exposed before able to work free at 06.10 on 18 February after jettisoning several torpedoes to reduce the boat's weight. The relieved captain, crew and their Italian passengers returned to port, docking in La Spezia on 28 February.

February proved to be a dry month for U-boat sinkings. Seven U-boats claimed a total of three ships, one of them a destroyer, hit and sunk out of thirteen attacks logged, but no Allied verification of any of these claims has been found. However, this changed during the following month. On 9 March Admiral of the Fleet Sir Philip Vian led the Royal Navy's 15th Cruiser Squadron – Force B – from Alexandria, comprising the two light cruisers HMS *Cleopatra* and the flagship HMS *Naiad*, accompanied by nine destroyers. The squadron was tasked with rendezvousing with warships bound from Malta and also intercepting an Italian cruiser reported as torpedoed and damaged. Unfortunately for them as they sailed westwards in response to what would ultimately prove to be false intelligence, they sailed within visual range of *U-565* north-north-east of Sidi Barrani during the following day, the boat operating since late January against Allied supply lanes westwards from Alexandria, albeit with no success as yet.

Aboard Oblt.z.S. Jebsen's boat, heading south, the watch led by the IIWO were the first to spot the smoke of the enemy warships. Jebsen was immediately called to the bridge as the distant masts began to take shape on the horizon. The U-boat was on a direct interception course and Jebsen immediately ordered her dived and began planning his attack. Two destroyers were first to come into clear view through the attack periscope as all four bow tubes were readied for underwater firing as the remainder of the enemy squadron became visible, yielding bigger prizes. Despite the target ships zig-zagging, they maintained a general westerly heading and shortly afterward Jebsen fired three torpedoes at the nearest cruiser. The target was the *Dido* class anti-aircraft cruiser HMS *Naiad* that flew Vian's flag. Hit twice, the cruiser sank a little after 20.00. taking eighty-two men with her. Meanwhile Jebsen had taken his boat down to 120 metres and then 180 metres as depth charges were hurled in their direction by the probing destroyers. Ultimately, *U-565* escaped, HMS *Naiad* being the sole success of the patrol that ended six days later in La Spezia and Jebsen's first combat success.

Jebsen had in fact decided to end his patrol, radioing FdU Italian that he was suffering from eye trouble, listed by FdU Italian as 'night-blindness', perhaps exacerbated by the blinding glare of the Mediterranean sun on the water during daylight hours when viewed through a periscope lens. Jebsen's was not the only such medical problem during March 1942, Kaptlt. Franz-Georg Reschke of *U-205* suffering the same condition and aborting his patrol on the last day of the month, while Kaptlt. Heinrich Driver of *U-371* was forced to break off a patrol due to 'eye trouble and exhaustion'.[3]

Conditions were in fact extremely difficult for the Mediterranean boats. Not only did they have clear and often smooth waters to contend with which allowed the enemy – particularly aircraft – to spot them more easily than in the turbid waters of the Atlantic, but the interior of the boats frequently became stiflingly hot, the boats forced to remain deeply submerged for long periods of time. Men often were using breathing equipment as a matter of routine while aboard. Stomach problems were found to be common amongst the German crewmen as they insisted on retaining their heavy German diet in a region where the climate did not favour such food. Aircraft posed frequent problems for U-boats at sea. With the sheer volume of German, Italian and Allied aircraft operating within a relatively small geographical areas U-boats were frequently forced to crash-dive or skulk underwater, the difficulty of identifying friend from foe when at altitude rendering all aircraft a potential threat. Likewise, aircrews were often unable to distinguish between friendly and enemy submarines. Thus, while patrols in the Mediterranean were generally fairly short by comparison with Atlantic boats, they were nerve-wracking in the extreme and a high rotation level was maintained with captains and crews back to Germany and other combat assignments.

Coupled with the problems posed by the Mediterranean waters them-selves, there was also the spectre of enemy offensive minelaying in obvious choke points and counter-mining by their own forces as well as extensive defensive fields. On 14 March *U-133* left Salamis at 17.00 on its second patrol. Hermann Hesse had been replaced as captain while the boat had been in Salamis following its last voyage during which Hesse had passed Gibraltar and sunk HMS *Gurkha*. He had transferred from the command of *U-133* to a staff post and from there to company commander at the 2 ULD training school.[4] His replacement was the 24-year-old Oblt.z.S. Eberhard Mohr, formerly a naval artillery officer until he transferred to the U-boat service in April 1940. Watch Officer aboard *U-111*, Mohr then took command of Type IID training boat *U-148* before transferring to 23rd U-Flotilla and *U-133* during March 1942. At 22.08, a radio message was received at FdU Italian from the Senior Officer of 23rd U-Flotilla: '19.00hrs. *U-133* hit a mine and sank. Scene of accident 1000m from Cape Turlo. Two escort vessels at the scene.'[5] The entire crew of forty-five men died after striking what tragically transpired to be a mine from a defensive field laid by German units.

March also saw three U-boats of 29th U-Flotilla deployed against Convoy MW10 travelling from Alexandria to Malta. Admiral Vian had sailed with four fast supply ships – HMS *Breconshire*, MV *Clan Campbell*, MV *Pampas* and MV *Talabot* – bound for the besieged island carrying mainly ammunition and fuel, escorted by the cruisers HMS *Cleopatra*, *Dido*, *Euryalus* and *Carlisle* plus destroyers, while aircraft patrolled overhead and three submarines provided a screening force to the north. Seven 'Hunt' class escort destroyers sailed from Tobruk to take up the position of ASW 'sweepers' ahead of the convoy's path. Almost immediately they suffered at the hands of Kaptlt. Fraatz's *U-652*, HMS *Heythrop* being torpedoed off Sidi Barrani on the morning of 20 March. The floundering vessel was later sunk by HMS *Eridge*, after which the remaining six destroyers joined the convoy, raising the total of its destroyer escort to sixteen ships.

Meanwhile six German Junkers Ju52 transport aircraft had sighted the convoy while flying en-route to North Africa and reported its position. The *Regia Marina* sent the battleship *Littorio* along with with two heavy and one light cruiser plus twelve destroyers towards Vian's force and what is now called the Second Battle of the Sirte took place off the Gulf of Sirte. Prepared for the Italians' arrival, the Axis forces were kept off the four crucial supply ships with guns, torpedoes and smokescreens.

After four hours, and amidst vicious air attack, the battle was over inconclusively and with no U-boat intervention. *U-73*, *U-205* and *U-431* had all been directed to support Italian submarines and surface forces dispatched to intercept. However, poor visibility and storms rendered the U-boats ineffective and the battered convoy successfully reached the bealeaguered island fortress on 23 March. Ultimately it was a doomed effort, however, as fresh *Luftwaffe* air attacks mounted by Ju 88 and Me 109 aircraft sank sank all four transport ships – two just off the coast and the remainder in Valletta harbour before much of their cargo could be off-loaded, only 5,000 tons of a total 26,000 tons being salvaged. A further casualty was the 'Hunt' class destroyer HMS *Southwold* which struck a mine and sank while assisting the sinking *Breconshire* off the coast of Malta, the destroyer's back being broken by the blast.

While the U-boats had taken no part in the destruction of Convoy MW10, *U-73* had suffered severe damage to its stern and radio gear after being bombed by British aircraft, the boat miraculously limping back to La Spezia surfaced across the breadth of the Mediterranean Sea, docking on 26 March and facing four months of work in the shipyard, again illustrating the much slower pace of work achieved in Mediterranean ports than in Germany or even occupied France.

Fraatz's *U-652* had also repeated its successful sinking of HMS *Heythrop* with the destruction of the 'J' class destroyer HMS *Jaguar* off Sidi Barrani on 26 March in the early hours of the morning. Another detonation was heard aboard the U-boat but Fraatz was unable to confirm if he had the other vessel, a tanker that *Jaguar* was escorting. However, Kaptlt. Reschke's *U-205* was also on the scene and he fired a single torpedo that sank the British oiler SS *Slavol* which HMS *Jaguar* was escorting toward Tobruk nearly three hours after the destroyer had been hit. Fraatz returned to Pola, while Reschke in turn put into Messina on 4 April.

The first U-boat sinking of April was a case of mistaken identity that could have had far more tragic results. On 7 April Kaptlt. Egon Reiner von Schlippenbach's *U-453* sighted a large motor vessel. Immediately diving to firing position, von Schlippenbach attacked with torpedoes a little after midday, hitting the target and damaging the 9,716-ton MV *Somersetshire* almost as the German captain realised his mistake. 'Schlippenbach torpedoed hospital ship – only identified after firing as attacking against the sun. Ship not flying flags.'[6] Fortunately the ship, which was vividly painted in white with large red crosses on the sides and funnel, was not fatally damaged and in fact was carrying no patients at the time. She was returning from repatriating wounded soldiers to South Africa, Australia and New Zealand, destined for more active duty when *U-453* struck. The torpedo hit in the starboard bow and seven people were killed in the blast. The *Somersetshire* began to settle by the head almost immediately and developed such a list that her thirteen usable lifeboats were lowered in order to take off the Royal Army Medical Corps personnel and 114 crewmembers. Indeed Italian forces sighted the ship and reported it sinking off Mersa Matruh. However, before long it became apparent that the ship was not going down and while the sixty-four medical staff that served aboard, as well as two stewardesses, were put aboard a Greek destroyer, the crew reboarded the ship and managed to limp into Alexandria using just the port engine and assisted by tugs the next day.

It was von Schlippenbach's second erroneous attack in his two Mediterranean patrols thus far, but one for which he did not receive a reprimand this time as it was reckoned the sun behind the ship had left only a dark silhouette, hiding the obvious Red Cross livery. Mirroring the sinking of SS *Athenia* by *U-30* at the outbreak of war, Hitler personally approved a proposal by OKM that the sinking be officially denied and von Schlippenbach altered his War Diary accordingly.

During April a new plan of attack in the eastern Mediterranean was devised by Kreisch and Oehrn.[7] Using *U-81*, *U-331*, *U-561* and *U-562*, Operation '*Morgenstern*' (Morning Star) involved the laying of minefields outside British harbours, followed by shore bombardment and the harassing of local transport shipping. The four boats, under Operational Order 4, were scheduled to lay twelve TMB mines off Haifa, eight TMC mines off Beirut, twelve TMBs off Famagusta and twelve TMBs and eight TMCs off Port Said. (TMB mines were designed especially for submarine use, deployed via the torpedo tubes in the same manner as a torpedo although up to three could be loaded into each tube simultaneously. TMC mines were more powerful versions of the same basic design, though with an increased length only two could be carried per tube.) The War Diary of FdU Italian also made specific mention that *U-81* and *U-331* were to be stationed off the formerly Vichy-controlled Syrian ports, now in Allied hands.

Kapitänleutnant Friedrich Guggenberger's *U-81* spearheaded the assault, departing Salamis on 4 April. Since his sinking of HMS *Ark Royal* and subsequent award of the Knight's Cross, Guggenberger had achieved little. A single patrol in February against British supply lines to Tobruk had yielded no successes, despite an attempted attack on a British cruiser at one minute to midnight on 15 February, two torpedoes exploding prematurely. This time *U-81* sailed directly for Haifa where it laid twelve TMB mines at the harbour mouth during the night of 15 April. Sailing north, the following evening Guggenberger sighted and attacked two targets travelling in convoy within three-quarters of an hour of each other. His first was the 1,150-ton French anti-submarine trawler *Viking*, torpedoed ten miles southwest of Beirut, the second the substantial 6,018-ton British tanker ss *Caspia*, again sunk by torpedo attack. Retreating towards the south, Guggenberger was near Jaffa the following day.

North from the Arab port lay a small electrical power station which Guggenberger sighted and shelled during the evening of 17 April. As a pall of smoke enveloped the area, *U-81* departed, sailing south to repeat the attack against an oil refinery at the harbour of Haifa. One hundred shells fom the 8.8cm deck gun landed on target, once again spreading flames, smoke and confusion ashore. Nor were these his only successes. Between 16 and 22 April, Guggenberger destroyed eight small Egyptian sailing vessels, each around 100 tons displacment, by gunfire and ramming, damaging a ninth on 17 April and sowing further panic and alarm along the eastern Mediterranean seaboard.

U-81 suffered damage to a hydroplane while operating in the shallow coastal waters on 21 April and returned to Salamis, docking eight days later, a fresh painting adorning the conning tower showing a man with, somewhat ironically considering that the population of Jaffa was almost entirely Arab, exaggerated Jewish features fleeing exploding shells and the word 'Jaffa' painted alongside.

Guggenberger's was not the only successful '*Morgenstern*' patrol. *Kapitän-leutnant* Freiharr Hans-Dietrich von Tiesenhausen's *U-331* had also left Salamis on 4 April, successfully laying eight TMC mines off Beirut nine days later.[8] During that night, *U-331* surfaced and edged into the harbour, attacking a moored freighter that was being unloaded by barge. Though a large column of fire and smoke was seen by von Tiesenhausen, the Norwegian ss *Lyder Sagen* was undamaged as the barges appeared to have taken the brunt of the explosion. A second torpedo attack later that night also yielded no result, a torpedo being seen to run on the surface and strike the estimated 4,000-ton target but fail to explode. Nonetheless during the following night *U-331* attacked three small sailing vessels with her deck gun off the Lebanese coast and claimed them destroyed, as well as shelling and destroying an electrical power station at Beirut. During this period, however, a crewman was injured, losing a finger and forcing *U-331* to begin the return to Salamis.

The remaining two '*Morgenstern*' boats were less successful with surface operations, but yielded more from their minefields. *Kapitänleutnant* Horst Hamm's *U-562* laid its twelve TMB mines off Famagusta on 13 April, two British ships being sunk on 29 April – the 157-ton sailing vessel *Terpisthea* and the 81-ton steam tug *Alliance* which was towing her. Hamm then sailed into Turkish waters (the British authorities later claiming that he had violated international law by entering a Turkish harbour), sighting a British ship in the process of loading before following it out to sea and launching an attack. Regardless, the attack failed and *U-562* returned to Pola on 11 May. To the south *Kapitänleutnant* Robert Bartels' *U-561* laid twelve TMB and eight TMC mines off Port Said on 15 April, which later accounted for the 6,692-ton Greek ss *Mount Olympus* and the 5,062-ton Norwegian ss *Hav* during the following month. The Norwegian ship was carrying 7,380 tons of barley from Port Said to Beirut when the explosion occurred amidships on the starboard side. Two men were killed, the body of mechanic Alfred Lund, on duty in the engine room at the time, was never found while the body of Able Seaman Einar Enerud was found outside the breakwater during the next day. Several men were injured, three of them being taken to the British hospital ship *Aba* in the harbour. *Hav* immediately began to sink with flooding in number one, two, three and four holds and the engine room. Another Greek freighter, ss *Fred*, was also damaged by one of Bartels' mines. Though the results of this field would take weeks to be known, April had ended successfully for the Mediterranean U-boats.

The successful trend appeared to continue into May, *U-372* reporting two armed trawlers attacked and probably sunk near Tobruk, though they remain unverified by Allied sources. *Kapitänleutnant* Wilhelm Dommes aboard *U-431* also attacked four ships between 18 and 27 May. The first was a grounded steamer, a hit abaft of the bridge being plainly seen, though again the victory has never been verified. His second attack though yielded firm results. On the evening of 20 May *U-431* attacked Convoy AT46 near Sollum and sank the 4,216-ton British tanker ss *Eocene* with torpedoes. A week later two more ships were reported attacked and hit whilst in convoy within the same region, though neither has been confirmed.

However, May also heralded further losses for the Mediterranean U-boats, one being involved in a difficult entanglement with Spanish neutrality, another sunk by aircraft and a third destroyed after a fifteen-hour hunt by destroyers northeast of Tobruk. The former, 29th U-Flotilla's *U-573*, became the centre of a diplomatic incident. *Kapitänleutnant* Heinrich Heinsohn had taken his boat from Pola on 19 April to operate in the western Mediterranean waters, one of three boats charged with inter-cepting Allied naval forces engaged on resupplying Malta, particularly the

American aircraft carrier USS *Wasp* which flew off Spitfires to reinforce the island's defences.

During the early afternoon on 1 May he was sighted and attacked by Hudson 'M' of 233 Squadron RAF east of Gibraltar while on the surface. The Hudson pilot, Sergeant Brent, dived from 1,700 feet and straddled the U-boat with three 250lb depth charges from a height of only 30 feet above the waves as *U-573* vainly attempted to crash dive. The U-boat's decks were still awash when two of the charges exploded against the starboard side of the conning tower. *U-573* managed to submerge, but a large patch of spreading oil showed the British crew that they had successfully damaged their target. Moments later the bow of the U-boat appeared almost perpendicular to the waves, sliding back beneath the waves before re-emerging once more as *U-573* was brought painfully to the surface, gradually assuming an even keel. Seeing little alternative, unable to manouevre his stricken U-boat out of range of the circling Hudson, Heinsohn prepared to surrender, his crew emerging on deck and raising their hands to the aircraft above. The circling Hudson broke off its planned machine-gun run and remained above the stricken U-boat while attempting to summon assistance.[9] However, Brent was forced to break off his patrol with fuel running low, and was thus unable to capitalise on the capture, enabling *U-573* to attempt to get underway before British reinforcements could arrive.

The engine was nursed into life and *U-573* headed for the Spanish coast at Cartagena, where it arrived during the following day assisted by two Spanish tugboats. Spanish authorities allowed it a three-month period for repairs, an irregular concession as international regulations forbade such a lengthy repair time. With the U-boat publicly in harbour the British Embassy in Madrid sent several strong protests to the Spanish foreign ministry. It soon became apparent that the shattered boat was irreparable, even within the allotted extended time period. With Heinsohn and his crew interned, a compromise was reached whereby the *Kriegsmarine* sold *U-573* to the Spanish Navy for 1,500,000 Reichsmarks, minus its torpedoes. Thus on 2 August 1942 at 10.00, the Spanish Navy officially took over *U-573* which was renamed *S01*.[10]

On the same day that Heinsohn reached safety in Spain, *U-74* on its second patrol in the Mediterranean was sunk by combined naval and air attack. The boat had departed La Spezia on 23 April with Oblt.z.S. Karl Friedrich having taken over from the previous commander Eitel-Friedrich Kentrat who had brought *U-74* past Gibraltar in December. *U-74* was spotted running surfaced by PBY Catalina 'C' of 202 Squadron RAF east-south-east of Cartagena. Flight Lieutenant RY Powell dived into the attack as *U-74* began to submerge, seven depth charges following the boat under, dropped ahead of the swirl left by the boat's churning propellers.

There was no visible result, but Powell continued to circle the area until the destroyers HMS *Wishart* and *Wrestler* arrived. Before long they had established ASDIC contact with the hidden enemy and repeated depth-charge attacks were crowned with an upwelling of oil and wreckage – no trace of Friedrich or his forty-five crewmen was ever found.

The end of April saw only eighteen boats still active in the Mediterranean, several of them consigned to shipyard repairs that could stretch for weeks if not months. In return only three merchant ships had been confirmed sunk that month. Also ashore, the administrative structure of the flotilla had changed. With FdU Italian directly providing operational instructions for U-boats of both the 23rd and 29th U-Flotilla that also frequently changed deployment from western to eastern waters, the two units were to be amalgamated during April, the 23rd U-Flotilla ceasing to exist as a combat unit from May 1942. All boats would now come under the 29th U-Flotilla, K.K. Fritz Frauenheim assuming control, replacing K.K. Franz Becker who returned to a staff position at BdU, this time as liaison for the commander of all Atlantic-based Italian submarines. Frauenheim too would move on, his place taken in July 1943 by K.K. Gunter Jahn who commanded the 29th U-Flotilla until its dissolution in September 1944.[11] Like Frauenheim, Jahn was an experienced U-boat commander who had been awarded the Knight's Cross, this time as captain of *U-596* in the Atlantic.

While the western Mediterranean proved perilous as British air power began to take control during May, five other boats, *U-83, U-205, U-431, U-565* and *U-568,* concentrated against the Libyan coast. On 22 May, OKM ordered all available boats to assemble off Tobruk to act in support of Rommel's land offensive launched on 27 May against the Allied garrison and onward toward Egypt. It was, however, a vain effort.

Besides Dommes' largely phantom victories, Kaptlt. Hans-Werner Kraus' *U-83* claimed a steamer torpedoed near Sollum, another unverified victory. Kraus was also scheduled on 28 May to participate in landing a joint German/Italian commando team in an amphibious assault in the Gulf of Bomba east of Tobruk, but technical problems aboard the boat necessitated its return to Salamis by the end of the month. Kraus had reported to FdU Italian that his boat was non-operational in the Gulf of Bomba on the scheduled day, forced to withdraw for bottom repairs, a diver having discovered amongst other problems a badly-bent blade on the port screw. However, due to constant enemy air activity diver repairs on more minor problems were aborted and the boat forced to head home.

Kapitänleutnant Joachim Preuss's *U-568* was less fortunate after attempting to attack a large convoy sailing from Alexandria at the end of May, with a strong escort that included destroyers the HMS *Eridge, Hurworth* and *Hero.*

At daylight on the 27th, the convoy was in the Gulf of Sollum. Tobruk radio was then broadcasting a continuous stream of air-raid warnings. As the convoy was such an obvious target for attack, all ships were reconciled to a day at action stations.

In the early forenoon an aircraft reported sighting a U-boat to the northeast. [The aircraft, a British Blenheim bomber, sighted *U-568* and attacked with bombs, rupturing one of the boat's fuel tanks. Author's note.] The U-boat was no longer a threat to the convoy; consequently some surprise was felt when the senior officer weakened the air defence by detaching *Hurworth* and *Hero* to investigate. In fact he knew that the Axis offensive had commenced and that the aerial activity was in support of the land battle but had omitted to inform his command.

Some hours later, *Eridge* was ordered to reinforce the other destroyers which had gained contact with the U-boat but had expended most of their depth charges. We were not sorry to exchange a slow convoy for the possibility of offensive action but, on sighting our consorts, were disappointed to find that they had lost contact. We waited until they had completed an unsuccessful search; then, being the senior officer, I assumed command. I guessed that the U-boat's Captain would try to get as far as possible from a hostile shore so I ordered a search commencing in a northerly direction from the U-boat's last known position. This was successful, *Hero* first regaining contact, followed a few minutes later by *Hurworth*. Both ships then carried out an attack at the end of which neither had any depth charges. *Eridge*, now the only ship with any charges, had not made contact but the others kept signalling their ranges and bearings of the target which were plotted on a large scale chart. These placed the U-boat to the south and enabled its course and speed to be estimated. *Eridge* steered an intercepting course until the submarine detector picked up an echo. Conditions in the Mediterranean were notoriously poor for submarine detection but, as the range decreased on this occasion, the echoes cracked in the receiver like pistol shots.

Eridge then carried out two attacks with her charges set to detonate at 250 feet. A few dead fish floated to the surface but the U-boat maintained her course and speed so I concluded she was much deeper, possibly at 500 or 600 feet. The next attacks were carried out while the sun was setting and daylight slowly fading. The charges were now set to detonate at maximum depth and so deep were the explosions that the surface of the sea merely vibrated. At these depths, attacks were unlikely to be accurate so many charges would be needed to ensure significant damage. These were no longer available so, conditions still being good enough for two ships to maintain contact, I ordered *Hero* to proceed at full speed to Tobruk and replenish. She was capable of more than thirty knots; nevertheless, she would be absent for several hours.

The attacks continued while a full moon rose serenely out of the sea, forming a perfect background for the U-boat to make a torpedo attack from the darker northern sector if we should lose contact. Eventually, *Eridge* had only one salvo of five charges left and I decided to retain these in case the U-boat decreased her depth. But our best chance of a 'kill' depended on maintaining contact until exhausted batteries forced the U-boat to surface. Echoes from her hull were still loud and clear; nevertheless we waited with increasing impatience, willing *Hero* to return. In fact, she never did. On approaching Tobruk she had been diverted to the west to investigate a report, which subsequently proved false, of a seaborne assault in the British rear.

About midnight, a new noise began to impinge on the high pitched transmissions of the detector. It was repeated at intervals and sounded like the sigh of air escaping from a pair of bellows. We needed a few minutes to realise its significance. The U-boat was blowing her tanks in the process of surfacing!

All guns were trained along the bearing on which she was expected to appear. This lay in the darker sector so the destroyers would be clearly silhouetted against the moon in the southern sky. As we were expecting her to try to escape on the surface while fighting with gun and torpedoes, it would be imperative to open fire before her own weapons could be used. Everyone was very conscious of this during the exciting, anxious wait before a dark smudge gradually materialised against the darker background. The searchlight was immediately illuminated showing the U-boat wallowing gently in the slight swell which was pouring off her hull and sparkling in the moonlight. Speed was increased to fifteen knots to counter a surface escape and the guns ordered to open fire. But use of the main armament was an error because the vivid flash of the four-inch guns temporarily blinded everyone on the upper deck. 'Cease-fire' was promptly ordered but by the time vision was restored, the U-boat had vanished. Searches ahead by radar and submarine detector proved negative; neither could propeller noises be heard although a look-out thought he had seen the U-boat ahead. So speed had to be maintained while the instruments tried to verify his report. The results being negative again, the engines were stopped; at the same time *Hurworth* reported she had lost contact. The initiative had now passed to the U-boat which might even exchange the role of hunted for hunter. She also had a choice from several additional courses of action, either submerged or on the surface, and her prospects of escape would be greatly improved unless we guessed what she was doing. If she had moved ahead, she would hardly risk turning close across the bows of either destroyer so our speed would have been sufficient to keep her in sight. But if she had remained where she had surfaced, *Eridge* would have passed her while those on the upper deck were blinded. She would then have an opportunity to move in any direction between east and west on a southerly semi-circle and that, being astern, could not be covered by our primitive fixed radar. On the other hand the moon was now in our favour and propeller noises should be audible. But she was neither seen nor heard. So had she dived into our wake where the turbulence caused by the propellers would be masking the detectors' transmissions? This seemed a reasonable conclusion so I ordered both destroyers to reverse course and carry out a southerly search. How invaluable *Hero* would have been at that moment!

Then followed an endless, anxious thirty minutes. The detector's transmissions flowed monotonously without any corresponding echo. Each lack of response seemed to emphasise with increasing insistence that the wrong action had been selected. If so, the U-boat would be getting further away with every passing minute and any alternative search would be futile. So we pressed on doggedly until, just as we were beginning to despair, the detector received the whisper of an echo at an extreme range. It could have come from a wreck or a shoal of fish but as *Eridge* drew closer, the echoes became so clear that doubt no longer existed. It was the U-boat! Soon afterwards, *Hurworth* reported that she too had gained contact.

The U-boat steered south for about an hour. Then she suddenly doubled back on her track and started to zig-zag in a northerly direction. But conditions were still so good that the submarine detector had no difficulty in holding her. Our main concern was still the lack of charges.

At 04.00 *U-568* surfaced for the last time. She came up gently and silently without any fuss. One moment the sea ahead was empty; the next she was rolling sluggishly in the slight swell. A second later she was gripped in the beam of our searchlight which revealed several seamen tumbling out of the conning tower. They could have been her gun's crew, so fire was opened to deter them. This time we did not repeat our mistakes. *Eridge* maintained her slow speed while only her close range weapons raked the U-boat's hull from which riccochetting tracers described curious patterns in the air. As *Eridge* surged alongside, the final pattern of five charges was released. These were set shallow and detonated with a mighty crash, drenching the U-boat under a great gush of water. Men were now leaping into the sea so fire was checked and the whaler sent away with a boarding party with a slight hope of getting onboard to prevent her being scuttled. But the U-boat was so obviously foundering that the whaler soon turned to the more humanitarian role of saving life. To the best of my recollection *Eridge* alone picked up the U-boat's entire company which, upon reaching Tobruk, was divided between *Eridge*, *Hurworth*, and *Hero* for the passage to Alexandria.[12]

In May 1942 Victor Oehrn was transferred from Rome to Libya as the fall of Tobruk to Axis forces appeared imminent and all available strength was concentrated for what was seen as the final decisive push. Malta had virtually ceased to exist as a viable base due to the continual heavy German and Italian bombing, allowing most Axis supply convoys and aircraft to cross the Mediterranean to North Africa unmolested and thus allowing Rommel to build up his meagre forces.

Flag Officer German Naval Command Italy will direct operations for FdU for duration of naval operations from his headquarters in Libya (Derna).

1. U-boats will be controlled from Rome.
2. Oehrn is to be assigned to Derna.[13]

He expected to be gone from Rome for only ten days: indeed before departing he asked Renate von Winterfeld, secretary to the senior *Kriegsmarine* officer in Rome V.A. Eberhard Weichold, to marry him upon his return. However, after arriving in Derna and witnessing first hand the fall of Tobruk, Oehrn was appointed *Kriegsmarine* liaison officer to *Feldmarschall* Albert Kesselring, responsible for army operations in the Mediterranean. His tenure at FdU Italian was effectively over, the post of Kreisch's chief of staff taken over by K.K. Schewe.[14]

On 20 June Tobruk had finally fallen to the Germans and seven days later FdU *Italian* ordered boats sent against troop and supply transports from Syria, Palestine, Port Said to Alexandria in a final onslaught to prevent reinforcement in the face of the *Afrika Korps*. On land Rommel had captured a huge amount of booty in the battered town, enough to equip 30,000 men for three months and more than 10,000m³ of petrol, desperately needed for his mobile units.

At sea Kaptlt. Hans Heidtmann's *U-559* featured in an OKW communiqué of 12 June, stating that the boat had 'especially distinguished itself' off the Palestinian coast in an attack on a convoy destined for Tobruk. Indeed Heidtmann, whose boat suffered persistent troubles with its starboard diesel throughout the patrol, had encountered Convoy AT49 west of Alexandria on 10 June and torpedoed two ships, damaging the British fleet oiler SS *Brambleleaf* and sinking the Norwegian freighter MV *Athene*, carrying 6,000 tons of fuel initially bound for Alexandria but rerouted to Tobruk in the convoy alongside four other transport ships and six escorts. The convoy had been initially sighted by *U-81* – which had recently survived a near miss by seven torpedoes fired from HMS *Turbulent* – which shadowed while transmitting beacon signals to gather other available boats, *U-431*, *U-453* and *U-559* soon on the scene. The first to be hit was the British SS *Brambleleaf*, the convoy commodore ordering *Athene* to take the oiler's place in front as it dropped out of formation. Nearly three hours later a single torpedo hit *Athene* between the poop and amidships, destroying most of the deck and flooding fuel from the ruptured hold over the boat deck and poop, also covering crewmen there. The fuel ignited shortly afterward, hastening the abandoning of the ship, several crewmen forced to leap overboard, never to be seen again. The SS *Athene* burned fiercely before sinking later that day, the seventeen survivors being picked up by the convoy escorts. Both *U-453* and *U-431* attacked the convoy again later that night, the men aboard Schlippenbach's

U-453 hearing a heavy detonation after a torpedo run of nearly five minutes but with no confirmed success while Dommes' *U-431* hit and sank 2,073-ton British steamer ss *Havre*.

June appeared to herald a veritable bonanza of success for the 29th U-flotilla. German U-boats claimed a total of nineteen ships sunk, a further six hit and at least damaged. Italian submarines added another four ships claimed – all warships bar one small schooner, though the only confirmed warship sinking was in fact the mistaken torpedoing of the Italian destroyer *Usodimare*. The reality of German success amounted to thirteen ships sunk and two damaged. However, several of the U-boat sinkings were from the scattered remnants of convoys running toward Malta, an island deemed, rightly or wrongly, of crucial importance to the Mediterranean war.

Two Malta convoys – five escorted merchant ships codenamed 'Harpoon' from Gibraltar and twelve ships codenamed 'Vigorous' from Alexandria – were savaged by combined German and Italian air and sea power. Only one of 'Harpoon's' merchant ships reached Malta for the loss of two destroyers and serious damage to three more as well as a cruiser by combined Italian and German naval and aircraft attacks. All of the 'Vigorous' ships were forced to turn back with losses of one cruiser, three destroyers and two merchant ships, the latter to aircraft attack.

After the 'Vigorous' convoy aborted its attempt to reach Malta, Heinz Schonder's *U-77* torpedoed and sank destroyer HMS *Grove* from the convoy on 12 June, Dommes's *U-431* damaged two steamers fom the convoy the following day near Tobruk. On 14 June Reschke in *U-205* claimed a hit on a 'Vigorous' freighter, while the following day Dommes sank *LCT119* by gunfire. The final U-boat victory against the hard-pressed convoy was the torpedoing and sinking of anti-aircraft cruiser HMS *Hermione* by Reschke in the early hours of 16 June as the ship sailed to Alexandria after the attempted convoy operation.

In the east too, the Germans maintained pressure on the small supply ships sailing between Palestine and Egypt. Hans-Werner Kraus' *U-83* sailed to patrol the waters off Palestine and Lebanon, claiming three small freighters and four sailing ships and damage to another 6,000-ton freighter. For this and his claimed accumulated sinking of twenty ships – and in no small part to boost recognition of the Mediterranean U-boats – Kraus was awarded the Knight's Cross, sailing into Salamis flying twenty pennants, his boat's conning tower adorned with a Knight's Cross and the number '20' beneath it. As Kraus entered harbour alongside Wilhelm Dommes' *U-431* flying seven pennants of its own, a propaganda ministry film crew was on hand to film the event, later shown as a newsreel in German cinemas.

The sole loss to the 29th U-Flotilla was *U-652*, caught on the surface and bombed by a Swordfish of 815 Squadron FAA northeast of Bardia on 2 June. *Oberleutnant zur See* Georg-Werner Fraatz's boat was badly damaged in the attack, which rendered it unable to dive. A second Swordfish attack was ineffective as the depth charges dropped short. However, the boat was doomed and Fraatz was able to call for assistance from Guggenberger's nearby *U-81* which was searching for a reported downed German aircraft crew. Guggenberger was on the scene within two hours and took off Fraatz and his crew, Fraatz using one of *U-81*'s stern torpedoes to sink his crippled and abandoned boat.

By the end of June 1942 British hopes for the pursuit of a successful Mediterranean strategy appeared dashed. The Eighth Army had been virtually routed by Rommel's *Afrika Korps* and were preparing a last ditch attempt to hold Egypt at El Alamein. Malta had been bombed into near oblivion and many ships lost attempting to raise the siege and bolster the inhabitants, including the defeat of Operation 'Vigorous'. Malta had long featured in Italian plans of conquest, with German assistance pledged for a planned airborne landing – Operation 'Hercules'. However, the conundrum for Axis forces was that when the island bore the full brunt of their air forces in the Mediterranean it could not operate as a base from which to intercept convoys to Rommel in North Africa. However, when Rommel wanted to go onto the offensive, he required those same air forces in support, reducing the attacks against Malta and allowing a surprisingly resilient island to regenerate and interfere once more with his crucial supplies. Indeed it was only during April 1942 that General Siegfried Westphal, Rommel's Chief of Staff, estimated that enough stores had arrived on seaborne transport to supply the army in the field for one month.

Ironically, it was in fact the elation of the sudden victory over Tobruk and subsequent concentration on capturing Egypt that saved Malta. Mussolini, encouraged by Rommel, focussed his attention on capturing the Suez Canal, postponing the planned Italian airborne attack against Malta, in which Hitler had little faith anyway, remembering the poor performance of much of Italy's forces and the terrible casualties suffered by his own paratroopers on Crete. Only Raeder and Kesselring voiced their alarm at this decision, rightly concluding that the Axis position in the North African desert would never be secure until Malta was taken. Theirs, however, were lone voices.

On the Allied side there was worry at the highest quarters about the situation that the main Royal Navy base at Alexandria faced. Ironically, not from the fact that the desert land war lay perilously near to the port, but from a possible overreaction. On 25 June, Winston Churchill communicated his concern to General Auchinleck who took personal command of the Allied forces at Mersa Matruh that same day.

Karl Donitz, architect of Germany's U-boat strategy, firmly resisted the deployment of U-boats to the Mediterranean but was ultimately overruled.

Fritz Frauenheim, combat veteran and Knight's Cross holder, would become the first German U-boat flotilla commander in the Mediterranean in September 1941 with his appointment as chief of the 23rd U-Flotilla.

Victor Oehm (left) and Eberhard Godt. Godt was chief of the Befehlshaber der Unterseeboote (BdU) Operational Staff (BdU.Ops) and directly subordinate to Donitz.

Victor Oehm was the first Fuhrer der Unterseeboote (FdU) Italian, appointed as regional commander for the 23rd and 29th U-Flotillas. Unlike other FdUs, the Italian office held considerable operational authority rather than just fulfilling a purely logistical role.

The military port of Salamis under attack by German aircraft during
the invasion of Greece in I 941. The battleship Kilkis is aflame at the centre of the
photograph. To the left is the dry dock later used by the U-boat service.

A surfacing Type VII U-boat —
the only class of German submarine deployed in the Mediterranean.

Salamis under German occupation. The hulks of Kilkis and Lemnos are still visible, and on the left:
the U-boats' dry-dock. The U-boats tended to moor alongside piers seen in the background to the right.

A U-boat enters La Spezia harbour. The boarding gangway
can be seen on deck beside the 8.8cm deck gun.

U-596 enters Salamis harbour.

Sharing La Spezia harbour with major units of the Italian Navy (in this case the cruiser Balzano) proved to become a major hindrance to the rapid turnaround of operational U-boats as Italian dockyard workers were directed to their own nation's needs before those of the Germans.

Calm clear waters made for an often idyllic cruising environment but extremely hazardous combat conditions, with periscope wakes more than usually visible and shallow submerged U-boats easily spotted from the air.

Kapitanleutnant Friedrich Guggenberger's sinking of HMS Ark
Royal resulted in the award of the Knight's Cross as well as an
Italian medal for bravery, seen being bestowed here.

Guggenberger had sunk the prized Ark Royal, an event claimed in
the German press since the beginning of the war but finally achieved
after the arrival of the first U-boats in the Mediterranean

Kapitänleutnant Frhr. v. Tiesenhausen erhielt das Ritterkreuz des Eisernen Kreuzes für die Versenkung der „Barham"

Britisches Schlachtschiff „Barham" (31 100 t, 25 sm, 8—38 cm, 12—15,2 cm 8 — 10,2 cm, 16 — 4 cm, 8 MG, 4 Flugzeuge), von deutschem Unterseeboot unter Kptlt. Frhr. v. Tiesenhausen vor Sollum versenkt Foto: S...

Britischer Leichter Kreuzer „Neptune" (7175 t, 32,5 sm, 8 — 15,2 cm 8 — 10,2 cm, 4 — 4,7 cm, 12 MG, 8 TR IIII, 2 Flugzeuge), von deutschem Unterseeboot unter Kptlt. Driver vor Alexandria versenkt Foto: W...

Britischer Leichter Kreuzer „Galatea" (5220 t, 32,2 sm, 6 — 15,2 cm 8 — 10,2 cm, 2 — 4,7 cm, 8 MG, 6 TR III, ein Flugzeug) Foto: W...

Britischer Zerstörer „Thanet" (905 t, 36 sm, 3 — 10,2 cm, 1 — 4 cm, 4 MG 4 TR II), von japanischen Zerstörern vor Endau, Malaya, versenkt Foto: At...

Schiffsversenkungen einer Woche

(16-23. Februar 1942)

Vor Nordafrika:

Aus britischen Geleitzügen wurden drei Schiffe herausgeschossen und versenkt, darunter ein Transporter von 9000 BRT. Zwei weitere Frachter von zusammen 15000 BRT. wurden so schwer beschädigt, daß mit ihrem Verlust zu rechnen ist.

Im Mittelmeer:

Vor Alexandria wurde ein englischer Flottenverband angegriffen, wobei zwei feindliche Kriegsschiffseinheiten durch Torpedos schwer beschädigt wurden. In den Gewässern um Kreta büßte die britische Flotte ein U-Boot ein. Zwei britische Kreuzer, zwei Zerstörer und ein großes Handelsschiff wurden von deutschen Kampfflugzeugen angegriffen und durch Bombentreffer beschädigt.

Vor Norwegen:

Ein britisches U-Boot vernichtet.

Vor der englischen Küste:

Ein deutscher Sperrbrecher beschädigte ein feindliches Schnellboot so schwer, daß mit dessen Untergang gerechnet werden kann. Bei den täglichen Kontrollflügen der deutschen Luftwaffe über dem britischen Seegebiet erhielt ein Handelsschiff Volltreffer, während ein britischer Bewacher versenkt wurde. Im Versorgungshafen Great Yarmouth wurden erhebliche Zerstörungen angerichtet.

Im Karibischen Meer:

Bei dem kühnen Angriff auf eine amerikanische Tankerflotte in der Nähe von Aruba und Curacao wurden drei Tanker mit zusammen 17400 BRT. versenkt, die Hafenanlagen und Raffinerien dieser Inseln durch Artilleriebeschuß schwer beschädigt. Auf der Reede des britischen Hafens Port of Spain von Trinidad versenkte ein deutsches U-Boot zwei Schiffe, darunter einen Tanker.

Vor der USA-Küste:

Weitere 17 Schiffe mit 102000 BRT. wurden durch deutsche U-Boote versenkt. Damit erhöht sich der bisherige Erfolg unserer Unterseeboote im westlichen Atlantik auf 80 Schiffe mit insgesamt 532000 BRT.

'Ships sunk during one week'; Die Kriegsmarine magazine makes huge play of Royal Navy losses including the sinking of four major British warships between 16 and 23 February 1942 -three of them in the Mediterranean. HMS Barham is at the top, flanked by a portrait of her victor, Kaptlt. von Tiesenhausen.

The state of the crews' chins leads one to believe that
this photograph (taken in La Spezia) is as a boat was leaving for a patrol.
The hats were not standard issue...

Donitz's relations with his U-boat personnel were helped enormously by
frequent personal appearances to welcome home returning crews and, where
possible, to see them off on patrol. The loyalty with which he came to be
viewed was almost unparalleled within the Kriegsmarine.

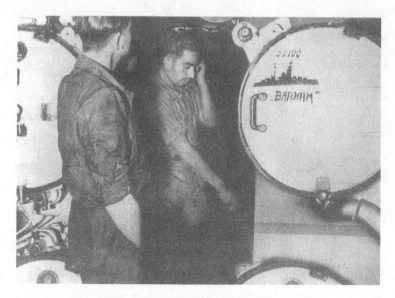

The torpedo crew aboard U-331, however,
have their own way of marking a successful attack.

Relaxing beneath the Mediterranean sun, but maintaining the ever-present lookout.

Gun actions were a regular occurrence in the eastern Mediterranean
in particular, where many vessels were so small or of such shallow
draught that they were unworthy - or difficult - torpedo targets.

A U-boat crew in Pola on the Istrian Peninsula. Considered and subsequently dismissed
as a replacement port for Salamis at one point, it was nonetheless one of the
four main U-boat bases in the Mediterranean.

Loading a TMB mine aboard a Type VIIC U-boat. This was the primary mine used during such operations as 'Morgenstern' aimed at British ports in the eastern Mediterranean.

U-407 newly transferred to the Mediterranean from 9th U-Flotilla at Brest and still bearing the flotilla's 'Laughing Sawfish' emblem.

U-73 puts to sea. Kapitanleutnant Helmut Rosenbaum is second from the right, saluting.

Stalking HMS Eagle. Rosenbaum speaks on the U-boat's intercom while the boat moves at depth, the shallow depth gauge visible on the right showing maximum and probably exceeded.

Success! The sinking of HMS Eagle earned Rosenbaum the Knight's Cross on 12 August 1942.

The gun crew of a Type VII U-boat standing down as
their boat cruises on an idyllic sea.

In time crews were made to kneel on
deck on the outer casing when the
boats were leaving or returning to
port in order to lessen potential
casualties caused by mines laid in the
approaches. This particular crew
seems more relaxed than that as they
near their voyage's end.

After fuelling, taking on board stores and ammunition, the boat was finally cleared for sea with crewmen assembling for last minute checks and an on-deck inspection

U-372, the sinker of the British submarine depot ship HMS Medway.
The boat is pictured here entering port, but at its first operational home,
Brest in France, prior to the boat's transfer to the Mediterranean.

U-596 enters La Spezia 12 March 1943. The camouflage pattern,
designed to break up the boat's silhouette, was one peculiar to
Mediterranean U-boats and was made by dark grey patterning over the
familiar light grey used by the Kriegsmarine.

Crewmen of U-617 loading stores in La Spezia in preparation for sailing in March 1943. Spoilage was a problem in the Mediterranean heat as the boats possessed only basic refrigeration aboard. Behind them is the Italian cruiser Taranto.

U-73 (left) and U-S61 photographed together in La Spezia on 5 September 1942. The larger flak platforms, built to accommodate increased weaponry, at the rear of the conning towers can be plainly seen.

Type VIIB U-83 enters La Spezia. The boat bore the 'Viking Ship' squadron emblem of KGlOO as its commander had served in the Luftwaffe during the early years of the war.

Deck watch alongside an auxiliary lookout. Not only were vigilanr lookouts crucial for signs of enemy targets but also for survival against aircraft, perhaps the greatest threat to U-boats from the beginning of 1943 onward.

Kapitanleutnant Josef Rother and his LI Leutnant (Ing.) Stubbe aboard U-380. Rother was tasked with rescuing trapped members of the Afrika Korps in May 1943; he returned with four men.

A Type VII U-boat in choppy water. Late-war flak armament had added considerably to the size of the conning tower. This boat also shows the addition of the snorkel, lowered into its deck nacelle.

U-81 at sea displaying the twin-barrelled 20mm flak gun (foreground) and a pair of twin Breda machine guns added locally for extra firepower.

Albrecht Brandi (right), one of the most highly-decorated U-boat commanders of the Second World War - but also one of the most optimistic with his claims of success.

The captured officers of U-S9S.
(Left to right) Jurgen Qμaet-Faslem, Friedrich Kaiser, Emmerich Freiherr von Mirbach and Horst Eberhard von Horstig, photographed aboard the American ship Brazil en-route to POW camp in the United States.

The crew of U-616 enjoy final cigarettes ashore in Toulon harbour before beginning a war patrol.

Oberleutnant zur See Siegfried Koitschka at the end of U-6Uls patrol. The strain of U-boat operations within the Mediterranean is etched clearly on his face.

Freshly scrubbed, the crew of U616 are inspected by Kapitan zur See Leo Kreisch, FdU Italian.

A U-boat at sea. The swastika flag flew for only three years within the
Mediterranean - a campaign that, though ultimately futile,
cost the Royal Navy a heavy toll in major warships.

Please tell Harwood that I am rather worried about reports of undue despondency and alarm in Alexandria and of the Navy hastening to evacuate to the Red Sea. Although various precautionary moves may be taken and *Queen Elizabeth* should be got out at earliest, I trust a firm, confident attitude will be maintained.[15]

However, within two days the Allied front line had once more been forced back, this time to within 40 miles of Alexandria at the small town of El Alamein, the Allied trenches running between the Alamein railway station south to the Qattara Depression. With German aircraft beginning to bomb the port, Admiral Harwood ordered the evacuation of the Alexandria naval base, the ships retreating to Beirut, Haifa and Port Said. A plan had been previously formulated in which an orderly evacuation would take place over a three-week period. However, the timetable for this meticulously-ordered withdrawal was ignored and the entire operation decended into chaos as it was carried out over the space of only 48 hours. Among the ships withdrawing to Beirut was the 14,650-ton submarine depot ship HMS *Medway*, carrying 1,135 men, 114 torpedoes and a huge supply of spare parts for the 1st Submarine Flotilla as well as the flotilla's kit and personal belongings.

The ship, the first of its kind designed for the Royal Navy, was carrying Captain P Ruck, commander of the 1st Submarine Flotilla, and sailing under escort from the cruiser HMS *Dido* and seven destroyers. Heinz Joachim Neumann's *U-372* sighted the procession, taking *Medway* to be a large cargo ship. At 08.24 on 30 June two torpedoes out of a salvo of four hit the ship in the engine and dynamo rooms. Despite the provision of special torpedo protection in the form of a 1in torpedo bulkhead 13 feet inboard amidships, the ship immediately began to sink and within 20 minutes was gone.

Thirty men were lost with their ship, a WRNS officer, Third Officer Audrey Sylvia, later Mentioned in Despatches for giving up her lifebelt to a rating whom she found having difficulties in the water (both she and the rating survived). Despite forty-seven of the ship's stored torpedoes later floating clear and being recovered, the loss of the *Medway* was devastating for British Mediterranean submarine operations. Eventually a small depot ship HMS *Talbot* was moved from Malta to replace her at Beirut, changing her name to HMS *Medway II*. Neumann meanwhile had dived immediately to 125 metres after firing and retreated unscathed from the scene, though he did not realise at the time the true significance of his target.

Ironically the entire British retreat was proved to be, in hindsight, premature as the high tide of Rommel's advance across North Africa finally broke on the last-ditch Allied lines at El Alamein. Alexandria was soon once again the home to the Royal Navy's eastern Mediterranean fleet.

Chapter 5

Attrition

In mid-1942, minelaying became a priority for FdU Italian. Coupled with fields laid by S-boats, the U-boats' ability to penetrate closer inshore was considered essential to blockading the Allied ports. On 10 June 1942 *U-561* had been ordered under 'Operational Order 5' to take on board mines to lay off Port Said amongst the retreating British forces. Bartels was ordered to proceed to Augusta via Messina to reload for the mission, Salamis unable to provide minelaying gear. *U-561* docked in Augusta, north of Syracuse on Sicily's east coast, on 2 July.

That same day instructions were issued for all U-boats operating in the eastern Mediterranean from FdU Italian, reflecting the uncertain status of French shipping:

> There is a possibility that French naval forces may leave Alexandria. Do not stop them if they are on a westerly or northerly course. On the other hand, they are to be attacked if they set course for Port Said or the Syrian coast.[1]

Fresh plans were made to intensify the pressure against the retreating British units that had evacuated Alexandria. One-quarter of the U-boats was to be assigned minelaying duties, with one tube loaded with mines and the remainder free for torpedoes. Minefields were planned for Haifa, Port Said, Cape Ras (Beirut), Jaffa, Tripoli and Larnaca.

On land July witnessed ferocious fighting over the Alamein positions. Mussolini had arrived in Derna on 29 June to await his triumphal entry into Cairo at the head of the Axis troops, but the final step proved too far for Rommel's thinly stretched forces. At one point he was down to only thirteen combat ready-tanks as the tide of battle ebbed and flowed until by the month's end both sides had fought themselves to a defensive stalemate.

At sea *U-77*, *U-97*, *U-375*, *U-562* and *U-565* all experienced success in the eastern Mediterranean alongside the Italian boats *Perla* and *Alagi*. *Oberleutnant zur See* Friedrich Bürgel sank the first ship of the month a little after midday on 1 July. Bürgel and his crew had already sunk two Greek freighters west of Haifa on 28 June, the destruction of the 786-ton British freighter SS *Marilyse Moller* marking the end of his patrol, *U-97* docking at Salamis on 4 July.

Kapitänleutnant Jürgen Könenkamp's *U-375* sank the Norwegian freighter SS *Hero* in the early hours of 6 July. The steamer, in Admiralty service, had departed Beirut the day before, carrying general cargo for Port Said. Sailing in convoy with a three-ship escort she was hit by two torpedoes fired from *U-375*, the first striking the forward hold, the second hitting the after part of the ship 30 seconds later. The 1,376-ton *Hero* was practically blown to pieces, sinking in less than a minute. Only fourteen crewmen who had been on deck managed to save themselves by jumping overboard, being picked up half an hour later by an escort vessel although the ship's master, Captain Nielsen, died of his wounds shortly afterward. An unsuccessful three-torpedo attack against a freighter on 23 July was followed later that month by Könenkamp attacking two sailing ships south of Cyprus, destroying them by gunfire and ramming. *U-375* returned to Salamis on 3 August.

Kapitänleutnant Wilhelm Franken's *U-565* operated off the coast of Palestine before heading south to Egypt and sinking three sailing vessels by gunfire northeast of Alexandria. The first was a 120-ton Egyptian schooner carrying oil, abandoned by her crew and sunk by gunfire, the others described as large fishing boats, the crews of which were taken aboard the U-boat. He continued this run of sinkings into August, when he destroyed another large fishing boat with gunfire before returning to Salamis on 4 August with periscope damage suffered during an aborted attack on the last day of July.

Kapitänleutnant Heinrich Schonder's *U-77* rampaged through the coastal waters between Cyprus and Lebanon from the second half of July and into August, sinking a total of eight sailing vessels by gunfire, including the harbour defence ship HMS *Vassiliki* on 22 July, the ship, built in 1879, on passage from Beirut to Famagusta. On 21 August Schonder returned to Salamis, sailing once more four days later to Pola where the boat would be overhauled before a scheduled patrol in October. Schonder was awarded the Knight's Cross on 19 August for his success and transferred back to Germany to take charge of the Type IXD-2 boat *U-200* then under construction. His place aboard *U-77* was taken by Oblt.z.S. Otto Hartmann, former IWO aboard *U-97*.

As the land war fought itself to a standstill, Allied attentions once more turned to resupplying Malta. The near disastrous attempts made in March through to June had allowed the Admiralty to conclude that only a fresh attempt using a large, fast-moving convoy could save Malta, which teetered precariously close to starvation, the island's Governor General estimating 7 September as the expected date of forced capitulation. Elsewhere the debacle of Arctic convoy PQ17 had led to a temporary suspension of convoys to the Soviet Union, allowing the Home Fleet to be used to bolster the next race for Malta. Operation 'Pedestal' was set for early August.

The convoy – codenamed Force K – would consist of fourteen large, fast merchant ships, all carrying fuel, ammunition and food except for the British tanker *Ohio*, the largest tanker capable of making over 16 knots then in existence, that would be filled solely with 11,500 tons of kerosene and diesel, escorted by British warships. The largest escort group was named Force Z and comprised the battleships HMS *Nelson* and *Rodney*, the carriers HMS *Victorious*, *Eagle* and *Indomitable* as well as three *Dido* class cruisers and fourteen destroyers. A further group of four cruisers and eleven destroyers – Force X – would provide close escort. In the Mediterranean a screening force of eight submarines patrolled north of Sicily and south of Pantelleria where the Sicilian narrows posed a particular geographical threat to 'Pedestal'. Additionally, the aircraft carrier HMS *Furious* was also east of Gibraltar, preparing to fly off thirty-eight Spitfires for Malta.

Ranged against the convoy were 200 Axis fighter aircraft (in fact nine less than could be provided by the Allied carriers), 280 bombers, sixty reconnaissance aircraft, twenty-three S-boats, six cruisers, eleven destroyers and twenty-one submarines. The main Italian battle fleet also lay in the background, although it had not yet proven equal to the task of challenging strong British naval forces.

Of the twenty-one Axis submarines, only three were German. *U-73*, *U-205* and *U-331* were deployed in the path of the convoy. Helmut Rosenbaum's *U-73* had sailed from La Spezia after four months of repairs and refit, including the installation of new engines. The boat made the familiar crossing of the La Spezia harbour basin from the flooded dry-dock to the pier that lay alongside the Arsenal to take on food and ammunition. Leaving the harbour Rosenbaum sailed west and joined his two flotilla-mates and accompanying Italian forces in a patrol line that stretched between Algiers and the Balearic Islands, planned to be ready in position from 10 August as Axis agents reported on the convoy's progress.[2]

However, von Tiesenhausen's *U-331* was sighted running surfaced on 8 August, three days after leaving La Spezia, by a Gibraltar-bound Hudson of 233 Squadron RAF. The Hudson dropped three bombs, jamming the U-boat's rudder. *U-331* dived but shortly afterward resurfaced to fight it out with the aircraft, successfully driving the attacker off. However, two of the boat's crew had been wounded during the exchange of fire, the IWO and Chief Bosun's Mate, so after repairs were made to the rudder *U-331* set course back to Italy.

Force K passed Gibraltar in dense fog during the evening of 10 August, the following day coming under the first of many aerial attacks. The Italian submarine *Uarsciek* attacked HMS *Furious*, claiming a hit but in fact missing as the carrier flew off its aircraft and turned back for Gibraltar. Nearby, Rosenbaum's *U-73* lay submerged in the path of the oncoming convoy. Rosenbaum's voyage to where he now lay had not been smooth. After slipping from La Spezia he had conducted numerous test dives in order to shake down the boat and its repairs and new crewmen. Several defects were quickly found, including leaks in the exhaust, the direction-finder coil, main bilge pump and attack periscope gland. The radio-location gear proved to be inoperative and the clutch on the main drive for the diesels kept slipping.

Not to be outdone by their boat, four crewmen soon became ill with gastric problems and high fevers. Though not unknown amongst the new and unacclimatised German crewmen, it was only by a slim margin that Rosenbaum decided to continue his cruise rather than abort and return home. The following day, matters had worsened with nearly a third of the crew suffering from the painful stomach problem. Nonetheless, Rosenbaum was determined to reach his allotted patrol area and not miss the possible target that he and the other captains had been briefed about by Kreisch.

By 7 August *U-73* was on station and most of the sick crewmen recovering, bar one sailor found to be suffering from bacillary dysentery and isolated as much as the cramped confines of the Type VII U-boat would allow. On the morning of Tuesday 11 August, after days of nothing sighted except a distant tanker and an unidentified submarine, warship propeller noises were detected to the west, the masts of a destroyer soon seen clearly on the horizon. At the same moment, the unmistakable silhouette of an aircraft carrier also appeared. It was the 22,600-ton HMS *Eagle*, an old carrier that had begun life as the unfinished Chilean battleship *Almirante Cochrane*, converted and launched in 1918. However, the 16 Sea Hurricanes aboard were valuable assets not only to Operation 'Pedestal' but also to Malta itself.

The entire convoy was steaming directly for the submerged U-boat, zigzagging but on a general heading that would pass *U-73* perfectly. Rosenbaum was able to choose his target, though a destroyer abruptly turning and heading directly for his periscope as *U-73* hung at shallow depth in the clear blue water alarmed him. Though permitted to attack any of the freighters, he had been instructed to target major warships first and fastened on the carrier, HMS *Eagle*, which was nearest. The approaching destroyer altered course as Rosenbaum lowered his periscope at the last minute, listening to the racing propellers pass astern. Once clear he again peered through the eyepiece at his prize target.

Rosenbaum calmly took his boat toward the convoy, slipping through the outer destroyer screen between the third and fourth destroyers in line, each at a distance of 400 yards as *U-73* passed, and preparing for a point blank attack on HMS *Eagle*, her Sea Hurricanes plainly visible on deck. At 13.15 at a range of 500 yards he fired a full bow salvo of four torpedoes. Immediately that the 'eels' were free of their tubes Rosenbaum ordered counter-flooding and took the boat down to the depths, all spare crewmen running forward to add speed to their descent. Four explosions were clearly heard, followed by the unmistakable creaking sound of bulkheads collapsing. All four torpedoes had hit. Among the men aboard the stricken carrier was Arthur Thorpe, a journalist from the *Daily Telegraph*:

We scrambled up the ladder to the upper deck with the ship listing over terrifyingly to the port side on which we were. The sea, normally ten feet below the rails, was surging ominously a bare two feet below them. We made the quarterdeck and grabbed anything we could to haul ourselves up the steeply sloping deck to the starboard side ... Looking round I saw the deck slanting more sharply than a gabled roof. Six-inch shells weighing over 100lbs tore loose from their brackets and bumped down the cliff-like deck.

Ratings on the port side saw them coming and flung themselves into the water to escape injury. Foolishly I asked the First Lieutenant 'Is she going?' He nodded. Several ratings, grasping the casing, clambered towards us. They fastened a stout rope to the deck. They slithered down into the thick oil welling out under the ship and coating the sea and drifted away. With perfect confidence in my lifebelt I did the same and let go.

I went under the wave but when I came to the surface I realised with horror that I had not put enough air into the lifebelt. My head was barely above water. With all the poor swimmer's dread of deep water I splashed and kicked clear of the ship. As I got free of the oil patch the sea became choppy and every wave washed clear over my head till I was dizzy. I gave myself up for lost.

No wreckage was near which I could grasp. Then as a wave lifted me I saw a glorious sight – a cork float 20 yards off with sailors clinging round it. I fought madly towards it ... Making another wild clutch, I felt my fingers grip.

Half a dozen ratings holding on tried to loosen the ropes to open the cork raft out. It was tied like a round bundle. But the oil on their fingers made the task impossible ... Another rating swam up and caught hold too. He told us his leg was broken. We helped him crawl on to the centre of the bundle ... I pulled myself up and saw the *Eagle* 200 yards away, lying on her side. Down the great red expanse of the *Eagle*'s hull men like ants were sliding down into the sea.

Suddenly I felt a shock at the base of my spine. I knew it was a depth-charge from a destroyer hunting the U-boat responsible. 'She is going' gasped one of the men. Then came a mighty rumbling as the sea poured relentlessly into the *Eagle*, forcing out the air. The water thrashed over her in a fury of white foam and then subsided. She had gone.[3]

The carrier took two officers and 158 ratings as well as the sixteen Sea Hurricanes of 801 Squadron FAA with her to the bottom, though HMS *Laforey*, *Malcom* and *Lookout* and the tug *Jaunty* picked up 927 of the ship's company, including Captain Mackintosh. The remaining destroyers hunted in vain for *U-73* but failed to touch the deep and slowly moving U-boat with their badly targeted rain of depth charges. For three hours Rosenbaum kept his boat at a depth of over 200 metres, water leaking through the various faults, but unable to be flushed from the boat as the bilge pumps lay silent. *U-73* became gradually heavier, the air inside fetid and rank as all non essential personnel lay in their bunks, breathing through potash escape gear in order to stay alive and conserve what oxygen there was.

Six hours after *Eagle* went down, and three since the last depth charges, Rosenbaum edged his boat to periscope depth. A fault in the hydroplanes made it difficult to control his depth, but an all-round look through the periscope showed an empty horizon. It also showed a broad oil leak from the U-boat's stern, the presence of so much oil from *Eagle* in the water fortunately having hidden the tell-tale trace from the hunters above. Finally the boat surfaced, fresh air flooding the humid interior and Rosenbaum sent his contact signal to FdU Italian, ending the message with: 'Hit *Eagle* four torpedoes 500 yards. Sinking noises clearly heard. Depth-charged, no damage.'[4]

The loss of HMS *Eagle* was a serious blow to Operation 'Pedestal' though they faced days of further incessant enemy attacks. The two remaining U-boats would have no more success against the convoy, Rosenbaum incorrectly claiming a destroyer possibly hit on 13 August as he trailed the 'Pedestal' ships. Franz-Georg Reschke's *U-205* failed to make contact, picking up some Italian airmen on 14 August, one of whom was slightly wounded, and five more the following day who had more serious injuries. Unable to treat them properly on board, Reschke headed to Cagliari to disembark his passengers and from there to Messina for replenishment.

Italian submarines, as well as MTBs and aircraft, carried out the remainder of the attacks on Force K. In total the Italian submarines sank two merchant ships and the cruiser HMS *Cairo*, damaging three more merchant ships and the cruisers HMS *Kenya* and *Nigeria*. By the time that the last ship, the indomitable British tanker *Ohio*, reached Valletta harbour there were only five merchant ships left out of the original fourteen. One aircraft carrier, two cruisers and a destroyer had been sunk, two other carriers, HMS *Indomitable* and *Victorious*, two cruisers and a destroyer damaged. In return the Italian submarines *Dagabur* and *Cobalto* were destroyed as well as thirty-nine aircraft claimed shot down. In fact the convoy should have been completely destroyed by Italian naval forces, the Cruiser Division comprising three light and three heavy cruisers and seventeen destroyers planning to attack Force K, but they had been denied German air cover by Kesselring who doubted the Italians' ardour for battle. Without protection, the Italians withdrew.

Ultimately the shattered remains of the 'Pedestal' convoy that did arrive in Malta revived the island's flagging ability to resist. Wartime opinion attached great importance to the revitalisation of Malta as a British base at this point but, though still a thorn in the Axis side in the Mediterranean, many post-war studies have shown that in fact the forces based on Malta had only a relatively small role to play in the defeat of the *Afrika Korps*, no matter how symbolic their stand. The same 'running sore' that plagued the German and Italian forces crossing the Mediterranean to supply Rommel's *Afrika Korps* also took a heavy toll and commitment from the Royal Navy and Allied merchant shipping, one felt by many to not be commensurate with its strategic importance. In reality Rommel's supply problems were more to do with the distance between the North African ports where the material was unloaded and the front line, there often being ample supply in the harbours but an inability to transport it to the front line other than by inefficient, vulnerable and fuel-consuming overland truck traffic. Both Tripoli and Benghazi were the ports used by the Axis forces in Libya, before the fall of Tobruk. Although Tobruk offered a closer disembarkation port to the lines at El Alamein, it was also within striking distance of British forces at Alexandria. Coupled with penetration of the Italian naval code net (since July 1941) and the *Luftwaffe* and *Heer* Enigma code used in the Mediterranean which allowed the precise targeting of tanker traffic and advanced knowledge of convoy routes and times, fuel was always going to be a problem to the *Afrika Korps'* advance – logistics not being one of Rommel's strong points as a commander.[5] Nonetheless, by the end of August the island of Malta was functioning as a base for British submarines, surface ships and aircraft and the Axis supply arteries were threatened by whatever interference it could achieve once more.

Elsewhere the final two sinkings by U-boat were in the eastern Mediterranean. During Operation 'Pedestal' the Admiralty sailed a second 'decoy' convoy from Alexandria, codenamed 'Drover'. Aware from agents that the convoy had put to sea, FdU Italian directed the six U-boats deployed in the eastern Mediterranean to intercept – *U-77, U-83, U-97, U-372, U-375* and *U-565*. For Kaptlt. Heinz Joachim Neumann's *U-372* it proved a disastrous patrol. After sailing from Salamis on 7 July the patrol had been barren, the U-boat was in the area of the heavily defended 'Drover' convoy west of Jaffa late at night on 3 August when it was detected on radar aboard Wellington 'M' of 221 Squadron RAF. Flight Sergeant Gay and his crew made visual contact a little after midnight, dropping flares over the startled German. *U-372* immediately crash-dived before the Wellington could attack, but Gay circled the area and called for surface support. Two destroyers, HMS *Sikh* and *Zulu*, rapidly arrived on the scene, the former quickly fixing the boat's position with ASDIC, delivering six depth charge attacks while *Zulu* stood by. *U-372* weathered the storm and the battered boat surfaced quietly after the attacks petered out and tried to use its higher surface speed and low silhouette to make a surfaced run for it. However, a lookout atop the *Sikh*'s crow's nest sighted the boat and both destroyers opened fire with their main guns, forcing Neumann back underwater. Throughout the rest of the morning the two destroyers repeatedly depth-charged the boat, two more destroyers HMS *Croome* and *Tetcott* arriving to add their weight to the attack with their fresh stocks of depth charges. Eventually at approximately 13.30 *U-372* clawed its way to the surface where the crew scuttled their boat and abandoned ship, all of them rescued by their attackers. Amongst the bedraggled crew was one extra passenger – an *Abwehr* agent Neumann had been scheduled to put ashore near Beirut before switching to anti-shipping operations.

Another of the boats ranged against 'Drover' suffered at the hands of enemy aircraft. *Oberleutnant zur See* Friedrich Bürgel's *U-97* was bombed and severely damaged north of Alexandria on 4 August, though Bürgel was able to limp away to safety. The boat limped slowly back to Salamis from where it was transferred onwards to La Spezia and the more sophisticated dockyard facilities there.

On the afternoon of 17 August, Kraus' *U-83* attacked the troop ship SS *Princess Marguerite* north of Port Said, erroneously believing her to be an auxiliary cruiser. The 5,875-ton passenger liner had been requisitioned in September 1941 by the Ministry of War Transport for use as a troop transport and at midday on 17 August was *en route* as part of a small convoy from Port Said to Famagusta carrying 125 crewmen and 998 British soldiers. Despite air cover and an escort of three destroyers and the armed merchant cruiser HMS *Antwerp*, the *Princess Marguerite*, was hit by Kraus' two-torpedo spread, the torpedoes igniting the ship's fuel tanks. The crippled liner was soon ablaze, exploding munitions adding to the chaos aboard as she began listing to port. As the ship was brought to a stop Captain Richard A Leicester gave the order to abandon ship, though burning oil on the water surface made the evacuation hazardous. Within 45 minutes the ship sank, killing fifty-five soldiers and five crewmembers. The survivors were rescued immediately by the British destroyers HMS *Hero* and *Kelvin* and later landed at Port Said. To avoid loss of morale in the United Kingdom, news that the *Princess Marguerite* had been sunk by enemy action was withheld from the public until 22 January 1945.

However, Kraus was not to escape lightly. Retaliation came swiftly in the form of British aircraft that caused extensive damage to the bow and flooding within the forward torpedo compartment. Smashed glass lay all around the control and radio rooms and the creeping odour of chlorine gas from flooded battery cells began to be detected. Men were instructed to don their potash breathing gear as they frantically fought to get their boat operational again. The aircraft were unable to finish their task though and Kraus limped from the scene, transmitting calls for assistance that resulted in the destroyer *Hermes* sailing from Crete and taking the boat in tow while German aircraft covered their retreat first to Messina for immediate repair and then onwards to La Spezia for two months of dockyard work. During this period Kraus, awarded an Italian medal for bravery, was rotated back to Germany to take command of the new long-range Type IXD-2 boat *U-199. Oberleutnant zur See* Ulrich Wörishoffer, formerly IWO of *U-565*, took his place as commander of *U-83*.

In the Aegean on 22 August Kaptlt. Wilhelm Franken's *U-565* was also hit by aircraft and severely damaged only eight days into his cruise. In response to his radioed appeals for assistance the Admiral Aegean requested and was granted air cover to be provided by units of X *Fliegerkorps*. The boat entered La Spezia harbour three days later.

Könenkamp's *U-375* scored the final success of August, torpedoing an unknown steamer estimated at 4,000 tons displacement on the evening of 26 August. Könenkamp fired a full bow salvo of four torpedoes and observed a hit after 5 minutes and 46 seconds, with a high column of churning water marking detonation. In fact he had hit the 6,288-ton steamer ss *Empire Kumari*. Ironically the ship was originally German, having been built as the ss *Sturmfels* for the Hansa Line, but seized by the Royal Navy on 25 August 1941 at Bandar Shapur, Persia as part of Operation 'Countenance'. Despite being scuttled by her German crew she was refloated and requisitioned by the Ministry of War Transport as ss *Empire Kumari*. Sailing from Haifa to Port Said as part of Convoy LW38 the ship had 450 tons of bagged potash aboard when the torpedoes struck. Three men were killed in the explosion; the damaged ship was taken under tow by the corvette HMS *Gloxinia* and later by the British tug HMS *Brigand* and Haifa harbour tug *Roach* into Haifa harbour. The crippled steamer arrived there on 27 August but sank while at anchor off the breakwater during that same evening. Her master, eighty-four crew and four gunners had in the meantime been taken off by HMS *Gloxinia* and landed at Haifa.

The rate of success experienced by the Mediterranean boats was meagre to say the least. Though they had accounted for three major warships since June as well as the depot ship *Medway*, they had only managed to sink eight merchant ships (including the scuttled *Empire Kurami*) that were over 200 tons displacement. In return the Mediterranean U-boat strength had been gradually reduced to fifteen boats by the end of August. Of these *U-83, U-97* and *U-565* were severely damaged and were expected to take considerable time within the struggling dockyards before they could sail again. Indeed by 1 September 1942, thirteen U-boats had been lost in action. Elsewhere this horrendous casualty rate may have forced a dramatic re-evaluation of the policy regarding U-boat deployment within the region, but acting in support of Rommel as they were, their tenure was firmly endorsed by Hitler.

On 29 August, at Hitler's *Werwolf* headquarters near Vinnitsa in the Ukraine, the subject of the Mediterranean received scant attention, though Raeder once more lobbied for a swift invasion of Malta:

> The opinion of the Naval Staff regarding the importance of the capture of Malta remains unaltered. The capture of Gibraltar remains a most desirable objective for the future. It is particularly important to seal off the Mediterranean completely in case a long drawn-out war requires us to secure our European *lebensraum* as thoroughly as possible. We now have 15 submarines in the area. Heavy damage was again caused by enemy bombers ... The C-in-C Navy continued to regard a possible attempt of the Anglo-Saxons to occupy Northwest Africa and get a foothold in North Africa with the aid of the French as a very great danger to the whole German war effort. Therefore Germany must maintain a very strong position in the Mediterranean ... The Führer concurs in this opinion ... He does not conceal his increasing dissatisfaction with the Italians, and alludes to plans which he is not yet able to discuss.[6]

On the night of 30 August Rommel launched his attack against the Allied line at Alam Halfa. Facing him was a reshaped British command, Auchinleck having been replaced by General Harold Alexander as C-in-C Middle East and the Eighth Army put under the command of General Bernard Montgomery. Facing the German and Italian assault were prepared defences including extensive minefields through which they had to manoeuvre and fight, all the while under ferocious attack from a reinvigorated Desert Air Force. Also, unbeknown to the Germans, Montgomery was privy to priceless intelligence yielded by penetration of the German *Luftwaffe* Enigma code – Rommel reporting his plans to Kesselring, his regional commander, who in turn transmitted them on to Germany using his *Luftwaffe* network. This, coupled with the recent breaking of the *Heer* 'Chaffinch' cipher, which provided a complete breakdown of the strength of the *Afrika Korps*, allowed the British Eighth Army to prepare with almost unprecedented knowledge of enemy plans and dispositions. By 3 September, with barely one day's fuel supply remaining, Rommel was forced to withdraw. Though it is fair to say that Montgomery's cautiousness and insistence on fighting a logistical war in which he could guarantee material superiority robbed the Allied forces of a chance to pursue Rommel and inflict more grievous injury to his forces, the *Afrika Korps* had been defeated.

At sea the planned U-boat onslaught against the British supply routes continued. On 1 September Flag Officer German Naval Command Italy ordered:

> Western Mediterranean boats – concentrate on destruction of Gibraltar forces south-east of Balearics. Main targets are aircraft carriers and heavy units. Plus any transports for British landing attempts in Africa.
>
> Eastern Mediterranean boats – communications lines between Port Said and Alexandria. Alternative targets: traffic off ports on Syria and Cyprus to Port Said and Alexandria.[7]

Within a week the latter were give permission to exercise greater individual choice when FdU Italian transmitted 'free action' allowed to all eastern Mediterranean boats following the reversal at Alam Halfa. However, despite the new instruction, September yielded little for the U-boats. Könenkamp's *U-375* once again claimed a heavy toll on sailing traffic as well as a small freighter, the 558-ton Palestinian SS *Arnon*, torpedoed and finished off with gunfire as she sailed in convoy with three sailing vessels. On 6 September he engaged an Egyptian schooner off Khān Yūnis, the U-boat coming under sluggish and inaccurate fire from shore batteries as it pounded the 108-ton *Turkian* with gunfire. Schomburg's *U-561* also claimed two sailing vessels sunk off Syria by gunfire, while Reschke's *U-205* claimed a hit against an unknown destroyer on 4 September north of Alexandria after a torpedo running time of 5 minutes and 48 seconds. Despite the sound of one detonation clearly heard aboard *U-205* as it lay submerged in the mid-afternoon heat, the attack has never been confirmed by Allied sources. In total, the combined claimed and confirmed tonnage despatched during September by the Mediterranean U-boats reached 1,073 tons. To the west *U-331* trailed two large ships on 12 September before recognising them as Swedish Red Cross ships heading for Greece.

The following month, October, saw no improvement, though four U-boats entered the Mediterranean during the night of 10 October, the 'Tümmler' group consisting of *U-458*, *U-593*, *U-605* and *U-660*, the first reinforcements since January. U-boats patrolled the western areas of the Mediterranean with three in the east. It was felt by Kreisch that this deployment offered the maximum protection to Rommel's rear should the Allies attempt a landing behind his forces, while also leaving the possibility of aggressive interdiction of Allied supply routes. However, Hitler himself ordered the boats redirected following credible evidence of the British aircraft carrier HMS *Furious* and an accompanying Task Force preparing to leave Gibraltar. He feared an attempted attack on Sardinia or further fighter transfers to Malta and ordered all available forces sent to the western Mediterranean to emulate Rosenbaum's success against HMS *Eagle*. Kreisch acquiesced and all bar one U-boat were directed to head for their new patrol area, two of the three that were due to be relieved from the waters off Palestine ordered to replenish at Messina and reinforce the other seven U-boats. A further seven Italian submarines were stationed between the Spanish mainland and Ibiza.

During the evening of 28 October lookouts aboard *U-81* and *U-605* both sighted the enemy task force of HMS *Furious*, two cruisers and six destroyers, which was indeed on a resupply mission to Malta to fly off aircraft bound for the island, moving at high speed. Soon *U-565* and *U-431* were also in contact, both boats attempting an attack as the British sped by. Dommes' *U-431* loosed a four-torpedo bow salvo but missed, while Franken's *U-565* logged a similar attack, all of which hit but failed to explode. With the British moving at 21 knots, the U-boats were soon left behind and the pursuit was abandoned.

However, Kreisch planned an interception for the return voyage of HMS *Furious* but once again, despite making contact, the U-boats were unable to strike a blow against the British ships. Thus a single sailing vessel claimed off Lebanon by *U-77* and two failed attempts against the carrier HMS *Furious* were the only recorded German U-boat attacks during October 1942.

The one remaining U-boat in the eastern Mediterranean during the abortive hunt for HMS *Furious* was *U-559*. The boat, which had been at sea since August with only a brief break in Messina, was considered unsuitable for the hunt in the east as the boat was in some need of repair. It was felt that it could remain off the Palestinian coast, tasked with intercepting shipping 'anywhere' until its offensive capabilities were completely exhausted. On 30 October while northeast of Port Said, *U-559* was on the surface in the darkness of early morning. Hans-Otto Heidtmann's boat, one of the first to enter the Mediterranean as part of the 'Goeben' group, was then picked up on radar aboard a Sunderland. Identified as a 'possible submarine contact' the Sunderland shadowed Heidtmann's boat until surface forces could arrive. HMS *Hero* was the first destroyer to arrive on the scene though a thorough ASDIC search revealed no trace of *U-559*. More radar-equipped aircraft soon joined the hunt, as the 12th Destroyer Flotilla – HMS *Pakenham*, *Petard*, *Dulverton* and *Hurworth* – slipped from Port Said some 70 miles distant to assist.

A little after noon the four destroyers rendezvoused with the still searching HMS *Hero* when a Wellesley aircraft of 47 Squadron RAF reported a periscope and the clear shadow of a submerged U-boat seven miles from the destroyers. The aircraft dropped flares and three depth charges on *U-559* as all five British destroyers raced to the location, HMS *Dulverton* almost immediately obtaining a clear ASDIC contact. Over the following ten hours the ships launched nineteen separate attacks using 150 depth charges until *U-559* was forced to surface. The U-boat had been lying at extreme depth but with several leaks filling the bilges with water and the air onboard barely breathable as the crew lay motionless within their battered boat. Heidtmann's final option was to drag his boat to the surface before flooding rendered that impossible and attempt a escape on the surface now night had fallen.

As soon as the conning tower emerged from the sea HMS *Hurworth* immediately picked up *U-559* on radar and blinded the emerging lookouts with its searchlight. The U-boat was too close to be engaged by the destroyers' main weaponry and so *Hurworth* and *Petard* opened fire with 20mm and 40mm cannon, raking the conning tower and pitching several dead bodies over the side, one of whom was possibly Heidtmann himself. With escape clearly impossible, the crew started to abandon ship while scuttling *U-559*. It is possible that Heidtmann was already dead by this stage, but the boat's evacuation was hurried and confused and amidst the chaos the radio crew neglected to ensure the destruction of their all-important Enigma machine and codebooks. Almost immediately Mark Thornton, captain of HMS *Petard*, saw an opportunity to capture the boat before it went under. He brought his destroyer nose to tail against *U-559* while a number of men jumped onto the German deck and attempted to attach a towline. The first and second attempts failed, but a third was more successful and with *U-559* secured by a thick manila rope other men began to arrive onboard from whalers that had been lowered to carry a boarding party (though one had been distracted by the task of rescuing shocked German survivors). HMS *Petard*'s second-in-command, Francis Anthony Blair Fasson, had been aboard one of the whalers but had stripped naked and dived overboard to swim to *U-559* while the whalers became bogged down amongst the Germans. Fasson climbed aboard and immediately ran for the conning tower, followed by Able Seaman Colin Grazier and NAAFI Canteen Assistant Thomas Brown. Fasson, with a sub-machine gun and a torch, led the two other men into *U-559*, making straight through the jumbled interior to Heidtmann's quarters forward of the control room. Once there he smashed open cabinets, and used nearby keys to unlock several drawers from which he took what looked to Brown like 'confidential books'. Brown began taking the documents to the control room ladder where he passed it up to willing hands above, returning several times to get more from Fasson who continued to ransack the radio room as water slowly edged up to knee deep. Fasson in the meantime had found a box which he attached to a lifting line rigged by Brown in the control room, cautioning the men above to lift it carefully as the 'instrument' was 'very delicate'. It may well have been the U-boat's Enigma machine. However, at that moment the scuttling took hold and the stern began to sink rapidly. Aboard *Petard* Thornton ordered engines reversed to try and pull the towline taut and lift the boat's stern, but the destroyer was perilously close to hitting and capsizing one of the whalers which was clearly collecting the captured documents, so instead the towline was ordered cut. Men above decks began to shout for Fasson and Grazier, who had joined him in the control room, to abandon ship but as they jumped clear Brown urged the two men to climb out before he was swept off the sinking U-boat, the two men being trapped by inrushing water and plunging to the depths with *U-559* and the precious 'instrument' that they had been unable to get clear of the boat. Neither man was seen again.

In total forty-one of the forty-eight German crew were rescued and the haul of captured documents included a short signal codebook for sending weather reports and another for reporting enemy ships and other tactical information to FdU Italian. These were priceless to British codebreakers who had been unable to penetrate the U-boats' 'Triton' Enigma code net that utilised the four-rotor machine introduced at the beginning of 1942. It remains one of the most important captures of U-boat intelligence materials of the war. The two British seamen killed, Fasson and Grazier, were both awarded the George Cross posthumously, though their real achievement would not be publicly known for thirty years. Canteen Assistant Brown was awarded the George Medal for his role in the recovery – and then promptly discharged from the Service when it was discovered that he had lied about his age in order to serve, in fact only being sixteen years old. The disappointed Brown, reduced to a civilian, was killed in early 1945 while attempting to rescue his sister who was trapped inside a burning building, never living to receive his medal.[8] Heidtmann, his exact cause of death unknown, was posthumously awarded the Knight's Cross on 14 April 1943.

Chapter 6

Operation 'Torch'

A SENSE OF VIRTUAL STALEMATE was felt throughout the Mediterranean-based U-boats following their poor performance in October. The enemy was conspicuously absent from the western Mediterranean, patrolling boats failing to encounter anything other than ceaseless aircraft patrols. FdU Italian conceded that perhaps it was the relatively limited endurance of the Type VIICs that was proving a constraint on the length of patrols, limited as they were to a radius of action determined by fuel and food consumption – the storage and durability of the latter problematic in the Mediterranean heat. In view of the paucity of enemy encounters it was decided to place the 1,554-ton depot ship MV *Bengazi* at the disposal of the 29th U-Flotilla. The ship was to be stocked with enough food to last ten crews one month at sea, 500,000 litres of fuel and forty electric torpedoes as well as lubricating oil. The ship was to be commissioned into the *Kriegsmarine* at Cagliari where it would also be based. In addition, the 1,300-ton steamer *Favor* was to be equipped with the same quanitity of fuel, food and lubricating oil and would be stationed at an as yet undecided base in the Balearic Islands. The *Favor* lacked the ability to carry torpedoes but it was felt her fuel capacity could be increased by an additional 500,000 litres in barrels in the ship's holds. The 29th U-Flotilla was instructed to fit out the new ships quickly, the *Bengazi* being expected in La Spezia on 8 November, and *Favor* the following day.

The pressure applied to the failing U-boats was being steadily ratcheted up as Rommel's hard-pressed *Afrika Korps* suffered further reverses, their dire supply situation allowing no respite. On Saturday 24 October the battle of El Alamein had begun, heralded by a 1,000-gun bombardment by the Eighth Army before Montgomery launched his anticipated attack. At that time Rommel was in Germany on sick leave, returning to North Africa the next day to reassume command. But it was a forlorn hope. A counter-attack on 27 October was thrown back by the Allies who began Operation 'Supercharge' on 2 November – the final British breakout from their El Alamein positions. Only thirty-two operational German panzers faced Montgomery's overwhelming forces. The following day Rommel ordered his forces to retreat, although Hitler ordered his once favourite commander to stay where he was with his now familiar 'stand or die' rhetoric. Agonising over whether or not to disobey a direct order from his commander-in-chief, fortunately sense finally prevailed and the following day Rommel ignored his order and again ordered a general retreat, thereby saving the remains of his army.

On 6 November, Adolf Hitler issued a proclamation that was passed on to the U-boat crews.

From *Führer* to FdU and all boats.
The existence of the *Afrika Korps* depends on the destruction of the Gibraltar force. I expect a ruthless, victorious operation.
Adolf Hitler.

There was little to be gained by such exhortation and events soon overtook the Mediterranean boats once more. On Sunday 8 November 1942, the long-planned Operation 'Torch' began as Allied troops surged ashore in Morocco and Algeria.

The Allied invasion had several aims: the destruction of the *Afrika Korps*, the cowing of Spain to prevent it being persuaded to enter the war on the Axis side, to provoke antagonism between Vichy France and Germany as German forces were predicted to invade Vichy, to expose Italy to the threat of direct attack from an Allied-controlled North Africa and, of course, securing of Allied convoy routes across the Mediterranean. Both the military and diplomatic groundwork for 'Torch' had taken months of careful planning, as United States and British forces were working in true cooperation against French units of indeterminate loyalties. Stalin in Moscow also had to be convinced of its rationale, pressing as he was for a more direct assault against German-held Europe and the opening of a 'Second Front' to take pressure off the Soviet Union which was soon to be embroiled in the rubble of Stalingrad.

In overall command was the relatively inexperienced General Dwight D Eisenhower, though what he lacked in combat experience he more than compensated for with acute political acumen, vital for the often rocky relationships between various Allied nations. During April 1942 Admiral Andrew Cunningham had been appointed to head the Royal Naval Staff Mission to Washington and proved an ideal opposite number to the equally blunt American, Admiral Ernest King. It was therefore Cunningham who was given command of the Allied Expeditionary Force for the invasion of North Africa and he would direct the 'Torch' landings from his headquarters in Gibraltar, beginning a long and successful friendship with Eisenhower.

German forces had unwittingly already bumped into the large convoy traffic assembled for Operation 'Torch', both U-boats and Condor reconnaissance aircraft sighting large groups of shipping at sea. However, although they regarded an attack in the Mediterranean as highly possible, they had no idea where the blow might actually fall. Hitler believed that the Allies would not risk inciting anger in France by attacking Vichy French possessions in North Africa, and therefore reasoned the most logical area was near Tripoli or Benghazi in Libya, attacking at Rommel's rear as the 'Desert Fox' retreated from El Alamein. Therefore on 4 November Dönitz was asked by OKM to redirect seven Atlantic Type VIICs into the Mediterranean. Dönitz in turn hurriedly formed the 'Delphin' group from six boats already at sea – *U-407*, *U-617*, *U-259*, *U-596*, *U-755* and *U-380* – reinforced by *U-595* out of Brest.[1] All seven boats successfully passed Gibraltar during the new moon between 8 and 10 November and once again the strength of the Mediterranean U-boat presence would reach twenty-five boats.

The BdU War Diary provides an excellent example of the orders given to U-boats transitting the waters of Gibraltar, dated 28 October 1942:

Additional Order to Operational Order No.53 for *U-595* and *U-755*.

I. Operation: To sail through Straits of Gibraltar into the Mediterranean during the new moon period in the first half of November. Further operations in the Mediterranean comes under FdU Italian.

Operation to be given up only:

1) If mechanical damage necessitates return.

2) Failure of Radar Interceptor.

3) In case repeated attempts to break through meet with failure. (See III 5)

II. General: Breakthrough will succeed without trouble only if the enemy has no forewarning of the attempt, therefore:

1) Strictest secrecy must be maintained by Officers and men until report is given that they have passed through.

2) Boat must remain unseen when in the Gibraltar area.

III. Operational Plan:

1) Boats to put out between 30 October and 1 November.

2) Report passing north of 42° N.

3) Between 42° N. and 39° N.

a) Radio limited only to matters of tactical importance.

b) General freedom for attack, but no convoy operation or requests for attack clearance.

4) South of 39° N between 15° W and 0° E,

a) Radio silence except for danger reports. Situation report only in case it is important for other boats.

b) Liberty to attack only battleships and carriers.

5) Both boats to break through in one night, according to plan on 9 November. Report of breakthrough to be given 'Operation ... carried out' with 2 digit number, whereby the number divided by 2 gives the evening during which the breakthrough was carried out.

Example: 'Operation 36 carried out' means: Breakthrough accomplished on night of 18-19 November. In case another attempt is necessary a 2 digit number will be given which when divided by 3 will give the date. Example: 'New operation 60' means: Breakthrough accomplished on 20–21 November.

In order to receive messages on the day before the attempt is made, boats are to switch to the longest wave length possible at mid-day and listen for the first 15 minutes of each hour, that is 12.00–12.15, 14.00–14.15 German Standard time, etc.

In case operation is unsuccessful the first night, another attempt will be made the next night. In case this also fails, boats will sail westward and try again on the 5th night.

IV. Experience gained from the last breakthrough in October 1942: Course followed was between middle of the Straits and the 200 metre line along the African side. Patrol boats unable to be seen. Searchlights from Gibraltar from time to time. Due to continuous air patrols Enge sailed through submerged.

V. In case the operation fails because of Radar Interceptor breakdown or three unsuccessful attempts have been made, boats are to sail westward and report after passing 15°W. On return cruise boats must report first when north of 43°N.

For the Officer Commanding U-boats

(Chief of Operations Division).[2]

By this stage Kreisch at FdU Italian was aware that the Allies were preparing for a major operation in the Mediterranean. An Italian agent reported a huge convoy, including three aircraft carriers, one battleship, a liner and at least forty freighters leaving Gibraltar on 5 November, followed by another equally impressive number of blacked-out ships later that night. The strongest probability that now occupied the minds of Kreisch, Weichold in Italy and as far up the chain of command to Adolf Hitler was a planned amphibious assault near Bejaia east of Algiers.

Dönitz recorded the to-and-fro of argument and counter-argument regarding the despatch of his precious boats against the looming Allied threat in the Mediterranean both east and west of Gibraltar:

Reports of giant massing of forces for landing operations in the western Mediterranean led to the following decree of Naval High Command:

1) Immediate investigation and reports, how many more boats for Mediterranean and when.

a) From operational areas.

b) From harbours of western France. Available by the end of November.

2) All boats in question are to be equipped for Mediterranean operations when they put out.

(Naval High Command 2271/42 Secret)

The teletype reply after consideration of these questions to Naval High Command on 7 November.

I. Only Type VIIC will be committed for operations in the Mediterranean. The following boats of this type will be off Gibraltar at the time in question:

a) *U-259* ready as reserve boat in area AM on 12 November, *U-411* (C.O. on first war cruise). On 16 November, *U-91*, *U-86*, *U-566*, *U-693*, *U-92*, *U-752* and *U-134*, of which *U-98* and *U-564* have Captains on first war cruise. *U-613*, *U-413* and *U-623* (all have had one war cruise), on 23 November *U-264*, *U-445*, *U-623* and *U-603* (all one war cruise). All other boats of Type VIIC in operational areas are either returning, damaged or short of fuel and are destined to go back to Spezia.

b) For the following period, boats from harbours of western France will be off Gibraltar: On 22 November *U-553*, *U-600* and *U-257*. Between 26 and 28 November, *U-373*, *U-432*, *U-254* and *U-221*. Between 29 November and 1 December, *U-610*, *U-757*, *U-455*, *U-569* and *U-615*.

II. Boats of Type IX (not considered suitable at present).

a) From operational area on 13 November, *U-510*, *U-130*, *U-173*, *U-103*, *U-108*, *U-155* and *U-515*. On 15 November, *U-519*, *U-185* (first war cruise).

b) From harbours of western France on 17 November: *U-66*, *U-176* and *U-164*. On 3 November, *U-513*, *U-507* and *U-517*.

III. In connection with I and II, it is noticed that none of the boats are equipped with charts of the Mediterranean, recognition signals etc., which would not hamper operations in open sea areas. The time of the proposed breakthrough of the Straits, 15 November is very unfavourable due to the phase of the moon, not only for the actual passage through the Straits but also the approaches thereto. The English are aware of the passage of *U-755*, *U-595*, *U-617* and *U-407*, *U-596* and *U-380* through the Straits and defences are bound to be strengthened. High percentage of losses must be reckoned on.

In consideration of the high number of misfortunes in the Atlantic War on the one side and the possibilities of success in connection with large numbers of boats in the Mediterranean on the other hand, German High Command received the following statement on 7 November.

U-boat situation 7 November:

a) Transfer of more boats to the Mediterranean: The effect of English activities in the Mediterranean are easily noticeable in the Atlantic. Defences of the convoys most recently attacked were much weaker than before, evidently because of greater escort power in the Mediterranean. Numerous slow ships sailing alone, lead us to believe that this is the case.

The same can be applied to ships in the North Sea. BdU believes therefore that greater prospects of success are in view in the Atlantic due to the decrease in number of screening vessels.

b) A great number of boats had to return to port after the last convoy action. Boats putting out at the time can go prepared to the Mediterranean. A great number of boats will be ready to sail from W. France on 20 November since many boats already at sea are low on fuel, the number of boats in the N. Atlantic will shrink, even though no more are sent to the Mediterranean. The favourable character of this area cannot therefore be answered by desired strength at this time.

c) Wariness of the English will already be sharpened in the Straits of Gibraltar by former operations. It can no longer be assumed that all the single ships, which pass through the Straits one after the other, will be unnoticed. The result will be increased watchfulness which will probably lead to losses of ships which are passing through, especially when the boats happen to pass through at an unfavourable phase of the moon. Heavy air patrols will limit freedom of movement of the boats. Warships and transports are unusually strongly protected and the possibility of losses is correspondingly high.

d) It appears that the prospects of success in the Mediterranean are slight.

e) In considering the transfer of more boats to the Mediterranean, the past situation must be regarded and prospects of small successes in the Mediterranean must be weighed against the more favourable chances in the North Atlantic, keeping in mind the overall situation. Transfer of boats to the Mediterranean is justified only if small success and heavy losses in the Mediterranean can be seen to offset decrease in the tonnage of ships sunk in the Atlantic.

With the predicted clash in the Mediterranean, Dönitz ordered some of the latest technological advances in U-boat weaponry supplied to the 29th U-Flotilla. The first fifty improved magnetic firing pistols produced, the Pi39H – generally shortened to Pi2 – were sent directly to La Spezia and Pola, though their limited number required that captains were told to use them only against targets of crucial importance. Dönitz ordered the Torpedo Development Division (TVA) to hasten their depatch of the new pistols, noting his message within the BdU War Diary, copied to the TVA and FdU Italian:

1. The situation in the Mediterranean makes use of Pistol 39H extremely important to Mediterranean boats. Reasons:
   a) Principal targets are battleships, aircraft carriers and large transports. Greatest damage possible is desired from single shots.
   b) According to air observation the worthwhile targets in the Mediterranean

are protected by anti-torpedo nets. The only workable solution is use of the 39H pistol.

c) This would also dispense with premature ignition and faulty shots in an area where not only do we find high seas and heavy swells but also ships of deep draught.

d) Operational torpedoes of greater destructive power are more urgent in the Mediterranean than in the Atlantic because of the intense situation in Africa.

2. BdU has ordered the 1st consignment of 50 39 H type pistols for the Mediterranean, also is trying to speed up the delay in their operation in the Atlantic.

BdU Secret 4733 A 4.[3]

Also a newly developed pattern-running steering unit – the *Federapparat* (spring loaded), or FAT – was allocated to the two ports.[4] The first twenty-four G7a compressed air-driven torpedoes thus equipped were despatched immediately from Kiel; six to Pola and eighteen for Spezia. Dönitz's reason for this action was not only the possible concentration of shipping that would be found off Allied invasion points should the expected landing go ahead, but that conditions in the Mediterranean favoured the ability of being able to take long-range pattern-running shots that could expect some measure of success against such a concentration of targets, thereby avoiding the necessity of closing the heavily-defended enemy in clear blue waters. Small groups of torpedo specialists from Germany's torpedo testing stations accompanied the weapons in order to provide some instruction on their use to the U-boats' commanders.

The new torpedoes required minor modifications to be made to existing torpedo tubes so as there were again a limited number on hand, only *U-83*, *U-453* and *U-562* already undergoing maintenance in La Spezia and *U-375* likewise in Pola were to be thus equipped, each boat having only two bow tubes modified in order to enable them to put to sea as rapidly as possible.[5] The FAT torpedo was capable of running an adjustable circling path set to loop to right or left on long or short legs after a preliminary run of 500m up to 1,500m. The torpedo speed was 30 knots with a maximum range of 2,500 metres. As such it was a 'fire and forget' weapon and particularly suitable for firing against ships operating in large formations, increasing the chances of a hit. Combined with the G7a it did, however, leave the tell-tale trace of an approaching torpedo on the surface that the use of electric (G7e) torpedoes negated. Thus to maximise their effectiveness and attempt to keep them secret from the Allies for as long as possible, use of the FAT unit was restricted to night shooting.

The four boats were instructed to carry an armament load that comprised six G7a FAT-type torpedoes with the rest G7e with the improved Pi2 pistols in the following configurations: During daytime there were to be three G7e and one G7a FAT torpedoes in the bow tubes; at nighttime two G7a FAT and two G7e with Pi2 pistol in the four bow tubes. Dönitz noted in his War Diary that the use of FAT torpedoes by Atlantic boats was 'not foreseen' because of the weapons' commitment to the 29th U-Flotilla.

On the eve of the 'Torch' landings, from a total strength of eighteen boats, Kreisch arrayed his then available nine boats in the western Mediterranean into three consecutive lines of defence straddling the narrow entrance to the Mediterranean. The first line comprised *U-81*, *U-565*, *U-593* and *U-605*, the second *U-77*, *U-205* and *U-660*, the last *U-73* and *U-458*. Three boats from the east, *U-331*, *U-431* and *U-561*, were rapidly sailing toward the new operational area to bolster the lines against the predicted onslaught. Before the arrival of the reinforcements of the 'Delphin' group this represented the entire available 'at sea' strength of the 29th U-Flotilla. *U-83* and heavily damaged *U-97* were in the overstretched dockyard at Salamis, *U-371* and *U-375* in Pola and *U-453* and *U-562* in La Spezia, both due for conversion to FAT torpedo tubes as well as their normal refit.

As the nine western boats reached their allotted patrol areas they finally clashed with the approaching armada. During the afternoon of 7 November five of them encountered fast-moving British forces. The first was *U-77*, which after radioing a contact report was attacked and bombed by escorting aircraft, driven underwater and away with casualties amongst the crew. Horst Deckert's *U-73* experienced similar problems, driven under and depth-charged by escorting destroyers on high anti-submarine alert. During that evening Friedrich Bürgel's *U-205* was able to finally fire at the oncoming enemy. He loosed a full bow salvo of four torpedoes against what he estimated to be an 18,000-ton troop transport, though all torpedoes missed. Fritz Guggenberger's *U-81* and Kurt Diggins' *U-458* both attempted attacks on Royal Navy targets but failed, though Diggins claimed a hit on a light cruiser.

With British BBC broadcasts proclaiming an imminent attack on North Africa by Allied troops, Kreisch followed his instincts and ordered eight of the U-boats – *U-73*, *U-77*, *U-81*, *U-205*, *U-660*, *U-331*, *U-431* and *U-561* – to Bougie Bay where the attack was expected, leaving only *U-565*, *U-458*, *U-593* and *U-605* near Algiers. The huge logistical organisation of convoys involved in Operation 'Torch' and its subsequent support of landed troops led to the establishment of newly designated routes. The initial assault convoy was named KMF1 which, when separated into two separate spearheads for Oran and Algiers, was suffixed 'O' and 'A' respectively. The follow-up troopships and fast Motor Transport shipping carrying reinforcements continued with this pattern – troopships returning from North Africa bearing the reversed designation 'MKF'. For the subsequent slow series of convoys carrying supplies the designation became 'KMS' – the returning ships simlarly bearing the designation 'MKS'.

On 8 November, as Allied troops began landing, they met mixed receptions from Vichy troops. The three main points of attack were Casablanca on the Moroccan Atlantic coast and Oran and Algiers in the Mediterranean on the coast of Algeria. Spain remained a major factor in 'Torch' planning, as it might either join the Axis forces or be invaded by Germany. Should Spain become an Axis power, the Straits of Gibraltar could be closed and 'Torch' forces trapped in the Mediterranean. Hence the landing of forces on the Atlantic coast of Morocco. Coupled with the unknown attitude that Spain would adopt, negotiations that had been going on between the Allies and several Vichy leaders had not been completed in time to prevent bloodshed during the Allied landings.

In Berlin Hitler was justifiably suspicious of his wavering 'ally'. During February 1941 the anglophobic French Admiral Jean François Darlan had replaced Pierre Laval as Pétain's deputy and was also made minister of the interior, defence and foreign affairs actively promoting a political alliance between Vichy and German forces. However, Hitler harboured a healthy mistrust of Darlan's opportunism, remarking in an evening conversation during April 1942:

> I was struck by a formula used by Admiral Darlan in an appeal to the French. Side by side with matters of no consequence, he spoke of 'precautions for the future' as if he were referring to one of the objects of his policy. Unfortunately I haven't had an opportunity of asking him to explain this mysterious statement. In any case, I could have drawn his attention to the fact that he seems to be hatching certain ideas that were not unfamiliar to me at the time of my struggle. And I'd have added that the tricks of a small conjuror cannot deceive a master conjuror.[6]

That month Darlan was pressured into returning the majority of his responsibilities back to the more overtly pro-Nazi Laval while he retained the post of Commander of the French armed forces.

On 7 November Darlan arrived in Algiers to visit his son who had been hospitalised after a severe attack of poliomyelitis. The following day, following covert meetings and agreements made in Cherchell the previous October between Algiers resistance and American General Mark W Clark, 400 poorly-armed and untrained French civilians neutralised the Vichy coastal artillery at Sidi Ferruch and the XIX Army Corps of Algiers in about fifteen hours. To achieve that result, their forces, under the command of José Aboulker, Henri d'Astier de la Vigerie, and Colonel

Jousse, that night occupied most of the strategic points in Algiers and arrested Vichy military and civil leaders. One of the groups arrested General Juin, chief commandant in North Africa, as well as Admiral Darlan.

General Clark then spent three days convincing Darlan and Juin to order French forces to cease hostilities, on 10 November in Oran and 11 November in Morocco, allowing in exchange for Darlan to remain as head of a French North African administration – a move that enraged the Free French leader Charles De Gaulle and public opinion in both the United Kingdom and the United States where Darlan had been publicly portrayed as a sinister Nazi collaborator. However, as Churchill telegraphed to General Eisenhower who was soon on hand to personally oversee the bargaining with Darlan as well as his 'Torch' operation: 'Anything for the battle, but the politics will have to be sorted out later on.'[7]

The difficulties faced in enlisting the assistance of such unpopular a figure was not helped when President Roosevelt publicly explained that it was a 'temporary expedient' thereby igniting fresh hostility from Darlan and other Vichy commanders who had supported his shift to the Allied cause. It was only Darlan's (correct) conviction that he held the keys to military power within Vichy North Africa, and the subsequent German invasion of his country, that prevented another change of heart.

After the commencement of 'Torch' German offers of military aid should the Allies attempt to land on Vichy North Africa, made by the head of the German Armistice Commission at Wiesbaden to a French representative, were quietly ignored for vital hours until Vichy grudgingly accepted and German aircraft flew to airfields in Tunisia. Once Darlan was discovered to have virtually defected to the Allied cause, Germany felt freer to use all the power that it possessed in occupied France. Hitler had already ordered troops readied to begin Operation 'Anton' – the occupation of Vichy France, which had been prepared under the code-name Operation 'Attila' as far back as December 1940.

On 11 November, following Darlan's public defection, 'Anton' began, German troops sweeping south into Vichy France and Italian forces landing on Corsica and in Nice in violation of the armistice terms signed in June 1940. They stopped short of the French naval base at Toulon, shrewdly and publicly recognised by Hitler as an unoccupied zone still under the complete control of Vichy. Though Toulon was in the Italian occupation zone, German army commanders wanted to storm the port immediately, but were apparently stopped at pistol point about 30 kilometres away on 12 November by German naval liaison officers. Raeder had won a delay from Hitler in the eventual occupation of Toulon, not least of all because Admiral de Laborde had ordered his major surface ships to raise steam and looked ready to sail for North Africa. However, this diplomatic manoeuvring did nothing to assuage the shock felt by Vichy commanders, including Admiral Darlan who, fearing seizure of the fleet in Toulon, finally acquiesced to requests by General Clark to order the Toulon fleet to sail to North Africa.

During Clark's difficult negotiations the 'Torch' landings had been battered by French resistance. At Casablanca American troops landed at three points along a 200-mile stretch of Atlantic coastline with very little fighting, though the Western task force clashed with French warships, the battleship *Jean Bart* damaged and a cruiser, several destroyers and submarines either sunk or beached. Dönitz was compelled to rush as many U-boats as he could to the waters off Morocco, seventeen boats arriving to face determined Allied naval defences.

At Oran events were bloodier. Landings to the west and east of Oran were followed by an attempt to smash through the harbour boom and land American Rangers directly from the ex-US Coast Guard cutters *Walney* and *Hartland*, but both were disabled by Vichy gunfire and sunk. Royal Navy forces repulsed a Vichy attack outside the port, disabling three destroyers and sinking two submarines. American troops fought doggedly into Oran which fell on 10 November. In Algiers the outdated destroyers HMS *Broke* and *Malcolm* were used on a similar attack on the harbour boom, the former breaking through and landing more American Rangers directly at the harbour's edge. The city fell rapidly and was captured and with it Admiral Darlan who subsequently ordered Vichy forces to cease their resistance after Clark's stubborn negotiation. In the meantime, while German reinforcements had arrived unopposed from Sicily to Tunisia on 9 November, Pétain assumed official command of Vichy forces the following day, though he soon made sure to communicate clandestinely with Darlan his support for the Allied forces and confidence in Darlan's actions.[8]

Operation 'Torch' had achieved its immediate objective, but now faced a growing threat at sea as Winston Churchill wrote: 'Although French resistance had ceased at Oran and Algiers German reactions along the North African coast now rapidly increased, and our vital supply route by sea was soon threatened by a swarm of U-boats.'[9] By midday on the day of the 'Torch' attack, German commanders realised that they had misjudged the Allied objectives. There were no reports of any landings near Bougie Bay, or indeed east of Algiers. Though Kreisch continued to believe that the former would soon be attacked by the Allies, Weichold in Rome overruled him and ordered all boats heading there to return to the seas off Algiers. However, the majority were running submerged by day and they would have to surface and receive Weichold's signal before they could head back. Indeed Hartmann aboard *U-77* did reach Bougie Bay and made a brief signal to FdU Italian: 'No enemy forces.'

The boats were redirected to join the battle off Algiers and Oran by a radioed message from FdU:

> Landings of strong enemy forces at many points, principally at Oran and Algiers … Algiers apparently in enemy hands, stronger resistance at Oran. Innumerable transports, covered by aircraft carriers and battleships. Go to it! All out! Risk everything.

Confusion, however, was rife within the U-boats. Kreisch ordered several conflicting orders over the next 24 hours, including instructions that the scheduled new arrivals of the 'Delphin' group were to transmit the safe passage confirmation 'Yes' immediately after passing the 1° meridian in direct contradiction to Dönitz's instructions that they delay this message until near Algiers for fear of betraying both their own positions and those of the following boats. Dönitz was under pressure to follow 'Delphin' with further transfers but forcefully argued against it, citing an inability of available dockyard space in the Mediterranean and the unsuitability of moon conditions later in November.

Kreisch continued to issue detailed routing instructions throughout 9 November, including to two 'Delphin' boats who had radioed the brief passage signal, U-595 and U-617. The boats at his disposal were to form two groups. The first, codenamed 'Hai', comprised six U-boats that were to operate off Algiers: U-77, U-205, U-331, U-431, U-561 and U-660. The second group, codenamed 'Delphin' was to attack Allied forces at Oran and comprised eight boats: U-73, U-81, U-458, U-565, U-593, U-595, U-605 and U-617. The boats were also given instructions to change their target priority from major warships to troop transports and freighters.

Schütze aboard U-605 was the next to attack, following the initial clashes on the day of the invasion. On 9 November he reported an escort vessel shielding the carrier HMS *Furious* sunk, though no confirmation of this was ever made. In fact he very nearly sank nearby U-660 which was lining up its own shot on *Furious* when Schütze's four torpedoes raced by only metres above their submerged conning tower. Aboard U-660 Götz Bauer and his crew were at once terrified and furious to have come so close to oblivion at the hands of a comrade boat and later that night Bauer surfaced and sent a single word transmission to U-605– '*Scafskopf*' (literally meaning 'sheep's head' but more colloquially 'Fool!'). Bauer in turn was reprimanded by Kreisch in Rome who admonished him for breaking radio silence with 'stupid remarks'.

Von Tiesenhausen's U-331, which had just reached the area, sighted the Torch convoy northwest of Algier, in the same area as Schütze's attack, and attacked immediately. He hit the 9,135-ton American troop transport SS *Leedstown*. The ship had already suffered a hit from a *Luftwaffe* air-dropped torpedo as well as bomb damage and lay at anchor when von Tiesenhausen's two torpedoes hit, finally opening the ship's hull completely as she settled on the shallow seabed, the men aboard abandoning her and successfully saving most of the cargo and equipment aboard.

Fritz Guggenberger's *U-81* was next to successfully attack, sighting a small convoy in the early hours of 10 November and hitting the 2,012-ton British SS *Garlinge* and sending her to the bottom, also claiming a hit on an escort vessel, though this was not confirmed. Wilhelm Dommes' aboard *U-431* also struck that morning, hitting what he believed to be a *Leander* class cruiser and a destroyer, in fact just hitting and sinking the misidentified destroyer HMS *Martin*. Escaping the scene, Dommes' boat was plagued by mechanical problems, including a jammed forward hydroplane, loud knocking from the portside propeller shaft and difficulties caused by a leak within the attack periscope causing clouding after every submersion. Dommes broke away from the battle and headed to La Spezia for repairs though he managed another attack on his return journey, torpedoing what he thought was a 'Tribal' class destroyer and a tanker but was in fact the Dutch destroyer HNMS *Isaac Sweers*, which was sunk, his other shot missing the tanker SS *Dingledale* despite Dommes reporting the tanker hit and ablaze. The Dutch destroyer had recently refuelled at sea from a fleet oiler of Force R (two oilers and four armed trawlers) and was holding station to cover Force R until daybreak when she was hit on the starboard side by two torpedoes, one rupturing an oil tank and spreading burning oil over the ship and the water. The second torpedo hit the officers' quarters, killing all thirteen officers that were sleeping there. The survivors were picked up by the British armed trawler HMT *Loch Oskaig*, which was prevented from getting alongside the blazing ship by the flames and exploding ammunition.[10] Four other U-boats, *U-458*, *U-561*, *U-77* and *U-73*, all attempted attacks on British warships the same day as Dommes' victory, though all missed despite the distant echoes of detonations heard aboard at least two of the attackers. On the receiving end, both *U-73* and *U-561* were narrowly missed by torpedo and gun attack from the submarine HMS *Ursula* on 11 November.

In Rome Kreisch reorganised his forces once again. He regrouped the seventeen available boats nearest to the Oran and Algiers battles into three small packs: the first group of five, codenamed '*Hai*' was to blockade Algiers; the second, '*Delphin*', again of five boats was to blockade Oran; while the last seven U-boats comprised the '*Wal*' group that was deployed as a mobile strike force operating in the stretch of water between Cape de Palos and Oran, an expanse a little over 100 miles in width. Once again Kreisch altered his plan shortly afterward, abolishing the '*Hai*' group and depatching those boats to join '*Wal*' raising the number of boats operating as a mobile pack to twelve. For the commanders at sea the orders and counter-orders that spilled through their radio rooms created confusion and a growing sense of despair at what some bitter German POWs would later call Kreisch's professional ineptitude. Radio signals also held the U-boats on the surface for valuable minutes where the overwhelming power of the assembled Allied forces were able to bring to bear their full offensive might.

The battle commenced again on 11 November, this time with at least some result for German efforts, all achieved by boats newly arrived from the Atlantic as part of Dönitz's 'Delphin' group. Jürgen Quaet-Faslem's *U-595*, which had only just arrived in the Mediterranean, attacked and sank the 5,332-ton freighter ss *Browning*, from Convoy KMS2 though the captain estimated his target to be twice the actual size it was. The freighter, which had passed Gibraltar at midnight and was designated to land supplies that included TNT and a deck cargo of four bulldozers at Azrew, broke away from the main convoy in the early morning. ss *Browning* was at that point the Commodore ship as she sailed with five others in single file down a mine-swept channel leading toward the captured city of Oran. With only ten miles left to travel before dis-embarking at Azrew the ship shuddered under the impact of two of *U-595*'s torpedoes out of a salvo of three, a single crewman being blown overboard and killed by the impact. Fires immediately broke out and soon the ship was ablaze from stem to stern. Immediately abandoned by the forty-three crew, sixteen gunners and two navy signallers, subsequent explosions rent the hull into pieces as the survivors were rescued by HMT *Fluellen*. The retaliatory attack against *U-595* lasted for sixteen hours as the Royal Navy escorts battered Quaet-Faslem's boat with depth charges before he managed to gingerly slip away. Ernst-Ulrich Brüller's *U-407* also managed a significant sinking, finding and torpedoing the British troopship ss *Viceroy Of India*, a converted 19,627-ton P&O liner, south of Cape de Gata with a full salvo of four torpedoes. The liner shuddered to a halt and evacuation of the American troops aboard began. Unsure of whether she would go down Brüller attempted to finish the liner off with a single stern torpedo, the ship heeling over to port and sinking by the stern. Almost miraculously, only four lives were lost aboard her. Further west, Josef Röther's *U-380* also stumbled upon a troopship, this time the 11,069-ton Dutch ss *Nieuw Zeeland* which he hit with one of four torpedoes fired. The slowly sinking ship had been returning from the landing its troops and had only 214 crew members, twenty-nine gunners and thirteen service passengers aboard. Röther finished her off with a stern shot and all but sixteen men were picked up by HNMS *Isaac Sweers*, soon to be sunk herself by *U-431*, and HMS *Porcupine*. But the Allied response was fierce and not only was the loss of life from these valuable ships relatively slight, but escort forces drove the attackers off quickly, hammering them with ASDIC and depth charges and driving them deep. The screening force of British submarines also managed to harm the operational capability of the 29th U-Flotilla when HMS *Turbulent* torpedoed and sank the depot ship SS *Bengazi* at 16.00 off Cape Ferrato, Sardinia. A single torpedo slammed into the hull of the fully-loaded ship which took forty G7e torpedoes, a huge supply of food and considerable quantities of lubrication and fuel oil down with her. The following day HMS *Stork*, a *Bittern* class sloop, was also hit by a single torpedo fired by Hartmann's *U-77*. A full bow salvo was fired but one torpedo jammed in its tube — a hot runner that had failed to leave the boat and had to be dealt with by the torpedo crew. A single explosion was seen near the sloop's bridge by Hartmann, and the sloop's bow was smashed and crumpled, severely damaged by the blast. However, the sloop was able to limp away to be repaired while Hartmann came under depth-charge attack by other Royal Navy ships above.

Throughout the remainder of November, only one more ship would be sunk by U-boat attack, *U-81* sighting a small convoy of four freighters and five escorts returning from Oran as Guggenberger began his return to port with battle damage. A final attack yielded one detonation after three minutes and another thirty seconds later. Guggenberger claimed one ship sunk and another damaged, though he had actually hit the 6,487-ton SS *Maron* twice, the eighty-one men aboard being rescued by HMS *Marigold* and later landed at Gibraltar. The British freighter SS *Lalande* from the same small convoy was hit and damaged the following day by *U-73*, but successfully reached port.

U-boat attacks against the Operation 'Torch' armada had been less than impressive. In total they had managed to sink eight ships, two of them destroyers, and two troopships. They had also damaged the formidable U-boat hunter HMS *Stork* and the SS *Lalande*. Alongside the poor German showing, Italian submarines had accounted for only a confirmed four ships sunk or damaged, though they included a single attack by *Argo* on 12 November that accounted for the 2,376-ton auxiliary AA ship *Tynwald* and the 13,482-ton troopship SS *Awatea* off Bougie Bay. With quick and severe retaliation almost always present, U-boat commanders relied on sound more often than not to gauge success. Distant detonations were often claimed as torpedo hits when they could have been premature detonations, depth charges or a myriad other things. One of the newly-arrived 'Delphin' commanders, Albrecht Brandi of *U-617*, proved to be possibly the most 'optimistic' claimer of all. Between 19 and 23 November he claimed to have sunk two steamers, one destroyer, a cruiser and a battleship. In fact he had hit nothing that could be confirmed.

In return the U-boats were hammered. *U-81*, *U-458*, *U-561*, *U-565*, *U-593* and *U-596* were all forced to break off the action and retreat with battle damage and in varying states of mechanical failure, though all successfully avoided enemy forces and made port. More devastatingly, five U-boats were sunk. The first to go was Götz Bauer's *U-660*. After unsuccessfully attempting a four-torpedo attack on Convoy TE3 off Oran on 12 November, the U-boat was located by the destroyers HMS *Wescott*, *Verity* and *Wivern* supported by the corvettes HMS *Starwort* and *Lotus*. Bauer went deep and ejected several of the newly-installed *Bolde* ASDIC decoy cartridges from the boat but was unable to escape the tenacious ASDIC lock. After four hours of accurate depth charging, Bauer surfaced his flooding boat and ordered her abandoned and scuttled, two men being killed by surface fire as the crew abandoned ship. Their attackers rescued the survivors.

On 14 November a Hudson from 233 Squadron RAF sighted and attacked Herbert-Viktor Schütze's *U-605* north of Oran, attacking and sinking the U-boat with no survivors. Flying Officer Hugh Thomson RNZAF, the navigator aboard Hudson 'B', remembered:

I remember [pilot] John Barling pointing out this wake some miles ahead of us. It was a beautiful clear day and we could see for miles ... I have yet to understand why the U-boat was caught unawares. In such conditions we should have been sighted miles away. I can only assume that the lookouts were looking westwards towards Gibraltar, into the lowering sun and into the direction from which they would expect an attack.

A definite identification being made, it was nose down, bomb doors open and depth charges activated ... I, being down in the navigator's compartment, had a bird's eye view of the U-boat as we attacked. The conning tower was fully surfaced but the decks were awash as it commenced its dive. Our WOP/AG [Wireless Operator/Air Gunner] in the turret had another good view as we pulled away and as the depth charges exploded ... We could see in the attack area quite a lot of what appeared to be brown wooden slats and there was also quite a patch of oil.[11]

That same day Jürgen Quaet-Faslem's *U-595* was also sighted while running surfaced and was attacked by Hudson bombers, two from 608 Squadron RAF damaging the boat with all of their eight depth charges.[12] Two exploded on either side of the bow and one fell several yards astern, another hitting the deck and bouncing off into the water before exploding. *U-595* crash-dived immediately after the attack but considerable damage had already been sustained. Glass on the instruments was broken, the main lighting system failed, fuses were jarred from place, fire broke out in the electric motor room damaging the plumbing system, a vent was dislocated and water seeped into the stern. Lockers were broken open and food was strewn about. A hasty inspection showed that the entire electrical system was not functioning properly. Only one motor was still operational but failed to give sufficient speed to sustain trim. In short order *U-595* became heavy by the stern and, after having been submerged for about 20 minutes, was forced to surface. The boat lay at the mercy of enemy aircraft, though the two original attackers soon departed, a Junkers Ju 88 diving from the clouds and startling them. However, six other Hudsons from 500 Squadron RAF arrived later in the day and launched their own attacks. The U-boat's LI, Oblt.(Ing.) Emmerich Freiherr von Mirbach, estimated that *U-595* could remain afloat for only another two to three hours and Quaet-Faslem decided to make for the African coast and there run close to land, put most of the crew ashore, and then with a skeleton crew aboard, make for deep water where he intended to scuttle the boat.

Above them the Hudsons began their attack. Their first attempt with four depth charges exploded ahead of the wildly zig-zagging *U-595*, heavy flak from the boat badly damaging the attacking aircraft.

> According to one account, the 20mm anti-aircraft gun on the bridge was manned by a rating while officers and petty officers sought shelter behind the cowling of the conning tower. The captain let go a steady barrage of advice at the gunner who finally, in exasperation, shouted, 'If you're so damned brave, come out here and help me with the ammunition'. The executive officer, [L.z.S. Friedrich] Kaiser, eventually did come to his aid. [13]

A second stick of four depth charges straddled the boat's stern and the air crew saw what appeared to be the release of four torpedoes from the front tubes, possibly to reduce the U-boat's weight and attempt to gain some speed. The Hudson strafed *U-595* which again replied with accurate and sustained flak. A third attack undershot by 35 yards and the aircraft circled to launch a 100lb bomb which exploded five yards from *U-595*'s starboard beam causing the boat to roll heavily. With damage accumulating, Quaet-Faslem appreciated that his boat was doomed and ran inshore as fast as possible while his gun crew valiantly struggled with the attacking bombers. Navigator aboard Hudson 'X' Flight-Lieutenant Jim Paine remembered the battle:

> The U-boat was firing away merrily and must have upset the aircraft's aim somewhat. The CO asked 'How do I attack this thing?' I said 'Aim in front of the conning tower and go across it at 30 degrees to straddle it.' I, meantime, armed myself with an F4 camera ready to take the U-boat picture of the year, if my hands would keep steady. The gunner manning the U-boat's aft gun was a blond and his gunnery was very accurate. Streams of tracer came whistling at us and I yelled 'Use your front guns.' 'Not close enough' said the CO. Just then the rear gunner said, 'There's an awful smell of petrol about'. I checked the fuel gauges and found one that read zero. We had been hit in the tank! Then there

was a clunk and the port undercarriage looked a bit of a mess. We flew damn
near up the muzzle of the gun and broke off to see the depth charges explode
near the stern. I got my photograph; it's now framed on my wall.[14]

Another depth charge run dropped four charges short of the target as the
aircraft gunners knocked two men from the gun platform, the Hudson in
turn being hit by heavy flak, which caused extensive damage. The final
depth charge run overshot *U-595*, landing off the port bow before the
aircraft delivered one more 100lb bomb that exploded close astern. By now
it was obvious that *U-595* was headed at full speed for the coast and was
likely to beach herself, the sixth Hudson that had not taken part in the
attack circling out of flak range until *U-595* ran aground.[15]

Quaet-Faslem had ordered all Enigma material and other secret
documents jettisoned overboard, believing that once clear of their boat his
crew could make contact with Vichy forces ashore and get back to base.
However, the plan went slightly wrong as, alongside the magnetic and
gyro-compasses, the echo sounding device was non-operational until the
last moment when it suddenly sprang to life with a reading of only eight
metres. Quaet-Faslem ordered hard to starboard just as *U-595* ran aground
at Cape Khamis and could not be refloated. Several of the crew later
recalled watching Quaet-Faslem as he went to his locker, pinned his Iron
Cross on his breast, wrapped the ship's flag about his neck, and gave the
order to abandon ship, adding, 'Every man for himself'. The rubber boat
was broken out as the crew gathered a few personal belongings, donned
life jackets and jumped into the sea as von Mirbach set the seven scuttling
charges distributed between the control room, radio room, motors, and the
diesel room as well as in the magazine. All of the charges exploded
simultaneously. The crew made for shore as their boat exploded behind
them, all but one man reaching the coast together.[16] Quaet-Faslem later
described to American interrogators what happened next:

> We ran as close as possible to the shore and blew her [*U-595*] up. All of the
> crew escaped but one. I presume that the destroyer which was bearing down on
> us picked him up. After we left the submarine, the destroyer fired four rounds.
> Two of them landed between the submarine and the destroyer, and two of them
> landed on the shore inland from where part of my crew stood. The destroyer
> put a landing party overside which came ashore to look for us.

The Germans gathered on shore and began walking inland a few hundred
yards when a British biplane aircraft saw them. The pilot dropped a note
to the crew written partly in Italian and partly in German which read:
'Halt, or I'll spray you with machine guns'. The Germans ran and were
machine-gunned by the plane, though to no effect.

A little further inland we met a [Vichy] French officer who told us that we were close to Picard, French Morocco and that the Americans were not in control there. Thinking that the French were our allies against the Americans, I gave him all the arms we had brought ashore with us, which were six Browning pistols. While I was gone with this French military officer to his office in Picard, the leader of the landing party came ashore and spoke to the French sergeant who had been with the French officer. The sergeant told him that our pistols had been taken, and the leader returned to the destroyer. We telephoned the French Naval Lieutenant Commander at Mostaganem, who said that cars would be sent for us. The French officer said on his word of honour as an officer and a gentleman that we were safe while in the hands of the French, and that we stood under the protection of the French government.

While we were waiting at Picard, we ate and were guided by French Arabian soldiers to a large room in a building where these soldiers guarded us as we slept. About midnight we were surrounded by an American tank company. We were questioned and searched by the Captain of the company. Later in the night we were questioned by a Lieutenant Colonel in the American Army. In the morning of 15 November, 1942, I went with the Lieutenant Colonel to the beach where the submarine had been sunk offshore. About two feet of the super-structure were still visible above the water. Then we were brought to Oran, Algeria. The crew and officers were photographed by an American soldier with a green band around his left sleeve. Then the crew and the officers were separated.

From there we went to the French-Aero Club for dinner and to spend the night. During the night we were questioned and fingerprinted by an American Lieutenant. During the early morning of the 16th November 1942, we were brought to an American ship.[17]

This remarkable capture marked the only time that an operational U-boat crew was taken by Allied ground forces.

In American hands Quaet-Faslem made a grim impression on his interrogators who screened all crewmen in order to extract whatever useful intelligence they could.

Quaet-Faslem was among the less pleasant of the U-boat captains so far encountered. He was bitter, taciturn, and barely civil, and the hatred in his eyes was apparent to all who talked to him. All attempts at conversation with him were futile. He seemed sunk in grief and gloom, and interrogators got the impression that he was reproaching himself for the loss of his boat and its incomplete destruction. The impression that this might be the case was strengthened by occasional frank accusations and more frequent veiled insinu-ations by his crew about his carelessness, inefficiency, and cowardice.[18]

The following day Hudson 'S' of 500 Squadron RAF, which had attacked Kurt Diggins' *U-458* on 13 November, inflicting heavy depth charge and machine gun damage and forcing Diggins to limp back to La Spezia, sighted a surfaced U-boat north of Algiers. It was the newly-arrived *U-259* commanded by Kaptlt. Klaus Köpke on his second patrol. The pilot, Flying Officer Mick Ensor, judged that his aircraft had not been spotted with its white-painted underbelly at the height of 7,000 feet that they were cruising at. He swung the Hudson around and dived to sea level, making a perfect depth charge attack from astern. However, one of the charges hit the forward deck and exploded, throwing the deck gun and most of the conning tower into the air – and into the Hudson. 'There was a great "woomph" and I instinctively pulled up only to find the control wheel came back uselessly into my lap, and the trim lever I found to be useless.'[19] The Hudson was severely damaged, with windows blown out, the elevators and one rudder gone while the other flapped about on the point of disintegration. The wings were bent out of shape and the fuselage holed, though Ensor was able to temporarily nurse the aircraft higher, using the crew as mobile ballast. The Hudson was nearing an uncontrollable state when Ensor ordered the crew to bale out, a naval vessel sighted ahead to port. All four men jumped, though the navigator and one gunner were killed during their drop – the former when his parachute failed to open, the latter after being knocked unconscious as he left the aircraft and drowning once in the water. HMS *Erne* and *Leith* picked up the two survivors. Behind them *U-259*, and all forty-eight crewmen aboard, was gone.

The last U-boat sunk by the 'Torch' forces was a veteran of Mediterranean operations. *Kapitänleutnant* Hans-Dietrich Freiherr von Tiesenhausen's *U-331* was surprised on the surface by three Hudsons of 500 Squadron RAF and straddled with three depth charges that lifted the U-boat's bow from the water, blowing open a torpedo loading hatch and flooding the forward torpedo room. Von Tiesenhausen's boat was doomed and he ordered her abandoned. As crewmen scrambled on deck the Hudsons continued their attacks, a 100lb bomb landing amongst men leaping overboard and more depth charges and machine gun fire killing men as *U-331* lay stricken below. Abruptly, a white flag was raised, no doubt in an attempt to stop the slaughter of the men trying to abandon ship. The pilot of the leading Hudson, Squadron Leader Ian Patterson RNZAF, radioed the possible surrender of a U-boat to naval forces and then returned to base to refuel before heading out once more to circle *U-331*, this time in the company of a Hurricane fighter. The survivors of the German crew were seen to be sitting on the deck of *U-331* which was lying motionless in the water.

Abruptly, a naval unit of a Martlet escorting an 820 Squadron FAA

Swordfish and Albacore arrived and to Patterson's dismay immediately attacked. The Martlet strafed the unsuspecting Germans, wounding von Tiesenhausen and his IIWO and killing several other men. Once this attack was finished the Albacore dropped a single torpedo that destroyed *U-331* and more of the crew. As the furious Patterson flew his Hudson homewards, a Walrus flying-boat and the destroyer HMS *Wilton* arrived to rescue the seventeen remaining German survivors, including the wounded captain.

As successful as Operation 'Torch' had been for the Allies, it had been a debacle for the 29th U-Flotilla. Heavy losses and damage in return for relatively small return had once more proved the inability of Type VIIC U-boats to deal with a large, heavily defended and well-prepared invasion force. The loss of the *Bengazi* had merely compounded their woes. The smaller *Favor* docked in Cagliari, Sardinia, on 22 November, alongside Otto Hartmann's *U-77* which also put into the port to repair damage sustained after its attack on HMS *Stork*. The boat's torpedo data computer, hydroplanes and tube No 3 were unserviceable, the Junkers compressor, gyrocompass, diesel engine couplings partially or intermittently useable and a cylinder head leaking. The boat was urgently worked on and ready to sail shortly afterward as Kreisch ordered Hartmann to join seven other boats being rushed to the seas off Toulon in order to attack an expected French breakout from the port. The ships of the main French battle fleet still lay in harbour despite Darlan's summons to Oran.

While German and Italian forces had successfully taken Vichy France during Operation 'Anton', there remained the vital prize still not claimed by Germany. Hence, the purpose of Operation 'Lila' was to secure the French fleet that lay in Toulon harbour. However, the French were fully aware of their perilous position. Although at first the noted Anglophobe Admiral de Laborde had wanted to put to sea to attack the Allied convoys of Operation 'Torch' as the invasion developed he had been stopped by Darlan's defection to the Allied course. De Laborde had privately vacillated over whether to obey Darlan's summons to North Africa, particularly as the request had come with no direct endorsement from a silent Pétain. As German forces had taken control of Vichy France, he had secured an agreement that a so-called 'free zone' that followed the perimeter of the harbour was to be garrisoned by Vichy troops, a proposal endorsed somewhat reluctantly by the Vichy Minister of Marine, Admiral Auphan. However, on 18 November the German military command had demanded the withdrawal of the Vichy soldiers from the zone, to be replaced only with naval personnel. Auphan resigned and de Laborde prepared his fleet for the possibility of an attempted *coup de main* by German forces to capture them.

The order to seize the French ships was given on 27 November at 04.00 and troops of the *Wehrmacht*'s 7th Panzer Division and SS Regiment

'*Langemarck*' of the 2nd SS Panzer Division '*Das Reich*' entered Toulon within 40 minutes, one SS man being killed and two wounded. Rather than be taken by the *Kriegsmarine* the French immediately scuttled themselves apart from four submarines that put to sea and escaped the German U-boat cordon to join the Allies. In total one battleship, two battlecruisers, four heavy cruisers, three light cruisers, twenty-four destroyers, ten submarines, three seaplane tenders and sixteen miscellaneous other vessels were scuttled. The morning following the scuttling, 300 men collected from the personnel reserves of various French U-boat bases arrived in Toulon after having travelled there by slow train via Paris. Their purpose was to take over and man the French submarines present, though finding no serviceable submarines to man, they returned from whence they had come using express trains.

A new naval command was established at Montpellier, K.A. Zuckschwerdt and his staff arriving from Saint Nazaire where they had been *Seekommandant Loire-Gironde* to become *Kommandant der Seeverteidigung Languedoc*. Zuckschwerdt's brief was to encompass from the Mediterranean border between Spain and France to the Bay de La Ciotat, west of Toulon. As Toulon itself was only a German enclave within the Italian zone, it was provided with its own command – *Deutsche Marinekommando Toulon,* under the control of K.z.S. Rolf Gumprich. Into this valuable port came the heavy weapons of MAA612 and light artillery of MAA687 to protect the new *Kriegsmarine* acquisition.

Despite their meagre performance against harrowing odds during November, the following month would see the men of the 29th U-Flotilla called on to continue the attack against Allied forces in the Mediterranean. The writing was indeed on the wall for the Axis in North Africa, although after the great success of the 'Torch' landings, Allied follow-up movements had been characteristically slow, allowing strong German forces to entrench in Tunisia as Vichy forces had stumbled in confusion between loyalties to either side. Although Rommel continued to be hard-pressed in Libya, the battle for North Africa was not yet over and the defence of the German and Italian held coastline of the northern Mediterranean loomed large for the U-boats still in action.

At BdU headquarters Dönitz was despondent about the continual loss of strength needed within the Atlantic to the perilous waters off Gibraltar and in the Mediterranean. On 18 November he summed up his thoughts on the matter in the BdU War Diary following the directive from OKM to keep twenty-four U-boats with the 29th U-Flotilla and twenty more west of Gibraltar:

Estimate of U-boat Situation

1) The U-boat operation in the Mediterranean has met with the following

success since 8 November: 100,000 tons of merchant shipping sunk, including the presumed '*Viceroy of India*'. 1 cruiser, 2 destroyers, 1 escort boat. Damaged were: 1 carrier, 1 cruiser, 1 destroyer, 1 corvette. Against this we have losses and damage to 19 U-boats. 5 boats evidently lost (*U-259 – U-331 – U-595 – U-605 – U-660*). 8 boats heavily damaged and no longer seaworthy. 3 boats lightly damaged. That is to say, within 10 days two-thirds of the boats have either been destroyed or put out of action.

These heavy losses must be attributed to attack of the first line of the enemy forces during the landing operations.

2) Estimations of the prospects for the future are as follows:

    a) The large number of targets, which has resulted in our successes to date, will fall off after the main landing operation has been completed. Current supplies will be brought in with smaller but more heavily protected convoys. Possibilities of success will therefore fall off. Chance for success against ships in the roads is no longer to be expected, after the enemy has taken possession of the harbours.

    b) Losses to date have been attributable to air attacks. The air situation will however, become worse, rather than better after the enemy has taken over air fields and put them into operation. Already the boats must attack from set positions. FdU Italian requires boats to send their positions. That is indeed a misfortune. That is to say that the boats will continually be under the eye of the enemy air force from the time they leave port until they reach their targets.

    c) The experience gained from the operation so far indicates that U-boats have not hindered enemy operations where all safety precautions, including heavy air patrols, were used. This also applies to future landing activities of the enemy and attacks we make on him. The U-boat is destined for this operation and there is no way out.

3) Operations of 22 boats W. of Gibraltar and Morocco resulted in: 54,000 tons of merchant shipping, 1 cruiser and 1 destroyer sunk. Damaged were: 6 merchant ships. One U-boat was badly damaged and 3 had superficial damage. It has not been yet established whether any boats were lost. Almost half of the damage was done by one attack on the ships in the roads as they lay motionless. Success and losses were smaller in proportion to boats in the Mediterranean in view of large number of boats and the short time the action lasted.

Prospects for the future (as under 2) in the Mediterranean is just as valid in the battle against the supply lines of USA and England coming to Gibraltar area between or immediately west of the St. Vincent-Casablanca line.

    a) Good prospects of success can be seen only in areas outside the realm of air patrols. Such an area cannot be found on the route from England to Gibraltar. That we have learned from experience in our action against convoys.

b) Action against convoys from USA outside air patrol areas, that is, W. of the Azores, holds no promise either, since the enemy can scarcely be found in such a large area. The ratio here is fundamentally different than in the case of convoy attacks in the North Atlantic, where current information regarding time and course of convoy movements and establishment of intercept service, makes for successful operation on even single convoys in spite of the expanse of the area.

c) The area to the E. of the Azores would perhaps make possible more freedom for operation than the St. Vincent-Casablanca area if air patrols and air cover were less intense. Time and space do not suffice to offer large success against E. bound targets before they reach the coastal areas and nothing can be expected from W. bound convoys save occasional individual sinkings. These however are easier in other areas.

4) Action near the entrance to the Mediterranean can therefore be carried out only W. of the Gibraltar corner.

Moreover small prospects of success and large possibilities of losses must be considered here as well as in the Mediterranean, for U-boat warfare has not been thought feasible in this area for the past 2 years, due to the proximity of the coast.

5) In summary, BdU regards further operations against the supply of Africa in the light of high losses and small success. No comparison can be drawn to the proportion of high success at the outset and the special course of the enemy operations, and no weight can be placed on future enemy plans.

6) This operation of U-boats was decisive moreover in the course of the war on tonnage in the Atlantic in which BdU indulged as the principal U-boat action. The war on tonnage was perhaps the decisive contribution of the U-boats at the start of the war. The enemy has made clear to us that his principal worry is the battle in the Atlantic even today, that is to say, the continual weakening of his power through sinkings by U-boats. As already reported, BdU believes that the unusually high sinkings recently in the Atlantic has some bearing in connection with the African invasion. If these sinkings are accepted because U-boats have been withdrawn for action in the Gibraltar area and Mediterranean then the enemy must be right and must feel the ultimate outcome will be a strengthening rather than a weakening of his power. Similar comparisons have been set forth at the time of withdrawal of boats for the N. Atlantic and the first Gibraltar operation at the end of 1941 and beginning of 1942.

BdU is convinced that the sinking results which these boats found in the favourable American situation was even more important than the undisputed success in the Arctic, while the same sort of operation W. of Gibraltar has met with almost nothing but losses.

7) The management of the war in the Atlantic will be as follows:

a) In the Mediterranean there are presently 20 boats. Up to the new moon period in December there will probably be further losses so that in order to have 24 boats, about six to eight will have to be sent into the Mediterranean. Full use of 24 boats will not be possible because of the situation which finds improvements on the bases going slowly.

b) In order to keep 20 boats in the Gibraltar area about six boats must be sent there on 1 December and about eight on 15 December.

c) Without considering losses and damage, there will be about 30 boats in area outside the Mediterranean, the Arctic and Gibraltar, by 1 December. On 15 December there will be about 40 boats, which will be spread out in areas from Iceland to Capetown.

d) Without considering the coming and going or long periods of boats in the yards due to bomb damage, 20 boats in the Gibraltar area represent 1/3 of all available Atlantic combat boats. (60).

e) Out of 20 boats in the Gibraltar area about 30 will be at sea for this operation when we consider those underway to and from port. U-boats in the Atlantic have sunk 200 tons per boat per day at sea during the last month and during the last week the figure has doubled. Therefore the operation will at least reach 30 x 30 x 200 or 180,000 tons, perhaps more as a result of recent experiences and this cannot be outweighed by any possible success in the Gibraltar area. Decrease in sinkings due to withdrawal of boats to the Mediterranean is not once considered in this case.

8) According to the opinion of BdU this is a question of widest scope to consider. BdU is clearly convinced that the weight of the U-boat war must be carried out in the Atlantic, that only war against tonnage will be effective in the overall war and that any deviation from these fundamental concepts will only lead to damage of the total war effort. BdU requests that orders be modified to permit new revisions on the grounds of the above consideration.

Chapter 7

France

THE DISASTROUS RECORD OF November showed little sign of improvement during the final month of 1942. To reinforce the depleted ranks of the 29th U-Flotilla Dönitz was once again ordered to transfer four more U-boats from the Atlantic into the Mediterranean. Once again Dönitz voiced his now familiar concerns, clearly worded and delivered to his superiors on 18 November, but OKM refused to countenance his objections. Reluctantly Dönitz agreed, ordering *U-258*, *U-301*, *U-443*, and *U-602* (designated Group 'Taucher') to pass Gibraltar during the new moon from 4 to 9 December. Two of the four safely entered the Mediterranean, a third, *U-301*, encountering some difficulty.

U-301 put to sea from Brest on 3 December 1942, transferring from the 1st U-Flotilla to the 29th U-flotilla. The boat launched an abortive attack on three enemy destroyers southwest of Cape Ortegal during the early hours of 7 December during its cruise toward Gibraltar. Later that night several enemy destroyers were encountered west of the Strait and with the port diesel malfunctioning the decision was taken to postpone the breakthrough until the following night. *U-301* lay quietly on the seabed 19 miles off Cadiz to await nightfall again. The diesel was still out of action when at 19.00 on 8 December the boat surfaced and set full speed on the starboard engine for the entrance to the Strait. A group of destroyers escorting what was thought to be either cruisers or battleships was soon sighted and *U-301* opted to attempt to attack the capital ships. However, just as they were about to penetrate the destroyer screen in the darkness, the British ships made a sharp turn to the southwest. Almost immediately the slim sillouette of the Type VIIC was spotted and a destroyer prepared to attack at a range of only 300 metres. With no hope of escape on one engine, *U-301* dived as fifteen depth charges chased it under and shook the boat, causing minor damage.

After nearly two hours of cat-and-mouse manoeuvering, *U-301* shook off its pursuers and at 02.37 on 9 December, surfaced abeam of the Cape Spartel lighthouse. Lights on the Spanish coast were clearly visible and the boat was carried toward the African shore on a 4-knot current, *U-301* following the 200 metre depth line eastwards. At 04.32 Ceuta was spotted and the FuMB radar detector began to pick up enemy radar signals. The Gibraltar searchlights probed the darkness, punctuated by occasional starshells and flares fired to illuminate the narrow passageway. Finally at 05.10 with radar signals increasing dramatically, *U-301* dived to 160 metres. By 06.30 Gibraltar was abeam and 90 minutes later *U-301* was through and into the Mediterranean. *U-301* was ordered to proceed toward its operational area, but damage caused during the difficult passage through the Straits caused Kaptlt. Willy Roderich Körner to break off his patrol and head straight for La Spezia, reaching the Italian port during the forenoon of 14 December. The boat would not sail again until 20 January 1943. The last U-boat of the 'Taucher' group, *U-258*, aborted due to an 'illness' of the captain Wilhelm von Mässenhausen. Another boat ordered to replace the latter, *U-257*, also aborted citing an 'illness' of the LI as well a leakage in the stuffing boxes. By then it was too late to order another replacment boat until the period of the next new moon. By the month's end there would be twenty-three boats in service for the 29th U-Flotilla, though at least four were in the shipyards for repairs to extensive damage.

It was not only in the Mediterranean that the U-boats directed against 'Torch' had suffered. Once the invasion had been detected all available Atlantic boats had rushed to the heavily-defended waters west of Gibraltar. Despite some daring attacks mounted by a few inshore U-boats, the majority struggled in the face of superior Allied air and naval forces.

> In coastal waters, such as those off Gibraltar that were under constant and powerful patrol, the current type of U-boat, which was slow under water and which had to surface to recharge batteries found itself confronted with tasks beyond its capacity to fulfill.
>
> For that reason I regarded the employment of U-boats off the Straits of Gibraltar now with the same grave misgivings as I had done in September 1941 ... I did not believe that a continuation of U-boat operations off Gibraltar was justified, nor could I accept Naval High Command's opinion that the very sharp decline in sinkings in the Atlantic would 'be more than counter-balanced by the infinitely more valuable sinking of ships carrying supplies and reinforcements to the Mediterranean'.
>
> Naval High Command, however ... refused to allow me to transfer U-boats from the area west of Gibraltar, but agreed on 23 November to their number being reduced to twelve.[1]

On 1 December Kreisch still had fourteen boats at sea, three of them returning to port.[2] During late afternoon that day Könenkamp's *U-375* encountered what the commander believed to be a *London* class cruiser. It was in fact the 2,650-ton minelayer HMS *Manxman* on passage from Algiers to Gibraltar. The ship was carrying no mines, cargo or passengers and was zig-zagging on a northwesterly course on a calm sea beneath a characteristically blue Mediterranean sky. The minelayer was approximately 71 miles northeast of Oran when lookouts spotted a single torpedo pass close astern from port to starboard, running shallow. Seconds later, before any warning could be given, a second torpedo struck the ship on the port side abreast the engine room, causing the stern to lift violently.

Almost immediately all lighting failed and extensive flooding occurred, *Manxman* assuming a severe list to starboard as she slewed to a stop. To prevent another attack the ship's armament was fired into the water at 1,000 yards range whenever anything was heard, or even thought to be heard by the ASDIC operator. Depth charges were periodically dropped around the ship from a fast motor-boat in an attempt to create the impression in any submerged U-boat that destroyers had arrived. Finally, a little before midnight, HMS *Pathfinder* arrived and towed the crippled ship to Oran, where due to the excessive draught she was unable to pass over various wrecks in the harbour and so she was towed to Mers-el-Kebir where she was berthed alongside the repair ship HMS *Vindictive* to begin her lengthy repair which would last until 1945. It was a good start to the month for the 29th U-Flotilla and although two torpedoes fired to finish off *Manxman* both missed, *U-375* was able to escape unhindered from the scene without suffering serious retaliation.

Throughout the remainder of December it was the Royal Navy that bore the brunt of the 29th U-Flotilla's few confirmed sinkings. Hamm reported suspected damage inflicted on an enemy destroyer on 9 November north of Oran by *U-562* which was never corroborated, but at 23.30 that night Kaptlt. Philipp Schüler's *U-602* on its first Mediterranean patrol torpedoed the destroyer HMS *Porcupine* while it escorted depot ship HMS *Maidstone* from Gibraltar to Algiers. Three torpedoes were fired, though Frederick L J Peters, an engine room artificer aboard the depot ship, recalled that: 'Four torpedoes were fired, two passed our bows, one missed astern, and the other hit *Porcupine*.'[3]

The destroyer had been hit in the port side engine room, completely disabling her and killing the entire engine-room crew. The ship began to slowly sink as a salvage vessel raced to the scene, finding the ship with her stern awash and on the verge of rolling over. The crippled ship was taken quickly in tow as a pair of electric auxilliary pumps struggled to bring the flooding under control. Eventually the destroyer was beached at Arzeu, her back broken, and declared a total loss.[4]

Two days later, at 16.25, Oblt.z.S. Puttkamer's also newly arrived 'Delphin' boat *U-443* sighted the fast convoy MKF4, bound for the United Kingdom, 60 miles west of Oran. Two torpedoes arced toward the clustered ships, both hitting the escort destroyer HMS *Blean* and sending her under with eighty-nine men killed from the crew of 168. Puttkamer believed that his second torpedo had hit a steamer, though both had in fact impacted against the unfortunate warship.

While the Italian submarine *Ambra* delivered frogmen into Algiers harbour to disable four ships and the *Mocenigo* hit the cruiser HMS *Argonaut* on 14 November, it was Puttkamer who next distinguished himself by sinking the loaded freighter SS *Edencrag* that night from Convoy TE9, killing the master, James Gentles, ten crewmen and two gunners. The eleven survivors were taken aboard corvette HMS *Samphire* and later landed at Algiers.

Four days later it was the veteran Franken's turn as he sighted destroyers of Force H on an ASW sweep near the coastline to the west of Oran. Opting to attack the warships Franken hit HMS *Partridge* with a single torpedo. Elmer Russell Dobson, a Canadian, was aboard the destroyer when Franken struck:

It was just after eight o'clock. On British ships, breakfast was coffee or cocoa, not like on Canadian ships. I had just come off duty and was lying down with my life jacket as a pillow on the mess deck, one deck below, when all of a sudden, BOOM! We all scrambled to our feet. We knew what was happening. The ship had stopped. There was mass confusion. I grabbed my life jacket but I didn't have enough time, or breath, to blow it up. It was useless.

By the time I got upstairs, the ship was leaning over on its starboard side. I remember seeing the Captain. He'd been caught in the middle of shaving. He came out on the bridge with one side of his face lathered and yells, 'Stick by the ship, boys. Stick by the ship.' We yelled back, 'Fuck you!' It was every man for himself. I just walked down the port side into the water.

It was quite warm, not freezing like the North Atlantic. Besides I was too excited to be cold. We were wearing our clothes anyways. You don't undress during wartime at sea. And you never shower, maybe take a little sponge bath. A lot of times you can't even do that because of the scarcity of fresh water on board.

I swam over to the life raft and grabbed onto the line hanging from it. There were a lot of guys hanging on. Too many. The raft was sinking. The Lieutenant who was in charge, asks in his plummy accent, for a volunteer to leave. He had no intention of leaving himself. Because of my swimming ability I volunteered. I let go and made my way over to a two by eight piece of wood floating on the surface.

One of the chaps from the engine room was struggling. He was a British guy. I never knew his name. He couldn't swim very well so I swam the two by eight over to him and he grabbed on. Then the two of us paddled our way over to the other destroyer ... The ship sank in just seven minutes.

The sea was covered in bunker oil. Pretty near the whole ship's company was bobbing in the water. It was chaos. I tried to keep my head up but you couldn't avoid swallowing some oil. That's why I ended up the way I did. It brought on the arthritis.

Then there were the depth charges. The *Partridge* went down so fast they didn't have time to set them to safety so they were going off underneath us. I opened my mouth and hollered to release the pressure building up inside my body. A doctor told me later that saved my life.

We never saw the submarine. It fired one torpedo. The engine room took a direct hit. Of the three Canadians working there I was the only one to get out alive. One chap, a nice young kid from Chatham, Ontario went down with the ship. We'd been out the night before. At the time I should have notified his parents to see what I could do to console them. I never did and it's preyed on my conscience ever since. The other guy was adrift, absent without official leave, so he wasn't even on board. In one sense, you could say he was lucky.

We were in the water maybe a couple of hours in total. The British chap and I swam until we reached the other destroyer. They had nets out over the side and with the help of the crew we were able to get aboard. That's all I remember.[5]

Three days later the penultimate November sinking achieved by 29th U-Flotilla would also be one of the largest.[6] In the early hours of 21 November, Hamm's *U-562* sighted Convoy KMF5A as it passed into the Mediterranean bound for Algiers. The convoy commodore ship was the 23,722-ton requisitioned P&O liner ss *Strathallen*, on her second journey to Algiers as she had taken part during the initial landings of Operation 'Torch', carrying 4,408 British and American troops and 296 Queen Alexandra's nurses and a crew of 430 men.

Hamm believed his target to be a large 14,000-ton freighter and elected to fire two torpedoes. The first passed across the bows of the *Strathallan* while the second one to leave the tubes struck. Hit on the port side in the engine room, neighbouring bulkheads were extensively damaged, allowing immediate flooding and sending the ship listing to port. Fires immediately broke out and Captain Biggs issued a tannoy address for all personnel to make their way to lifeboat stations. With panic among the tightly-packed troops below decks never far away, people began launching lifeboats and throwing rafts over the side, eyewitnesses recalling countless men jumping overboard, many in underwear. At least two engineer officers and two Lascar engine-room crew were killed in the initial torpedo explosion, but opinion has since remained divided over whether there were other lives lost. Private Vernon Minton of the 2nd Parachute Regiment was one of the men aboard when the troopship was torpedoed:

My regiment was billeted in the lower decks deep inside the troopship. We were told eventually that we were on our way to reinforce beleaguered troops in North Africa. We heard this enormous explosion in the early hours of the morning. The ship gave a massive shudder as the torpedo struck. It took us a long time to reach the upper decks with the bottleneck of soldiers all with one idea of getting out of the bowels of the stricken ship.

Once we reached the main deck an Officer asked for volunteers to go back into the engine room to man the pumps. My mate and I stepped forward and did what you were never supposed to do; volunteer that is . . . and went below. Funnily enough his name escapes me after 58 years. We made our way below and passed members of *Strathallan's* crew who were on the way up. During all this upheaval a very human touch took place which would probably have met with disapproval from the authorities but nevertheless was greatly appreciated at the time. The crew had 'liberated' some drinks from the bar and offered us a nip of whisky. In the early hours of the morning onboard a sinking ship below decks it was just what the doctor ordered.

Operating the pumps was hot exhausting work. We took spell about having a rest and breather. During a break I took a walk which was not easy because of the list to port. I found myself at an external cargo door with the sea inches below the line of door. While I was at these doors I spotted someone floating close by. He was only wearing a vest and must have stripped off his uniform. He was covered in oil. I managed to grab him but because of the oil I was unable to hang on to him. I don't know to this day what happened to that man, whether he survived or not. I rejoined my mate at the pumps and stayed there for a considerable period until a crew member told us to get up on deck as there was nothing more to be done.

On deck I helped free the last of the rafts. A cruiser sailed slowly past *Strathallan* and allowed us to jump onboard. We were taken below to the locker where the anchor chains were stored. Not what you would call the best of accommodation but believe me it was more than welcome. We thought *Strathallan* was going to sink at anytime which it did eventually. The cruiser turned around and began a anti-submarine sweep. They began dropping depth charges. The noise was horrendous. After every explosion the chains lifted off the deck and came down with an almighty bang. This coupled with the sound of explosions and with dark cramped conditions made it an altogether unpleasant experience . . . one I have never forgotten to this day.[7]

After the initial attack the nurses and 1,000 troops were picked up by the destroyer HMS *Verity* while HMS *Laforey* took the *Strathallan* in tow. With the help of the salvage tug *Restive* it was hoped that she might reach Oran, but her list increased and the remainder of the troops were taken off by escorting destroyers. In the early hours of the following morning the liner caught fire, and once it reached her cargo of rockets and ammunition, the rest of the crew were taken off by *Restive* after which the ship sank 12 miles from Oran. Given the number of people aboard it is miraculous that the number of casualties was so low.

Hamm was pleased with his success and headed back toward La Spezia after helping guide other boats towards the convoy. However, on 23 Decembers *U-562* unwittingly entered into an area east of the Spanish coast and south of the French coast that was prohibited to U-Boats, being allocated to the *Luftwaffe* for anti-submarine operations. Thus, during that morning *U-562* came under depth-charge and machine-gun attack from German aircraft patrolling the area. When Hamm finally reached La Spezia on Christmas Eve his boat was scheduled for over six weeks of costly repairs due to the damage caused by the *Luftwaffe* attack. Meanwhile Franken had arrived to harass Convoy KMF5, torpedoing and damaging the 16,297-ton British troopship and ex-Cunard liner SS *Cameronia* (sister-ship to the ill-fated SS *Lancastria* sunk by the *Luftwaffe* off Saint Nazaire in 1940), hitting No.7 hold and causing severe flooding as well as killing seventeen people.[8] The ship, however, reached Bône, Algeria and was later repaired.

The remainder of December was taken by one claimed hit with the new Pi2 pistol armed torpedo against a *Jervis* class destroyer by Schomburg aboard *U-561* and a staggering array of optimistic claims by Brandi in *U-617*. Between 28 and 30 December he claimed a steam tug, barge, destroyer and steamer sunk, with another two merchant ships damaged. This would aggregate over 10,000 tons to his score plus the warship of undetermined displacement. In fact the only hit substantiated by Allied records was the sinking of the 810-ton steam tug *St Issey* off Benghazi at which Brandi fired two torpedoes on the morning of 28 December. The barge that the Royal Navy tug was towing then became Brandi's next target, though both torpedoes apparently missed.

On the Allied side December provided a shock to their plans for the capture of North Africa, although one that was ultimately somewhat welcome. The embarassment caused to the British and American administrations by complicity with Vichy Admiral Darlan in the governing of North Africa was eliminated on Christmas Eve when he was shot by a young French monarchist Bonnier de la Chapelle. The assassin was arrested, tried and shot on dawn of 26 December, much to his surprise. To replace Darlan the Allies chose General Giraud who ably took control of the considerable authority that only Darlan could have mustered during the early days of 'Torch' and its difficult rapprochement between the French and Allies.

While the 'Torch' forces made slow progress towards Tunisia, their own advance made more difficult by the initial caution of their commanders upon first landing, as now they faced strong German and Italian forces entrenched before them. To the east Rommel continued to retreat into Libya with the Eighth Army in pursuit. Though the *Afrika Korps* was continually forced west away from the glittering prize of the Suez Canal, Rommel remained a dangerous and seemingly inexhaustible foe. Despite a brief mention in the FdU Italian War Diary of a 'probing reconnaissance of the Nile Delta', U-boat support for the *Afrika Korps* continued to centre on interception of 'Torch' convoy traffic as the build-up of Allied supplies for the advance from Algeria continued.

On New Year's Day 1943 Horst Deckert, commander of the veteran boat *U-73*, sighted Convoy UGS3 in the middle of the afternoon. It was Deckert's second patrol as captain of the boat following Rosenbaum's transfer to command the 30th U-Flotilla in the Black Sea. The convoy had formed at New York, a huge mass of eleven columns of forty-four vessels in total under escort by seven US Navy destroyers. Crossing the Atlantic without U-boat hindrance the convoy separated at Gibraltar, eleven merchant ships, including the Liberty ship SS *Arthur Middleton*, heading to Oran under escort by seven destroyers. The Liberty ship carried 6,412 tons of military cargo including munitions and explosives and U.S Army trucks on the foredeck, the landing craft *LC21* lashed to the stern deck. Nine miles from harbour the convoy slowed and formed a line in order to enter the confines of the harbour. At 14.28, as the Liberty ship cruised in an easterly direction parallel to the shoreline and with two British destroyers to port, two almost simultaneous explosions rent the bow of the ship. Deckert had hit the large freighter squarely and through his periscope he saw the ship explode after only 17 seconds as the sympathetic detonation of stored explosives blew her apart. One of only three survivors (all from the stern gun crew) from the eight officers, thirty-four men, twenty-seven gunners and twelve passengers remembered the sinking:

The concussion tossed me between the two bulkheads in the alleyway and within a few seconds, my senses returned and I stepped into my quarters to secure my life jacket. It was not there. I immediately stepped out on deck and, looking forward, saw that the whole fore part of the vessel, as far aft at #5 hatch, had submerged. In fact, only the poop deck was above water. I went toward the rail, which was already under water, and just managed to get clear just as the stern disappeared under the surface. I should judge, the SS *Arthur Middleton* sank within a minute after the explosion. The weather at the time was fine. There was practically no wind and the sea was smooth.

I managed to hang on to a barrel floating nearby and from this barrel, I sighted one of the doughnut rafts about 100ft. away. I swam to the doughnut raft and, shortly afterward, two other of the gun crew, namely Jankowski, First Class Seaman, and Andy Petrowski, First Class Seaman, joined me. I was on this doughnut raft with the other two men for about ½ hour.

Near where the SS *Arthur Middleton* went down the sea was covered with fuel oil and wreckage. Close-by was the navy barge, which had been on the afterdeck. The rest of the convoy had gone ahead and were about a mile to the eastward. However, there were two British destroyers close by. One was zigzagging but I do not believe dropped any depth charges. The other destroyer, which had been off our stern, port side, lowered a boat and came over to the doughnut raft. I and the two other navy gunners were taken in the small boat and placed aboard the British destroyer.

While I was on the doughnut raft, it would be quite easy for me to see if there were any survivors from the SS *Arthur Middleton*. I could see no-one in the water and there were no other rafts or lifeboats in sight.[9]

The same day as Deckert twisted the tail of the Allied navies once more, in Rome K.z.S. Leo Kreisch was promoted to the rank of *Konteradmiral*. Kreisch and his staff were faced with mounting logistical problems. The cost of the recent attacks against the Operation 'Torch' forces lay scattered between the various dockyards available to the 29th U-Flotilla. The most sophisticated of these facilities, La Spezia, was facing severe delays throughout January as the bulk of the Italian fleet had now transferred there and took precedence. Although conditions at Pola and Salamis were normal, they were incapable of handling the quantity of work required. Therefore, on 20 January 1943, the *Kriegsmarine* decided to use Toulon as a U-boat base, negotiating the use of the occupied port for repair and replenishment for the U-boat service with the Vichy government – no more than a formality, designed to maintain the pretence of a nation allied to the Axis powers rather than subjugated by them.

Initially the port was considered by FdU *Italian* as unprepared to house the 29th U-Flotilla whose transfer from La Spezia was being considered, the latter facilities now only capable of handling two U-boats simultaneously at best. Therefore three construction phases would be required to upgrade the French port, the first allowing the stationing of five boats with 450 men. The French *Arsenale de Toulon* was and still is one of the two major French naval bases. Situated east of Marseilles, the base was constructed between 1595 and 1610. Cardinal Richelieu, who demanded a strong French navy, designated Toulon France's primary Mediterranean naval base. The port itself lies to the north and northeast of the natural harbour (*Petite Rade*) which is turn leads to the head of the *Grand Rade de Toulon* (Large Roadstead of Toulon). A breakwater separating the *Grand* and *Petite Rades* protects the inner harbour from open ocean waves, while to landward hills shelter it from wind, notably the Mistral, a strong, cold northwesterly wind system that blows from Southern France into the Gulf of Lions.

The civil port of Marseilles was also to be used as a subsidiary base for the 29th U-Flotilla. With increasing Allied pressure on U-boats throughout France by bombing from burgeoning numbers of Allied aircraft, the bunkers already built in western France had reaped dividends in protecting the vulnerable U-boats when undergoing work in port. In North Africa the Allies had already acquired new airfields from which to begin similar bombardment of units of the 29th U-Flotilla so the same technology was to be applied to the French Mediterranean coast by German planners.

By December 1942 the Organisation Todt (OT) and local *Kriegsmarine* officials had agreed on Marseilles as the logical place to position the bunker, work beginning the following January, overseen by the construction firm Wayss & Freytag. Unfortunately the German occupation of Marseilles resulted in a brutal alteration of an area that bordered the city's docks. The city's old quarter, known as *La Panier* (the basket) was a medieval district with virtually unmapped streets and into which hundreds of refugees, many of them Jews from all over Europe, had come to seek anonymity and refuge. Almost immediately, and with the help of French police, elements of the SD security service began deportations, 6,000 arrested on the night of 22 January 1943, as part of an operation named 'Action Tiger,' of whom 4,000 were eventually deported to concentration camps. While much Jewish property was seized the occupation forces also oversaw the destruction of a large swathe of the houses and streets of the old quarter leading down to the waterfront.

Onto the now cleared Marseilles shoreline the construction of thirteen separate cells, capable of holding 20 boats in total was envisioned. However, the ground was found to be of relatively poor quality, requiring a wide foundation to be laid which would put the whole project at nearly two years before completion. For the construction of the foundation work the OT planned to use the technology already employed at the Deutsche Werft in Hamburg. Work began as planned and was not interrupted until 2 December 1943 when forty-six B 17 bombers raided Marseilles. The Chief of Marine Construction (*Chef des Amtes Marinebauwesen*) later wrote:

> In the air attack on 2 December the walls and locks for keeping the water out have been badly damaged. Therefore the target deadline for completion has been shifted back by at least eight weeks. The problems and delays caused by groundwater seepage cannot be overstated. Group Kommando West have enquired whether the building work can be simplified at all, whether the allocated space necessary for the Type VIIC can be also used for the smaller type (Type XXIII). Perhaps this would considerable lighten the necessary production and excavation work required and speeding up the possible completion date for the cells.[10]

However, the planned complex – codenamed 'Martha' –was never to be completed. Only some land workshop elements were finished by August 1944 when Marseilles was finally surrendered to the Allies.

In Toulon the Dock Castigneau was also earmarked for conversion into a concrete shelter, though the project would be severly delayed once more due to bombing damage in July 1944 with a recorded forty-nine direct hits on the dock area and foundation work. By the time these difficulties had been overcome, the plan was forced to be shelved permanently following the Allied landings in Southern France. Due to the problems that had been found with bunker construction in Marseilles, the War Diary of the 29th U-Flotilla recorded consideration being given to two alternative sites for the construction of bunkers. The first was at Cassis to the east of Marseilles, the second, and considered more favourable was at Villefranche-sur-Mer east of Nice, though neither proceeded beyond the survey stage.

Despite a promising beginning for the 29th U-Flotilla, 1943 proved to be more difficult than ever before for the U-boat crews. As Allied forces advanced from both Libya and Algieria they established numerous airfields along the North African coast from several of which anti-submarine missions could be flown, augmenting the base on Malta. The quantity of Allied merchant transport in the Mediterranean guaranteed a large escort presence which also heralded the establishment of dedicated hunter-killer groups.

> The service conditions were very difficult for our boats. With their airfields that stretched the length of the North African coast, radar equipped aircraft and coastal direction finder stations and well organised defences at sea, it required a lot of boldness and skill of our U-boat crews. And with such high casualty rates battling for every success.[11]

To replace *U-257* that had had to abort its passage through the Straits of Gibraltar, Dönitz despatched Oblt.z.S. Hans-Carl Kosbadt's *U-224* from Saint Nazaire to the Mediterranean. Kosbadt had sunk two ships on his previous war patrol (his first as commander) in the North Atlantic and passed Gibraltar on the night of 12 January. The following day Kosbadt was homing on the sixteen merchant ships of Convoy TE13 eastbound from Gibraltar when the Canadian corvette HMCS *Ville de Quebec* obtained a firm ASDIC trace on the stalking boat. The Canadian captain, A R E Coleman, signalled his intention to attack to the other four escorting corvettes and immediately peeled off to deliver an accurate depth-charge salvo that blew *U-224* to the surface bow-first. The Canadian opened fire with all available weapons, over 200 rounds hammering the U-boat as the corvette prepared to ram. *U-224* was wrecked by the corvette hitting squarely forward of the conning tower, rolling her over and sending the

U-boat to the bottom, a huge underwater explosion being followed by oil, smashed pieces of wood and torn clothing rising to the surface. Amidst the shattered debris was the sole survivor, IWO L.z.S. Wolf Dietrich Danckworth, who was picked up by the Canadian corvette HMCS *Port Arthur*.

Another relatively new arrival was also lost during January. *Kapitän-leutant* Willy Körner's *U-301* had suffered enough damage while entering the Mediterranean for the boat to be laid up in the yards at La Spezia since 14 December 1942. The boat sailed once more on the afternoon of 20 January, headed southwest for the Algerian coast. As the weather was misty around the harbour there was no escort provided, instead *U-301* sailed at speed from port, dropping several hand grenades to warn off any potential submarine threat before conducting a single 30-metre practice dive to test the seaworthiness of the boat. Körner set course for the northern tip of Corsica before the boat would swing south and make for its patrol area. At 02.00 the following morning a brief radio message informed Körner of an Allied convoy leaving Gibraltar bound for Algiers, Körner ordering full ahead as he raced to intercept. Although new directives from FdU Italian had forbidden surface travel during daylight, Körner was faced with no alternative if he hoped to intercept the convoy. Trusting to luck and the boat's surface speed, Körner headed south.

At 08.00 the U-boat's lookouts were changed, IIWO L.z.S. Georg Dettmer leading a Petty Officer, seaman and *Fähnrich zur See* Wilhelm Rahn onto the conning tower as a brief rain squall passed overhead. The rain soon passed and visibility increased with only a slight sea running in a gentle breeze. Suddenly a tremendous explosion to starboard catapulted Rahn into the air where he lost consciousness. The submarine HMS *Sahib* had sighted the surfaced *U-301* and hit it with three torpedoes. Rahn, who had joined the boat two days before she sailed, regained consciousness aboard the British submarine, the sole survivor of the attack. One other man of his bridge watch had been flung clear by the blast but was found to be dead in the water.

> Rahn was not at first aware of his boat having sunk and frequently asked in captivity whether there were other survivors ... He was [subsequently] mainly relieved that the torpedo which first hit his boat had not struck her in his lookout sector.[12] *

In return for the loss of two boats, the 29th U-Flotilla sank another three steamers, one ASW trawler and four sailing vessels hit by artillery and ramming by Schöneboom's *U-431* operating once more in the eastern Mediterranean between Cyprus and Haifa. The trawler, the 545-ton HMT *Jura*, was one of several ships escorting Convoy MKS5 when Mehl's

U-371 torpedoed and sank her, damaging the British steamer SS *Ville de Strasbourg* in a later attack against the same convoy.

Despite claims of two more freighters two days previously (neither confirmed), Albrecht Brandi attacked and sank the Greek SS *Annitsa* and the Norwegian MV *Harboe Jensen* on 15 January. At 10.31 *U-617* fired four torpedoes at a small convoy that consisted of the two merchant ships under escort by the armed trawler HMT *Southern Isles*. Brandi observed two hits on each merchant ship, that had what he labelled in his War Diary 'a great effect'. Both ships were sunk; one crew member from *Annitsa* lost and thirty-one survivors rescued by the trawler, another two picked up by a lifeboat from the *Harboe Jensen* who were in turn taken aboard the trawler. The Norwegian had suffered eighteen dead including the master, while five Norwegians and one Englishman jumped overboard and righted an upturned lifeboat which they used to save the two Greeks. Another Norwegian, Gunner Anders Falkensten, who had also jumped overboard, kept himself afloat on a plank and was rescued after about an hour.

In total Brandi had claimed a staggering eight ships sunk during this patrol, including a destroyer, and damage to two others. Three ships were confirmed: the two steamers and the tug *St Issey*. Two days later Brandi docked at La Spezia and was awarded the Knight's Cross on 21 January for a claimed total of fifteen ships totalling 58,700 tons sunk and six ships totalling 61,500 tons damaged. His actual achievement was to have sunk seven ships totalling 22,100 tons. The increased danger of surface travel and thus reliance on periscope vision and sound made confirmation of results difficult, something that was justifiably accepted in the Mediterranean theatre more so than other areas of U-boat operations. Nonetheless, the wish was plainly father to the deed for some commanders and crew. The last confirmed steamer sunk in January was by Schlippenbach's *U-453* which torpedoed and sank the Belgian SS *Jean Jadot*, carrying motor transport, gasoline, four tanks and 323 troops to Algiers as part of convoy KMS7. Three impacts were heard from four torpedoes fired, with six killed from the total complement of 403 men.

February, March and April continued to take a steady toll of the 29th U-Flotilla as they doggedly clashed with Allied naval and convoy traffic. Brandi added three more ships to his grim tally, sinking the fast minelayer HMS *Welshman* on 1 February. The ship, which had been heavily involved in the defence of Malta, went down while returning to Alexandria after laying a minefield west of Sicily. The *Welshman* was one of the four fastest ships in the Royal Navy, with a top speed of 40 knots, but was hit by a single devastating torpedo and sank, taking 154 crewmen with her.[15]

Four days later Brandi struck once more, attacking a small convoy of four steamers with four escorts that was travelling from Alexandria to Benghazi, finally launching his attack northeast of Tobruk. At 08.02 he fired four torpedoes, hitting the 1,350-ton Norwegian ss *Henrik* on the starboard foreship and another Norwegian, the 3,264-ton ss *Corona*. *Henrik* immediately started to burn, sinking by the bow in less than three minutes, two Chinese crewmen being killed from a complement of forty-six men. ss *Corona*, carrying 3,700 tons of military supplies including ammunition, was also hit on the starboard bow, the master immediately ordering engines stopped and the crew to abandon ship as he feared an explosion of the stored ammunition. Though there were no fatalities there had been some blast injuries and the majority of the crew were taken immediately to recently recaptured Tobruk from where a tug departed to take the crippled ship under tow. ss *Corona* had failed to sink and with escort *ML1012* remaining on the scene, the ship was taken in tow. The arrival of the tug that night eased the operation and some of *Corona*'s crew that had had been picked up by HMS *Erica* reboarded the ship, accompanied by a stoker from ss *Henrik*. ss *Corona* arrived in Tobruk harbour on late afternoon on 6 February where her master and fourteen crewmen reboarded her. The ship though had been extensively damaged; the forecastle deck line split to the keel and from the keel to near the port side of the deck, a collision bulkhead fractured allowing the forecastle deck to drop by one foot as well as myriad leaks in the ship's bilges. The freighter was beached, tied up to a wreck on her port side while the cargo was removed over the next two weeks. Eventually, battered some more by increasing winds and seas, the ship foundered in Tobruk harbour. For almost the first time Brandi's claims largely matched the results, though his estimated tonnage from the three ships sunk was 12,450 tons as opposed to the actual 7,264 tons sunk. The remains of the small convoy was also attacked by Johann Krieg's *U-81* two hours after Brandi, Krieg firing two torpedoes and hearing both detonate following long running times. However, there was no further confirmed sinking.

On 6 February Gunter Jahn's *U-596* and Hartmann's *U-77* joined the gathering attack against the 56-ship Convoy KMS8 bound from Gibraltar to Bône, Algeria. The convoy had already lost an escort vessel to the elements when HMS *Corncrake* sank while still in the Atlantic. After passing Gibraltar on 5 February, KMS8 came under determined Axis aircraft attack that sank the escort corvette HMCS *Louisburg* with an aerial torpedo the followinng day east of Oran. That morning Jahn fired four torpedoes toward the convoy, hearing three detonations on three steamers claimed at 5,000 tons each. Retreating submerged there was no way to verfiy the claims and they have never been identified. Early the following morning aircraft returned to drop flares over the convoy and at 02.00 Hartmann aboard *U-77* fired a spread of four torpedoes that hit the ships in positions 13 and 14 within KMS8. The first, 7,043-ton British ss *Empire Webster* carrying 3,000 tons of coal and military supplies, slewed out of position, three crew members and a gunner killed before the master, forty-nine crew, one gunner and eight soldiers abandoned ship and were rescued by HMCS *Camrose*. A final torpedo sent the burning ship under. The second ship hit, the 6,699-ton SS *Empire Banner* carrying 3,800 tons of military supplies, including tanks and trucks, suffered no casualties before sinking.

Gunners aboard the Liberty ship SS *Thomas Stone*, who had already claimed a German bomber brought down during the previous day's attacks, claimed to have seen two torpedoes race by their ship, a third hitting but failing to explode. They also, rather fancifully, claimed to have fired at and hit a U-boat that surfaced 500 yards off the ship's beam, later hitting a sighted periscope with several well-aimed shots. There were no Italian or German reports of damage caused by the merchant ship, although the corvette HMCS *Regina* supported by the minesweeper HMS *Rhyl* later accounted for the Italian submarine *Avorio* after they had been detached from KMS8 to escort an elderly former coal transport SS *Brinkburn*, whose crew had been overcome by fumes leaking from 1,500 tons of aviation fuel in canisters.

Elsewhere *U-596* torpedoed the 380-ton Landing Craft Infantry *LCI162* which exploded and sank on torpedo impact near Algiers, while both *U-205* and *U-407* reported attacks and hits against three steamers and an enemy patrol ship respectively, but without confirmation. Three other merchant ships were damaged by U-boat attack in the western Mediterranean during February, one, the 7,176-ton Liberty Ship SS *Nathaniel Greene*, finished off by *Luftwaffe* attack. The final confirmed sinking from the Algiers route was SS *Fintra*, hit and sunk by *U-371* while carrying ammunition unescorted toward the Allied port.

To the east, *U-81* claimed five small sailing and motor vessels destroyed by gunfire off Syria as well the torpedoing and damaging of the Dutch steamer SS *Saroena* escorted by an armed trawler as she carried 7,681 tons of crude oil from Tripoli to Haifa. Hit in the stern and set on fire by one of four torpedoes fired, two Chinese crewmen and three gunners panicked and jumped overboard where two of them drowned. The Dutch tanker was later beached near Beirut, the fire extinguished and the ship refloated, temporarily repaired and towed to Port Said pending more permanent work.

However, despite the confirmed destruction of seven enemy merchant ships and two naval vessels by German U-boats, February was a disastrous month for the 29th U-Flotilla with three U-boats destroyed. Admiral Cunningham had returned to his post as Commander-in-Chief, Mediterranean Fleet and used his naval forces with customary vigour against any and all Axis targets.[14]

On 17 February Friedrich Bürgel's *U-205* was detected by ASDIC aboard the destroyer HMS *Paladin* as the U-boat stalked a small convoy west of

Tobruk. The destroyer immediately followed the clear trace and dropped five depth charges that disabled *U-205* bringing the boat to the surface where the crew prepared to scuttle her and abandon ship. Immediately the crippled U-boat broke surface *Paladin* and another escort HMS *Jervis* opened fire, a South African Bisley bomber acting as air escort also joining in, attacking with machine guns and depth charges and forcing several emerging German crewmen to leap into the water. With wild gunfire hammering the boat – and also apparently killing four of *Paladin*'s own crew and injuring four others – the rest of the crew were seen to abandon ship as *U-205* lazily circled on electric motors. While forty-two survivors, including Bürgel, were rescued, two men from *Paladin* were launched as a boarding party to investigate the stricken U-boat. Sidney Constable and Kenneth J Troy both clambered aboard *U-205* and went below where they ransacked cupboards in the captain's area, radio and control rooms. There they recovered 'a large number of books' before leaving the U-boat. With a slim chance of capturing the boat intact, corvette HMS *Gloxina* attached a tow cable to the still-running boat, though *U-205* finally foundered and went down in 96 feet of water at Ras el Hilab Bay.[15]

Two days later veteran Kaptlt. Horst Hamm's *U-562* was sighted by Wellington 'S' of 38 Squadron RAF while the aircraft was covering the 'Roman' convoy comprising twelve motor vessels, three tankers and eleven escort vessels off the Libyan coast. The rear gunner, Sergeant J Brown, spotted *U-562* directly below his aircraft running at periscope depth in the clear water. The Wellington was, however, unable to turn and make an attack with sufficient speed to stop a torpedo launch and so vectored the destroyers HMS *Isis* and *Hursley* to the U-boat's position. A total of nine subsequent depth-charge attacks destroyed *U-562* which disappeared without trace.

On the morning of 23 February aircraft sighted the newly arrived *U-443* of Group 'Taucher' running surfaced off Algiers. A four destroyer Hunter-Killer group was immediately sent to investigate, HMS *Bicester* finding *U-443* on ASDIC near the reported location and attacking with ten deep-set depth charges. Although some wreckage was seen HMS *Wheatland* and *Lamerton* also mounted their own attacks on the strong ASDIC contact, followed by a second run by HMS *Bicester*. The destroyer then recovered two locker lids, a large cupboard door, splintered wood and some human remains, all that was left of Konstantin Puttkamer and his crew. It was a ruinous exchange rate for the flotilla – and one set to continue through to June 1943. Damage continued to be caused to the attacking U-boats as they struggled with increasingly effective escort forces, forcing them into yards for extended repair. *U-73* also suffered from a severe explosion and fire in her diesel room during an 'experimental trip' during February that required a return to port and four months of repair in La Spezia.

On land Rommel had retreated as far as the Mareth Line defences in southern Tunisia on the Gabes Gulf. All of Libya was now in the hands of the Eighth Army who crossed the border into Tunisia on 4 February. However, Rommel was not yet beaten. He could now transfer his forces between combat in the northwest against 'Torch' units or to the east if he desired. His supply lines were finally shortened to such a degree that his troops could receive replenishment – if it were there to be had. Leaving much of his forces to hold Mareth, on 19 February he delivered a sharp attack through Kasserine Pass with the aim of breaking through the Allied lines around Gafsa and recapturing Bône. Ultimately his stroke was unsuccessful, though he caused the Allied commanders considerable anxiety before the attack petered out.

With a vague interest rekindled in the North African theatre, Adolf Hitler proclaimed Rommel as supreme commander of all Axis forces in Tunisia, the newly-constituted 'Army Group *Afrika*'. Ironically this announcment arrived one day after Rommel began a general retreat from his offensive toward Bône. Despite a brief attack by General Hans-Jürgen von Arnim toward Medjez el Bab in Tunisia and another launched by Rommel against the Eighth Army, the offensive power of Army Group *Afrika* was finally broken. On 9 March Rommel departed Africa on his long-deferred sick leave, handing command to von Arnim as he flew first to see Mussolini and then onward to Hitler to convince them of the suicidal nature of continuing the Axis presence in North Africa. Both leaders were impervious to his pleas, Hitler barring him from returning to Tunisia until he was fit enough to 'take command of an operation against Casablanca' that existed only in the dictator's mind. Even the ever-optimistic Kesselring could not hide the imminent fall of Tunisia, though by that stage of the war Hitler had virtually forgotten Africa, written off as no longer worth his time. Subsequently, the Mareth Line was outflanked and Axis forces pushed steadily back from March until Tunis itself was ready to fall.

March 1943 marked a high point for the 29th U-Flotilla, mirroring the experience of the U-boat service as a whole. With the Allied advances in North Africa, on 8 March *Marinekommando Italien* directed Kreisch to concentrate his U-boat operations on the western Mediterranean for fear of an attempted amphibious attack against Sardinia. Kreisch directed that U-boats then becoming ready for sea in La Spezia (*U-380, U-407, U-371, U-755, U-97* and *U-565*) and Pola (*U-561, U-431* and *U-617*) would head west to counter this possible threat. The two boats readying in Salamis (*U-593* and *U-375*) would continue to hunt the Middle Eastern coastline between Syria and Egypt.

Twelve vessels were sunk in the Mediterranean by the flotilla aggregating nearly 47,000 tons. The largest single sinking was the

Norwegian motor tanker MV *Hallanger* torpedoed by Jahn's *U-596* during an attack against the 20-ship Convoy ET16 from Bône to Gibraltar moments after he also hit and sank the 7,133-ton British steamer SS *Fort a la Corbe*. The large Norwegian was travelling in ballast in position 52 of ET16 when the first torpedo hit in No. 8 tank on the port side. Two minutes later another hit No. 6 tank and eight minutes after that the third and final torpedo strike burst against the port side aft bunkers. Jahn was subsequently awarded the Knight's Cross. Convoys ET14 tand KMS10 had also come under U-boat attack during March, the former losing a ship to *U-431* and two others damaged by *U-596* while the latter suffered two ships sunk by *U-380* and *U-77* who also damaged a third.

On 9 March the first U-boat arrived in Toulon, *U-602* entering the harbour after unsuccessfully patrolling off the Algerian coast. By the month's end, *U-458*, *U-561* and *U-431* had also entered Toulon harbour, mooring at the former French Mourillon submarine base and inaugurating it into the use of the 29th U-Flotilla. But such a high tide meant that the fortunes of the Mediterranean boats could do nothing but recede. During the next two months the results gradually diminished. April saw five ships sunk by *U-755*, *U-593*, *U-565* and *U-371*, the most significant and costly to the Allies torpedoed by Franken's *U-565* when he sank American freighter SS *Michigan* and the French troopship SS *Sidi-Bel-Abbès* from Convoy UGC7 on 20 April north of the Habibas Islands. The latter was carrying 1,130 Senegalese troops destined for Oran from Casablanca, 611 lives being lost in the sinking. The *Michigan*, carrying 6,300 tons of military supplies and a deck cargo of gliders, was successfully evacuated before she sank, many of the rescued crew opting to remain in their lifeboats and assist the struggling Senegalese in the water. Franken was also awarded the Knight's Cross upon his return to port. Amongst the unconfirmed claims made by three other boats were more from Albrecht Brandi who claimed a heavy cruiser sunk and three destroyers at least damaged during April, as well as a hit on an *Orcades* class transport. None of them were ever confirmed. In port the problems were also intensified. Allied air raids had begun to hammer the dockyard and town of La Spezia, several Lancaster attacks by 106 Squadron RAF accurately hitting the docks and causing further delays to an already overstretched repair service. *U-97*, at sea from the Italian port since 10 April and under the command of new captain Oblt.z.S. Hans-Georg Trox, was directed not to return there but rather to proceed to Pola at the end of their patrol.[16] Another, *U-371* at sea since 7 April, was to dock in Toulon.

May yielded even less for the U-boats; *U-565* claiming a probable tanker hit, the new arrival Siegfried Koitschka in *U-616* claiming another possible hit on a tanker and confirmed damage by another new arrival, Huth's

U-414, on ss *Fort Anne* and sinking of the CAM (Catapult Aircraft Merchantman) ship ss *Empire Eve*. Both were a part of Convoy KMS14, attacked northeast of Mostaganem, Algeria, on 18 May.

One of the crewmen aboard Koitschka's boat *U-616* recalled their passage through the straits of Gibraltar and subsequent arrival in the Mediterranean:

We left St Nazaire not knowing our destination and we had been at sea for a few days before Koitschka announced that we were going into the Mediterranean! Our hearts sank at this announcement, because no U-boat had ever entered and returned from the Mediterranean and getting past Gibraltar, probably the hottest place in the world for any passing U-boat, was nearly impossible. But Koitschka, by now admired by the crew for his ability, toughness and a great sense of humour, took the *U-616* through on the surface at night with no trouble from the Tommies who must have been asleep. We operated off Oran and attacked a destroyer without success although we heard the torpedoes detonate. Torpedoes in the German Navy were always a source of trouble and could never be relied on. On 13 May we left the area to proceed to our base, La Spezia in Italy, but were attacked by a British aircraft. We dived in a shower of bombs but thought nothing of it but several hours later our hydrophone man reported the sound of propellers of fast moving warships and we went deep to avoid any unpleasantness.

We were soon down to 500 feet, moving at slow speed and keeping as quiet as a mouse, but our listener soon dampened our hopes of creeping away by announcing an enemy coming in to attack. At the right time we sped up and went hard a port, but the first pattern of depth charges came down on top of us with an ear-shattering, thunderous crash!

Our faithful U-boat staggered and creaked and threatened to implode but she regained her poise. Down came more depth charges but one ship of the group above seemed more persistent than the others and dropped her charges right on the target each time.

The boat was in a shambles; gauges smashed, air lines ruptured, the main compass in pieces and water spraying into the boat and still the charges came down relentlessly. The diesel engines were damaged as were the electric motors, several cells of the battery were cracked and the radio out of order and a charge that exploded quite close to the bows threatened to stave the hull of the boat in. After three hours we were thinking that we would have to go up and scuttle the boat but all of a sudden our tormentors went away. After the war I discovered that our attackers had been HMS *Haydon*, USS *Kalk*, HMS *Calpe* and the USS *Strive*. Our main tormentor turned out to be HMS *Haydon* whose captain wanted to stay and sink us but outranked by the captain of USS *Kalk* he had come under his orders and sailed for Gibraltar. On arrival at La Spezia it was found that our torpedo tubes had been slewed sideways by the depth charges and these had to be replaced. The nightmare of that attack stayed with me long after the war ended.[17]

Koitschka, who had learnt his trade as IWO on Erich Topp's *U-552* in the Atlantic, had been lucky. Within the period between March and May 1943 seven U-boats were destroyed in the Mediterranean or attempting to pass the Straits of Gibraltar. On 4 March when Hudson 'V' of 500 Squadron RAF was flying the ASW sweep 'Baffle West 2', the crew sighted a fully-surfaced *U-83* running in bad visibility. The U-boat had also spotted its attacker as it began to zig-zag violently and firing a light machine gun. The Hudson dropped three 100lb ASW bombs from 1,500 feet but missed the U-boat below. The pilot, Sgt. G Jackimov then armed depth charges and began a low-level attack on Kaptlt. Ulrich Wörishofer's boat, straddling her with three charges, white smoke then seen to billow from the conning tower. *U-83* then clearly began to sink on an even keel, at least fifteen men observed swimming away from the large oil patch that remained behind *U-83* as well as at least twenty-five bodies seen rising to the surface with the upwelling oil and large bubbles of air. Jackimov dropped two dinghies, but they were seen to 'appear to sink' upon hitting the water. After 30 minutes the Hudson left the area and nothing was ever found of the survivors from *U-83*.

Over three weeks later, on 28 March, Oblt.z.S. Otto Hartmann's experienced *U-77* was also sighted by its wash while heading home near the Spanish coast after a successful attack on Convoy ET14. Hartmann's lookouts obviously sighted the 48 Squadron RAF Hudson as the British crew watched it submerge while they prepared a depth-charge run. Only the periscope was visible when four depth charges straddled the track of the periscope wake, bringing a streak of oil and bubbles to the surface. Low on fuel, the Hudson was forced to depart but its message of a probably damaged U-boat brought Hudson 'L' of 233 Squadron RAF to the scene, the second aircraft finding *U-77* surfaced and preparing to return fire. Hartmann's boat had suffered severe damage and he had radioed his dire predicament to FdU Italian who advised Hartmann to head for Alicante in neutral Spain and claim the right under international maritime law to undertake repairs. Hurried diplomatic communications from Kreisch via Dönitz in Berlin then followed to urge the Spanish to send a vessel to rendezvous with *U-77* and, if required, tow it into port. Simultaneously Josef Röther's *U-380* was directed to meet with Hartmann and take off forty men, leaving a skeleton crew aboard to face internment in Spain and eventual repatriation. However, the arrival of the new aircraft as *U-77* lay alone between Ibiza and Calo de San Antonia, finished any hope Hartmann harboured. Despite fierce flak the British bomber dropped four depth charges, a single ASW bomb and fired 3,000 rounds of machine-gun ammunition at the devastated boat until *U-77* went down with thirty-eight men including Hartmann. Nine survivors later drifted ashore near Derna, Spain, and were eventually repatriated to Germany.

Kreisch once more appealed for reinforcements for his depleted ranks and Dönitz was compelled to order more U-boats to try and run the Straits of Gibraltar. '1 April. *U-303* and *U-414* have been transferred to the command of Senior Officer U-boat Mediterranean, and have departed for this area.' The two boats slipped through the Allied defences on the nights of 8 and 9 April before both heading to La Spezia after achieving nothing *en route.*

Further loss was suffered by Frauenheim's flotilla on 23 April when *U-602* vanished some time after 19 April when Kreisch had received Kaptlt. Philipp Schüler's last radio message from a position near the Algerian coast. Although unconfirmed the sinking was initially attributed to a Hudson of 500 Squadron RAF that depth-charged a U-boat near Oran on 23 April. During the attack the Hudson was hit by heavy flak and the pilot, R Obee, was killed, the remaining crew nursing the shattered bomber back to its airfield at Tafaraouri near Oran where they baled out. However, the Admiralty subsequently removed this accreditation of the sinking of *U-602*.

Again, Dönitz was called upon to reinforce the Mediterranean U-boats and despatched further units under the direction of Raeder in Berlin.

5 May

The serious situation in the Mediterranean has forced further withdrawal of boats from other areas. As ordered by ObdM, *U-447* and *U-659* have been instructed to try to break through during the present new moon period, without considering the amount of fuel consumed. They are to go to Toulon. Boats have been given all information available on conditions in the Straits of Gibraltar.

U-447 had an unsuccessful gunnery duel with a landing boat, during which she shot down a barrage balloon.

6 May

U-616 navigated the Straits of Gibraltar and joined the forces of FdU Mediterranean. There had been anxiety for this boat, but she had apparently waited for the new moon period to break through.

7 May

U-410 has passed through the Straits of Gibraltar and has joined the command of FdU Mediterranean

19 May

U-447 and *U-659* were ordered on the 5 May to proceed through the Straits of Gibraltar into the Mediterranean. If possible the period of the new moon was to be made use of. In spite of orders to report the boats have not done so up to now. According to an intercept message U-boats were reported on the 8 May in the area W. of Gibraltar. Probably the boats were destroyed by aircraft or by anti-submarine groups directed on to them by the aircraft. They must be considered lost.[18]

Friedrich-Wilhelm Bothe's *U-447* had indeed been sunk, caught by two Hudsons of 233 Squadron RAF as the U-boat prepared for its run past Gibraltar. Eight depth charges straddled the boat which was strafed with machine gun fire and never seen again. The loss of *U-659* was more peculiar. Operating as part of the '*Drossel*' group while still in the Atlantic, the boat was one of several attempting to intercept a southbound convoy near Cape Finisterre. In rough seas *U-659* was attempting a surfaced torpedo attack when it collided with *U-439* making a similar attack. Both U-boats sank, the commander, Kaptlt. Hans Stock and forty-three of his crew from *U-659* lost in the accident.

Of the boats that managed to run the Allied defences and reach the Mediterranean, *U-410* came closest to disaster. *Oberleutnant zur See* Horst Fenski's boat was attacked by a twin-engined aircraft in the morning of 6 May. The plane dived directly out of the sun and raked *U-410* with gunfire, dropping three bombs, which landed only five to ten metres ahead of the U-boat. Aboard *U-410* there was considerable panic, Fenski and others yelling contradictory orders, which resulted in men within the control room hearing the order to dive and *U-410* began to submerge, the conning tower hatch slammed shut with three men still on the bridge. At the last moment, Fenski, who was inside the conning tower, realised what had happened and ordered the boat to immediately resurface. By this time the three men topside were in water up to their armpits and as the boat surged upward once more Fenski flung open the hatch and rushed to the bridge, men tumbling out to man machine-guns as the plane prepared for another run. A concentrated burst of gunnery from the U-boat dissuaded their attacker, who appeared content to circle *U-410* out of firing range. Finally, three quarters of an hour later, the aircraft dropped a parting salvo of three bombs, all of which fell wide, and departed as *U-410* took the opportunity to submerge.

It was soon discovered that there was a five-metre fracture in the forward pressure hull between the torpedo tubes, through which a stream of water about 3cm thick was spurting. Additionally, all of the bow caps on the forward torpedo tubes had been damaged. Fenski immediately set course for La Spezia where the boat was placed into dry-dock, where it would stay until early August. During this period in dry-dock the opportunity was also taken to rebuild the conning tower by lengthening Platform I and mounting retractable twin Breda machine guns. The single 20mm cannon was removed.

Off Toulon on 21 May, the new addition *U-303* was torpedoed and sunk by the submarine HMS *Sickle* as the U-boat conducted sea trials, twenty of the crew being killed, the remainder, including Kaptlt. Karl-Franz Heine, being rescued by a German minesweeper. Only the day before, *Sickle* had missed with a six-torpedo salvo against another U-boat within the same area.

The other boat that had accompanied *U-303* into the Mediterranean, Oblt.z.S. Horst Walther Huth's *U-414* was also sunk. Detected by sonar aboard the corvette HMS *Vetch* while Huth stalked Convoy GTX1 off Oran on 25 May, the British captain was about to launch a depth-charge attack on the suspected U-boat contact when Huth removed any doubts and raised his periscope only 100 feet from the approaching corvette. The subsequent barrage of nine depth charges yielded bubbles of air and oil but no other trace of Huth or his crew. It had been the young commander's final mistake, experience that he had obtained as IWO aboard Hamm's *U-562* unable to save himself or his men.

The last sinking in May was Walter Göing's *U-755*, sighted and attacked on 28 May by Hudson 'V' of 608 Squadron RAF near Majorca. Göing opted to remain surfaced and returned fire at the approaching bomber which was equipped with newly developed air-to-surface rockets. Firing two of the projectiles, one failed to release from its rail, while the other hit dead centre on the hull of *U-755*. Circling for a second attack Flying Officer A K Ogilvie fired four rockets, three of which hit the U-boat below the waterline, their power sufficient to carry them through the cushioning water and thick hull. Göing's boat was destroyed and he ordered all men to abandon ship, machine-gun fire from the Hudson hastening them overboard. *U-755* gradually sank stern first, nine wounded survivors being rescued by the Spanish destroyer *Churruca* and later repatriated. Göing was not amongst them.

There was little to celebrate within the 29th U-Flotilla. Nor indeed within the Axis land forces still stubbornly fighting to the end. Pushed into a small corner of Tunisia, they were also increasingly beleaguered to seaward. Admiral Cunningham ordered the Royal Navy's Mediterranean Fleet that no Germans or Italians should be allowed to escape, signalling the fleet: 'Sink, burn and destroy: Let nothing pass'. On 4 May three U-boats were ordered by SKL to take fuel from Italy to Tunisia for Army Group *Afrika*, there being no available harbours or landing strips held by the Axis for more conventional transports. *U-380*, *U-407* and *U-561* were instructed to load cans of fuel in their pressure hulls, there not being enough time to effect conversion of the boat into a fuel carrier as had been attempted during the invasion of Norway in 1940.[19]

Three more boats – *U-458* and the soon to be lost *U-755* and *U-414* – were to undertake such conversion. Livorno, Naples and Reggio were the three ports designated as loading areas for the initial shipments, *U-380* the first to begin loading fuel and ammunition at Livorno. The boat had had its deck gun removed and all but two torpedoes taken off to make room for every available inch of stores. Additionally, half of the crew were ordered to stay behind as well, Kaptlt. Josef Röther having to choose which men as none volunteered to stay in Livorno. *U-380* sailed on Friday 7 May beneath a cloudless sky. Röther's destination was Tunis, but the city appeared to either be on the brink of falling or had indeed fallen when he subsequently ordered on 8 May to sail for Kelibia, Tunisia. This caused considerable anxiety for the captain as he possessed no map that showed this harbour, though coordinates soon followed that shed at least some light on the matter. Both Sidi Daoud and Kelibia had been designated as suitable harbours, though both lacked piers and so the unloading would have to be undertaken at sea into whatever dinghies were available. Naval Command Tunisia recommended redirection to Sidi Daoud, though SKL demurred and ordered Kelibia to prepare for unloading with whatever equipment was on hand and available. A pilot was organised to come on board *U-380* and show Röther the most suitable unloading point, and that night *U-380* arrived off the harbour submerged.

However, in the meantime events finally overwhelmed Army Group *Afrika*. On Sunday 9 May 1943 Axis forces signed an unconditional surrender in Tunisia to the U.S II Corps. It was a military disaster of the same magnitude as the recent debacle at Stalingrad and thousands of German troops shuffled into Allied POW camps. Aboard *U-380* there was further confusion. Surfacing and sweeping the coastline there was no sign of any pilot and on 9 May Röther was ordered to abandon his mission, jettison the ammunition and fuel and close the shore in order to embark as many soldiers as possible before proceeding to Empedode. The horrendous task of hauling tons of stores through the conning tower hatch in baking heat was eventually completed and Röther fired the two torpedoes at distant enemy destroyers for good measure, though to no avail. The boat nudged closer to land under cover of darkness and was bombarded with a succession of garbled morse light messages as Röther attempted to make sense of the prevailing confusion. Eventually four men – *Obergefreiter* Heinrich Pehn and *Gefreiter* Hans Handwerk, Ernst Schulz and Hans Renner – emerged from the darkness in a small rowing boat. Taken aboard *U-380* they told Röther that fifty more men waited ashore. However, with British warships searching the coastline, unleashing periodic bombardments of enemy forces, and British troops ashore the situation was too dangerous. Some badly-aimed shots from an enemy shore battery decided the issue and *U-380* edged away from land and submerged with its four passengers. With little alternative, Röther reversed course and headed for La Spezia where he docked on 16 May.

The conversion of the three fuel boats had been cancelled then restored and cancelled once again while Röther had been at sea. Likewise *U-407* and *U-561* had continued loading supplies in Naples until definite news of the collapse of Army Group *Afrika* forced an unloading.

With North Africa fallen, the Mediterranean came increasingly under Allied dominance. Spain had been deterred from entering the war on the Axis side and both ends of the sea were firmly controlled by the Royal Navy. Convoy traffic could now traverse the Mediterranean under cover of Allied naval and air forces for the entire length of the journey. Shipping from the east was no longer forced to take the longer route around the Cape of Good Hope but could instead use the Suez Canal which was also firmly in Allied hands since the conquest of Italian East Africa.

What was more, the 'soft underbelly' of Europe lay open to possible invasion from North African bases. Ominously for the Axis, on 13 May, the Royal Navy began its bombardment of Pantelleria Island, midway between Sicily and Tunisia and boasting an Axis airstrip that had already come under increasing air attack by Allied bombers. Between 8 May and 11 June, Allied aircraft dropped 6,313 tons of bombs on the Italian and German forces there. The operation to take the island called for the use of sustained aerial bombardment to crush enemy power on the island and therefore reduce the number of Allied ground forces needed to capture and hold it. Finally, on the night of 10 June men of the British 1st Infantry Division embarked to assault and capture Pantelleria. As their landing craft approached the island's harbour the next day, B 17s delivered a final pounding to the Pantelleria harbour area. Shortly afterwards aircraft spotted a white cross on the island's airfield. When the initial British assault hit the beach unopposed, its commander contacted Pantelleria's military governor who immediately surrendered the island and its garrison of seventy-eight Germans and 11,121 Italians. It was an example of the overwhelming force that the Allies were now capable of bringing to bear against their enemy in the Mediterranean.

The boats of the 29th U-Flotilla were to be faced with fresh challenges for the remainder of 1943, no longer operating in support of a ground war, but soon to be fighting defensive battles around Italy. Tactics and weapons were also under review, and on 10 May Dönitz recorded a lengthy summary and conclusions in his War Diary of the use of the new Pi2 pistol and the FAT torpedo. While the former met with complete approval, the FAT G7a torpedo was withdrawn from the Mediterranean due to boats being betrayed by the wake left behind the air-driven torpedo – seemingly regardless of whether used by day or night. Instead the deployment of FAT II torpedoes, using the G7e, was to be hurried to the Mediterranean to face the predicted onslaught.

Chapter 8

Operation 'Husky' to Anzio

ON 1 JUNE 1943 THERE WERE ONLY seventeen operational U-boats on the strength of the 29th U-Flotilla, two of them, *U-617* and *U-561*, at sea returning to port. Of the total strength, *U-97*, *U-565*, *U-73*, *U-617*, *U-596*, *U-380*, *U-616*, and *U-410* were stationed in La Spezia, *U-81* and *U-453* in Pola, *U-371*, *U-431*, *U-375*, *U-561*, *U-458* and *U-407* in Toulon and *U-593* in Salamis.[1] Those stationed in Italy found yard conditions deteriorating as they were grudgingly given yard space alongside the pressing needs of the *Regia Marina*, by men whose hearts were no longer committed to the Axis cause. The primary advantage of having the boats stationed in Italy, rather than Salamis or Pola, had been to allow access to the front line established across the entrance to the western Mediterranean against the invasion traffic bound for North Africa. The port also allowed relatively good communications with Germany for crew rotation and supplies. However, with the seizure of Toulon and subsequent renovation of the port for U-boat service, these advantages were somewhat nullified.

With the fall of North Africa the German high command became extremely doubtful of Italian attitudes to the war. Though Mussolini remained a staunch ally, the same could not be said of King Victor Emmanuel III and the fascist Grand Council. Fearing that they might depose Mussolini, OKM ordered the 29th U-Flotilla to officially relocate to the superior dockyard at Toulon during July, FdU Italian moving to Aix-en-Provence from where Kreisch could oversee the administration of the base, while Frauenheim assumed direct control of the port as head of 29th U-Flotilla until August 1943 when he was replaced by the Mediterranean combat veteran and Knight's Cross holder Gunter Jahn of *U-596*.[2] Coupled with the move, the post of FdU Italian was renamed FdU Mediterranean (*FdU Mittelmeer*) as of August 1943. His U-boats had been receiving steady upgrades in flak armament to reflect the steadily increasing effectiveness of Allied aerial power. The 29th U-Flotilla also began using its own dedicated Enigma code, named 'Medusa', or 'Turtle' to the Allies who broke it during June and were able to read it until

October 1944 when it was no longer deemed necessary as the last boats had gone.

The first two patrols of June 1943 were begun by *U-431* and *U-97* on the 5th of the month. Three nights later a new boat, Hans-Ferdinand Massmann's *U-409*, slipped through the Straits of Gibraltar. Massmann's transit had not been without incident, attacked five days after departing Brest by an aircraft of 48 Squadron RAF, driving off the attacker with heavy flak. A second aircraft attack east of Gibraltar after passing through the Straits was again held off sufficiently to allow the boat to dive to safety. Massmann brought *U-409* into Toulon harbour on 11 June.

The following day 27-year-old Hans-Georg Trox's *U-97* chanced upon the unescorted Dutch ss *Palima* sailing from Port Said to Famagusta and hit her with a single torpedo. The freighter, carrying ammunition, paints, acid and two trucks as cargo, sank with twenty-six men aboard, the surviving thirty-nine men rescued by a whaleboat and Greek destroyer and landed later that day in Beirut. Three days later Trox struck again, hitting and sinking the 8,995-ton British tanker MV *Athelmonarch* carrying 13,600 tons of aviation fuel to Alexandria from Beirut. The tanker sank northwest of Jaffa while under escort by the Greek destroyer *Aetos*, forty-seven survivors out of a total complement of fifty-one taken onboard the destroyer.

But the two sinkings along the eastern Mediterranean seaboard had brought Allied forces hunting for the U-boat, Hudson 'T' of 459 Squadron RAF sighting the surfaced *U-97* near Haifa on 16 June. Attacking out of the sun, Flight Sergeant D T Barnard hit *U-97* with four depth charges while some of the crew were apparently sunbathing on deck. One of the charges exploded after hitting the deck, the blast flinging the Hudson 400 feet into the air and causing severe damage to the wings and fuselage. Two others were judged near-misses and the fourth exploded ahead of *U-97*'s course. Several of the Germans were seen jumping overboard during the attack, and this increased as the U-boat began to sink by the stern. Barely aloft, Barnard circled *U-97* as the bow rose sharply out of the water and she slid stern-first underwater, the last few survivors swimming away from the suction created by a sinking vessel. British ships later arrived and rescued twenty-one German sailors, though Trox was not amongst them.

Krieg's *U-81* had also recently sailed from Pola to take up its eastern Mediterranean station, sinking the troopship ss *Yoma* north of Alexandria. The 8,131-ton liner was in Convoy GTX2 alongside ss *Amarapoora*, *Pegu*, *Kemmendine* and *Sagaing en route* from Sfax to Alexandria when she was hit by two torpedoes. Going down by the stern within five minutes, 451 of the 1,670 troops onboard, as well as Captain George Patterson and thirty-two crew members, were lost. The remainder were saved by the skilful actions of their minesweeper escort and another of the merchant ships in convoy. Krieg then sailed between Cyprus and Beirut, destroying three sailing vessels and torpedoing the 3,742-ton Greek freighter SS *Maichalios* sailing in ballast – for once underclaimed by a U-boat commander as Krieg misidentified her as the smaller Greek SS *Livathos*. The Greek was missed by an initial spread of two torpedoes, one of a second pair fired striking the stern and causing it to break off, the ship sinking rapidly with one crewman killed.

To the west Schöneboom's *U-431* attacked Convoy MKS15, claiming two cruisers hit but to no confirmed result. Likewise Albrecht Brandi claimed another destroyer sunk from a naval Task Force, but to no actual result. Horst Deckert in *U-73* torpedoed and sank steamer SS *Brinkburn* from TE22 on 21 June, damaging the large Fleet Oiler *Abbeydale* from Convoy XTG2 six days later. On the convoy's return route, designated GTX3, Freiherr Egon Reiner von Schlippenbach's *U-453* also damaged an oiler, hitting SS *Oligarch* 40 miles northwest of Derna.

On 22 June Gerd Kelbling's *U-593* found a military convoy designated 'Elastic' sailing from Azrew, Algeria, to Bizerte in Tunisia. At 21.31 Kelbling fired a spread of four torpedoes as the convoy sailed eight miles northeast of Cape Corbelin. The USS *LST333*, loaded with landing pontoons and troops, was struck by one torpedo. The explosion completely demolished the stern, killing twenty-five men of the onboard complement of 288, carried away the screws and rudder and stopped the engines although the robust ship showed no signs of sinking. After nearly 20 minutes, accompanying smaller LCTs *244* and *19* took the crippled ship in tow and proceeded slowly towards the beach, assisted shortly thereafter by the submarine chaser USS *SC503* which came alongside and took off thirty-two injured crew members and twenty-four injured passengers and brought them to Algiers. After five hours of towing, the mangled remains of the landing ship's stern ran aground near Dellys where the rest of the men aboard were taken off. USS *LST333* later sank during a salvage attempt on 6 July. A second LST had also been hit. USS *LST387* had also received a single torpedo hit but was towed to Dellys by landing craft and later repaired and able to return to active duty. Nonetheless, the torpedoing of these two Landing Ships was enough to hamper training for the planned Allied invasion of Sicily – Operation 'Husky'.[3]

The Allied forces spent the period between 22 June and 4 July rehearsing for the forthcoming invasion of Sicily. Even before the completion of the Allied campaign to clear North Africa, but on the heels of Operation 'Torch' resources began to be accumulated to enable a series of amphibious landings in the Mediterranean. During difficult negotiations between Churchill and Roosevelt and their military leaders at Casablanca in January, the ambitious Operation 'Round Up' – an invasion of Normandy and from there into the heart of Germany – was rightly deemed unfeasible. However, a primary objective for the Western Allies was to tie down Axis forces and thus relieve pressure on the Eastern Front, where Stalin continued to call for a Second Front. A secondary objective of finally pushing Italy out of the war was considered to be achieveable by an Allied assault on what Churchill euphemistically – and optimistic-ally – called 'the soft underbelly of Europe'. The Americans had been hard to convince, inclining towards increasing pressure in the Pacific and later attacking Germany directly. But the British prevailed and a large scale invasion of the southern periphery of Europe was planned. Sicily would be the first major step. Again the Allied supreme commander of the operation was General Eisenhower supported by Admiral Cunningham as the naval commander, General Alexander as land forces commander and Air Marshal Tedder as air forces commander. The rehearsals staged in the run-up to 'Husky' were not able to be undertaken at 'full scale' due to the proximity of Axis aircraft and U-boats. Nevertheless, three complete naval rehearsals and one combined rehearsal were conducted, so that by the time of the invasion all craft had performed their planned roles at least once. The loss of LSTs 333 and 387 caused some temporary problems for the Allies, however.

As the Allies prepared, the 29th U-Flotilla engaged Convoy KMS18B overnight on 4 July and well into the following afternoon. The convoy of ships was destined to join those gathering for the invasion of Sicily when Massmann in *U-409* launched the first attack, claiming an unsubstantiated steamer sunk. *U-375* attacked later that night when the convoy was almost midway between Oran and Algiers. Two freighters, the 5,634-ton MV *St Essylt* and the 8,765-ton SS *City of Venice* between them carrying 1,600 tons of stores, were sunk. The following afteoon at 15.43 Kelbling hit and sank British MV *Davis*, the 6,054-ton ship sinking with 4,000 tons of stores and fifty-two dead. Aboard the 6,054-ton ship were two LCTs destined for 'Husky', one destroyed during the sinking, the other damaged. MWS36 – the slow convoy from Alexandria to Malta – also suffered a casualty caused by U-boat attack when Schlippenbach's *U-453* found the ships northwest of Benghazi and torpedoed the 5,454-ton SS *Shahjeban* on 6 July. Four days later *U-371* damaged two large American ships from Convoy ET22A sailing from North Africa to Gibraltar; the Liberty ship SS *Matthew Maury* and tanker SS *Gulf Prince*. But that day events once more overtook German and Italian submarines at sea within the western Mediterranean as the expected blow fell on the coast of Sicily.

On 9 July, in stormy conditions hardly suited to the slow-moving invasion force, the armada sailed from North Africa for Sicily where the invasion began the next morning. Despite near-disastrous parachute drops preceding the amphibious landings, the attack went relatively smoothly in spite of often hideous conditions in the storm-tossed smaller landing ships and landing craft that ferried men to Sicily. On balance, despite the problems posed to the Allies by the severe weather it worked in their favour, lulling the Italian coastal defences into a false sense of security.

With two major landing points – General Patton's US Seventh Army in the Gulf of Gela on the south Sicilian coast and General Montgomery's Eighth Army south of Syracuse on the southeast coast – the armada of shipping stretched for miles, including 331 troopships and supply ships. They had concentrated in mid-Mediterranean east and west of Malta after converging from points as far east as Suez, Alexandria and Haifa and as far west as Oran where troop convoys (including Convoy KMS18B) had briefly stopped after their Atlantic crossing. But they were heavily defended by a massive naval presence that managed to deter nearly all submarine attacks over the ensuing days, though the *Luftwaffe* and Italian aircraft did succeed in braving the fierce flak and fighter cover to sink or damage several ships. Their numbers, barely 1,500 operational aircraft against an Allied umbrella of 4,000, guaranteed only limited success. Airfields on Sicily had been so heavily bombed during June that the squadrons had withdrawn to north and central Italy. Indeed Admiral Cunningham later remarked that it was '. . . almost magical that great fleets of ships could remain anchored on the enemy's coast . . . with only such slight losses from air attack as were incurred.'4

Indeed, despite once again being rushed to the new front, the U-boats achieved little throughout the remainder of July. Likewise the main Italian battle fleet remained virtually absent, vague notions of being held in reserve floated by the Italian command to Dönitz in Berlin, the *Grossadmiral* now head of the *Kriegsmarine* after Raeder's resignation in January. Italian submarines claimed eight successful attacks (in fact *MGB641* sunk and the cruiser HMS *Cleopatra* damaged), they lost eight submarines in return. The 29th U-Flotilla failed completely to breach the strong defensive cordon until 22 July when Krieg's *U-81* torpedoed and damaged the British SS *Empire Moon* off the eastern shores of Sicily and Brüller's *U-407* damaged the cruiser HMS *Newfoundland*, flagship of the support force, the following day by blowing off her rudders. The cruiser retreated to Malta, steering with her propellers. In reply, three U-boats were sunk in July.

On the morning of 12 July the destroyer HMS *Inconstant* escorting the troopships of Convoy MKF19 that were returning to Algeria after unloading their forces onto Sicily's battleground, detected Massmann's *U-409* on ASDIC and attacked. The destroyer hounded its quarry for two and a half hours, dropping forty-six depth charges, before *U-409* was finally fatally holed and brought to the surface. Massmann's boat was flooding rapidly and the young captain ordered all tanks blown as *U-409* began to sink uncontrollably. As the compressed air hissed into the diving bunkers displacing the water, the U-boat began an uncontrollable rise that culminated in it shooting out of the water bow first in front of the circling destroyer which immediately opened fire. Men began to spill from the boat which received several direct hits from the destroyer's main armament before sliding back underwater. Massmann and thirty-eight of his men were rescued, several having been wounded by gunfire.

During the course of that same night the British *MTB81* surprised a surfaced *U-561* near Messina. The U-boat had been recently put under the command of 26-year-old Oblt.z.S. Fritz Henning after the departure of Heinz Schomburg who had been transferred ashore to become supply officer for the flotilla. Henning was taken unawares and two torpedoes hit his boat which immediately sank. Only Henning and four other crew were later rescued by German coastal craft, the young commander later to be given command of *U-565* when its captain, Knight's Cross holder Wilhelm Franken, was rotated back to Germany.[5] Another patrol vessel, this time the USS *PC624*, destroyed *U-375* near the island of Pantelleria on the penultimate day of the month. Jürgen Könenkamp's experienced U-boat was sunk with no survivors.

In his *Wolfsschanze* headquarters on 17 July, Hitler had an anxious meeting with Dönitz, attempting to deal with the invasion of Sicily and the expected collapse of Italy as an ally.

> The C-in-C Navy declares that the attitude of the High Command in the employment of the Italian Fleet at the present time is infamous. In spite of all of his efforts, he was unable to get Admiral Riccardi to use his light forces to drive the enemy from the Straits of Messina, an intolerable situation since he has the forces available to do so ... At this point Field Marshal Rommel enters, and the Führer asks him whether he knows of any really capable persons in the Italian Army who are fully cooperating with Germany. Field Marshal Rommel replies that there is no such person ...
>
> The *Führer* asks C-in-C Navy whether he thinks it would be worthwhile to station more submarines in the Sicilian waters. The C-in-C Navy replies in the negative. Above all we must keep in mind that at the present time it is impossible for submarines to get through the Straits of Gibraltar. Perhaps this situation may be changed by autumn ... Even our S-boats have lost their effectiveness due to a tenfold superiority of enemy gunboat flotillas ...
>
> In conclusion the C-in-C Navy reports work on the anti-destroyer torpedo has progressed to a point where it will be possible to equip submarines therewith in the beginning of August.[6]

But despite Dönitz's previously-stated conviction, on 24 July OKM directed BdU to send three more U-boats through the Straits of Gibraltar to reinforce the 29th U-Flotilla. *U-614* sailed from Saint Nazaire and

U-454 and *U-706* from La Pallice within days of the new directive. None of them reached the Mediterranean – all three being destroyed by aircraft as they followed the latest orders for boats to stay surfaced and fight it out with their augmented flak batteries.

Despite a skilfully handled defensive battle on Sicily, the island was in Allied hands by Tuesday 17 August, though their often cautious advance had allowed a five-day orderly German naval evacuation of 100,000 troops and most of their vehicles and heavy weapons. Italy was now in a state of chaos by the successful invasion of Sicily. On 8 August the Italian King had stated that his country was officially in a 'state of siege', and Rome declared an Open City on 14 August. Mussolini's hold on power appeared to be at breaking point.

At sea Kurt Diggins' *U-458*, which had been rammed by an Allied escort vessel in early July and aborted to Toulon for repairs before sailing again on 14 August, was the next to claim damage inflicted to the enemy within the western Mediterranean, the American steamer SS *Cape Mohican* from Convoy MKS22 being torpedoed on 21 August. However, Diggins' presence was detected by the convoy's escort and destroyers HMS *Easton* and the Greek *Pindos* blew *U-458* to the surface with thirty depth charges, and opened fire on the damaged boat.

> Caught in the ships' searchlights she immediately came under fire so intense that eventually the order to cease firing had to be repeated more than once ... A number of men were seen by *Pindos* who got rather closer than *Easton*, to jump into the water and cling to the U-boat's side ...
>
> The U-boat at first lay stopped, but after about five minutes appeared to get underway. The crew had in fact abandoned her, leaving the engines running. At one time it looked as though the U-boat was going to ram *Pindos* but she passed under her stern and made to cross *Easton's* bows from port to starboard at a range of about 900 yards.
>
> *Easton* had only seen two or three men leave the boat which, with full buoyancy and on an even keel, was now, to all appearances attempting to escape, and she decide to ram ... Though caught in *Pindos'* searchlight, *Easton* went hard-a-port at the right time and struck the U-boat abreast of its forward gun. The destroyer shuddered, rose and plunged; the U-boat rolled over, her conning tower disappeared underwater to port abreast 'A' gun and then her bows were seen standing up high in the air very close to the starboard quarter.[7]

Diggins and thirty-nine survivors were later rescued by the destroyers.

Throughout August the U-boats claimed one cruiser, four destroyers and three steamers all hit and at least damaged, and a cruiser, destroyer and five merchant ships sunk in the western Mediterranean. In fact three merchants had been sunk and a fourth damaged. The British SS *Contractor*, carrying 6,110 tons of cargo including government stores and mail, was hit and sunk by Mehl's *U-371* on 7 August while in Convoy GTX5 southwest of Sardinia. The ship's ultimate destination had been Calcutta, and she took the master and three crew members with her as she went down.

Röther's *U-380* damaged the American SS *Pierre Soulé* escorted by three destroyers and one tug northwest of Palermo. The torpedo struck at the rudder post, lifting the ship bodily out of the water in a towering column of churning water. The rudder was blown off and damage caused to the shaft and engines, partially flooding the engine room and two holds. Understandably considering her to have been sunk, Röther withdrew although the American tug USS *Nauset* towed the ship to Bizerte. Later she would be repaired in a dry dock at Taranto, Italy. Fenski's *U-410* successfully attacked two ships from Convoy UGS14 on 26 August, a third claim remaining unsubstantiated from his three-torpedo spread. The American ships SS *John Bell* and *Richard Henderson*, between them carrying 12,200 tons of equipment and explosives, were both hit on their starboard sides and went down off La Calle, Algeria.

In the east Victor-Wilhelm Nonn's *U-596* destroyed several small sailing vessels off the Lebanese coast. Nonn, former IWO aboard *U-97*, was on his first patrol in command of the boat after he had replaced the departing K.K. Gunter Jahn. Jahn in turn had moved ashore and during July took command of the 29th U-Flotilla from Fritz Frauenheim. Jahn inherited a depleted flotilla that due to the uncertainties posed by events in Italy was also forced into a final relocation of staff from La Spezia to Toulon.

The imminent collapse of fascist Italy led Hitler to ready his forces for a possible occupation of the Italian peninsula. On 25 July the inevitable happened and after a vote of the Fascist Grand Council was carried to remove Mussolini as commander of Italian forces and pass that authority to the King, Mussolini resigned, and was promptly arrested and replaced by Marshall Pietro Badoglio. Immediately the aged Prime Minister opened secret negotiations with the Allied powers to surrender his country.

Within this charged environment and with suspicion between the Axis partners growing daily, Dönitz issued detailed verbal instructions to be passed on to V.A. Friedrich Ruge, *Befehlshaber Deutsche Marinekommando Italian*, on 26 July which included:

> If Rome is occupied the *Kriegsmarine* will immediately secure the Italian Fleet units in La Spezia, Taranto and Genoa, as well as the Italian merchantmen in all ports.
>
> The Commanding Officer of Submarines in Italy shall station U-boats off La

Spezia making sure, however, that the Italians do not become aware of this. Order: They will destroy the large ships of the *Regia Marina* if the latter should leave without our approval.[8]

On 3 September the Allies launched Operation 'Baytown', the invasion of Italy, with landings at Reggio, the tip of the 'boot' facing Messina, by Montgomery's Eighth Army. A covert armistice was signed with Badoglio, not announced officially by the BBC until a second Allied landing at midnight on 8 September by General Mark Clark's US Fifth Army at Salerno (Operation 'Avalanche').

Despite their prediction of such events, the shock of Italy's surrender still managed to catch much of the *Wehrmacht* off-balance. While German troops rushed to occupy key strategic points and begin disarming Italian forces, the U-boats failed to intercept the escaping Italian fleet. Only days previously Kesselring's Chief of Staff General Westphal had witnessed a visit by the Italian Minister of Marine Admiral Count de Courten during which he informed Kesselring that: '. . . the Italian Fleet would pull out on the 8th or 9th from Spezia to seek battle with the British Mediterranean Fleet. The Italian Fleet would conquer or perish, he said, with tears in his eyes. He then described in detail its intended plan of battle.'[9] On schedule the Fleet sailed from La Spezia on 9 September as Operation 'Avalanche' got underway, but not to do battle with the Allied invasion fleet. Instead the Italians headed for Malta to surrender, the planned U-boat cordon failing to intercept them. The Italians still suffered casualties; the battleship *Italia* was damged and the battleship *Roma* sunk by *Luftwaffe* Dornier Do 27 bombers experimenting with a newly-developed HS293 radio-guided bomb, and the sinking of the destroyers *Da Noli* and *Vivaldi* by coastal artillery and a mine respectively.

The 29th U-Flotilla, whittled down to thirteen serviceable boats, was faced with almost impossible conditions against overwhelming Allied strength that was also rapidly increasing in confidence. They were also coming under increasing pressure in port at Toulon with scattered harassing Allied air raids that would only intensify over the following months. In the whole of September the U-boats sank five merchant ships, one American minesweeper and the destroyer USS *Puckeridge*, one of Albrecht Brandi's three claimed destroyers. A further pair of ships was damaged. For Brandi's *U-617* it was to be their swansong.

On the night of 10 September the Leigh-Light equipped Wellington 'P' of 179 Squadron RAF detected a surfaced U-boat on their radar. Squadron Leader D B Hodgkinson lost height and approached on a direct path until the silhouette of the boat could be seen in the moonlight immediately ahead. At a range of half a mile the RAF crew switched on their blinding Leigh Light. Brandi later recalled the event to author Jochen Brennecke:

As the tropical night fell over North Africa and the narrow strip of the Straits I surfaced. Our batteries needed charging, but above all we needed some fresh air.

It was a lovely starlit night. All around us was peace, and nowhere was there even a shadow to be seen, nor even the rumble of a single aircraft. I handed over the watch to Count Arco, told him to set course for Mellile on the African coast and turned in. At the moment, so it seemed to me, our radar was of more importance than lookouts. Suddenly two terrific explosions rent the silence of the night. The U-boat staggered violently. I sprang up.[10]

Hodgkinson straddled the U-boat with six depth charges despite heavy flak. As the explosions subsided, the boat began steering erratically and leaking oil. Circling beyond flak range the aircraft called for reinforcements, which arrived in the shape of squadron mate Wellington 'J'. The latter's pilot, Pilot Officer W H Brunini, also attacked U-617 with six depth charges as the boat headed towards Spain. The boat disappeared momentarily in the blast after which the conning tower appeared to be aflame. In the fierce gun battle the Wellington's rear gunner, Flight Sergeant W Jones RAAF, was killed. But the damage had been done to U-617.

There was a crashing and splintering of glass and then the lights went out ... Pipes were bursting everywhere. The floor plates were flung out of their sockets, and as I rushed to the control room my foot got caught between two pipes that had been uncovered.

At last some order was restored and, at last, with some assistance I got my foot free ... With one lame diesel we tried to continue our way to the coast. I hope we should be able to lay the boat close in to the cliff and camouflage her with a few tarpaulins and some rocks.[11]

Brandi made for neutral waters, desperately trying to shake off the aircraft above as U-617 became increasingly stern heavy. With heavy damage, a persistent pursuer and dawn approaching, Brandi agonised over whether to abandon ship when the lurch of U-617 running aground decided the issue for him. He ordered the ship abandoned and set scuttling charges which exploded as the Germans made for shore in dinghies and swimming. Above them the Wellingtons had departed. In the early morning a Hudson arrived overhead, spotting the German dinghies and several men drying their clothes. U-617 was lying on its port side, down by the stern and shortly afterward Hudsons, Swordfish and three warships – HMS *Hyacinth*, *Harlem* and HMAS *Wollongong* – bombarded the wreck to ensure its destruction.

In the British communique these fireworks were celebrated as a sinking. Apparently all the bangs and noise had woken up the coastguards, for when all was quiet again and the British had departed, a Moroccan in Spanish uniform came trotting up. In his hand he brandished a long fearsome-looking flintlock, and from his gestures you would have thought he was at the head of a whole army.

'We were his prisoners' he shouted and he fiddled about with his old blunderbuss to such purpose that we really began to get quite nervous.

'Take the popgun away from the excited gentleman!'

In a moment it was done. Our Moroccan dithered and cursed in his own, unintelligible language, but what he was trying to say was obvious to us all.[12]

Brandi and his crew were eventually handed over to more even-tempered authorities and interned at Cadiz for two months. In November he was repatriated from Spain straight back to Toulon where Brandi took command of *U-380* in December after Josef Röther left the boat to take up a post ashore on the staff of 29th U-Flotilla.

Once more Dönitz ordered more U-boats to bolster the Mediterranean flotilla. This time, seven would be despatched from the Atlantic force, by this time itself depleted by fierce Allied countermeasures.

17 September

On orders of the Commander in Chief of the Navy seven further boats will be withdrawn for the Mediterranean. They are the following: *U-223, U-264, U-667, U-450, U-466, U-455* and *U-420*. It was intended to break through the Straits of Gibraltar in two groups but this cannot be done owing to the fact that the boats will not all be ready at the same time. *U-223* is still at sea.

Boats have been ordered to utilise favourable opportunities for attack while underway, but not to attack any convoys. If they are not successful in breaking through the Straits of Gibraltar at the first attempt, the boats are to withdraw, allow anti-U-boat activity to subside and attempt the break-through once more after two days. They are only to return if their 'Wanze' gear is faulty or if they have extensive engine trouble.[13]

The gauntlet of Biscay had to be run by the seven reinforcements, only one of which succeeded in breaching the Straits during September. The spearhead group of four – *U-223*, which had sailed already when the order came through, *U-264*, *U-455* and *U-667* – all sailed into fierce Allied ASW operations mounted as part of Operation 'Musketry' designed to sweep large swathes of the Bay of Biscay with aircraft equipped with Leigh Lights and radar. Only *U-223* made it, the rest aborting, *U-667* after sustaining considerable damage from six attacking aircraft, none of which were detected by the boat's 'Wanze' radar detector. On 26 September, Dönitz called off the attempt.

Boats *U-667, U-223, U-455* and *U-264*, withdrawn for the Mediterranean area, have been ordered, in view of the report by *U-667*, to give up their attempt to break through the Straits of Gibraltar and to withdraw to the west.

It is suspected that the enemy is using radar devices there, the wave-band of which (centimetric waves) cannot yet be intercepted by these boats. The appropriate receivers (Naxos) have, however, already been developed and will shortly be installed on all boats. The above boats are to refuel and then operate against convoys. *U-264* will, therefore, proceed to AK 80, *U-667*, *U-223* and *U-455* to BD80. A new attempt to break through is planned for the next new moon period.

Unbeknownst to Dönitz, Kaptlt. Karl-Jürgen Wächter's *U-223* had penetrated the Straits that night, entering the Mediterranean despite two heavy radar-guided air attacks on the way. Wächter took up a patrol station north of Oran. *Leutnant zur See* Gerhard Buske, a veteran of Mediterranean operations, was IWO during the voyage.

I had not entered the U-boat service straight away. First I was first on S-boats in 1941 then went to Flensburg *Marineschule* to march up and down sand dunes for months after which we were *Fähnriche*. That was then the first time that I went to the U-boats. It was two *Fähnriche* to one boat so that we could study how things were done. I was on *U-375*, *Kapitänleutnant* Könenkamp in the Mediterranean. I made two voyages with this boat, one to the eastern and one to the western Mediterranean. Then we came back to another school, *torpedolehrgang, artillerielehrgang, flaklehrgang* and so on. After that I was sent back to the Mediterranean as a *Leutnant*, I came aboard the boat U-Wächter, *U-223*.

The symbol that we had painted on the boat, the three dice, came from when the officers were playing dice. They shook the cup and threw and suddenly 223 came up and they all yelled 'that's our boat!' I wasn't on the boat then ...

I came through the Straits of Gibraltar on *U-223*. Then Wächter was gone in December, and the new commander Peter Gerlach came. So I made two more trips with Gerlach and then we were sunk off Palermo.[14]

Wächter sighted nothing until 2 October when he intercepted Convoy MKS27 bound for Sicily. His boat was equipped with the new 'destroyer killer' *Zaunkönig* homing torpedo and he fired four torpedoes, one of them a *Zaunkönig*, at 01.02. Although he claimed to observe a direct hit on a destroyer and heard three other detonations, the only confirmed hit was on the British steamer SS *Stanmore* carrying 2,500 tons of supplies that included explosives and 207 bags of mail. Badly damaged, the ship was later taken in tow and beached at Cape Tenes, Algeria, where she broke in two after the sacks of mail had been recovered.

Wächter's had been the third ship sunk since the month's beginning. *Oberleutnant zur See* Horst Arno Fenski in *U-410* launched a determined attack against convoy MKS26 on the 1st of the month, firing five torpedoes and observing one ship hit and sinking and four other detonations. Claiming four ships, he had actually destroyed the freighter ss *Fort Howe* and the tanker ss *Empire Commerce*, which, coupled with the other apparent successes earned him the award of the Knight's Cross on 26 November. However, his return to Toulon was not uneventful. While approaching the harbour, just outside the net booms, *U-410* accidentally collided with a German patrol boat and was badly damaged. Her entire bow was stove in and all the bow tubes badly damaged, though luckily none of the torpedoes in the forward tubes, which were all loaded, were detonated. The patrol boat was so badly damaged that it was later torpedoed and sunk. The damage to *U-410*'s bow necessitated extensive repairs, which lasted four months, during which time complete new bow tubes were installed. *U-410* also had her flak armament increased as part of a general upgrade for all Type VIIs. Twin 20mm cannons were mounted on Platform I and a quadruple 20mm *Vierling* on Platform II. While the boat lay in the yards, Fenski's crew went on leave twice, some for as much as eight weeks, while a new Engineering Officer, Oblt. (Ing.) Ferdnand Ritschel, came aboard.

Attacks during October against the invasion fleet gathered about southern Italy yielded the sinking by *U-616* of the destroyer uss *Buck* off Salerno on 9 October using a new T5 *Zaunkönig* torpedo. Hit in the bow, the destroyer's magazine exploded, killing 150 out of a crew of 247 men, the stricken warship sinking in less than four minutes. Koitschka also sank an LCT two days later. Elsewhere the 5,542-ton Norwegian tanker ss *Marit* was sunk by Nonn's *U-596* near Tobruk while Mehl's *U-371* accounted for the minesweeper hms *Hythe*, the destroyer uss *Bristol* sunk with fifty-two dead after another *Zaunkönig* strike and the Liberty ship ss *James Russell Lowell* damaged beyond repair, the keel found to have been twisted out of shape after the ship was towed to Colla, Algeria. There were also the familiar claims that could not be substantiated, including four steamers totalling 40,000 tons hit by Schönenboom in *U-431* in the early hours of 19 October and another the following day. Despite none ever being corroborated, 25-year-old Dietrich Schönenboom was awarded the Knight's Cross by radio on 20 October. He and his crew lived one more day to celebrate their success.

Wellington 'Z' of 179 Squadron RAF was patrolling in the darkness the following day when its radar registered a strong surface contact. Gunner Sgt. Len Neale remembered:

We carried on along the track until down to about 30 feet and a half mile from the contact. On went the Leigh Light to reveal a **** great cruiser or destroyer, we weren't too sure. It blasted away at us as poor old Don had to pull up at an alarming rate to climb over it! ... We did sustain damage to the aircraft rudder, but thank goodness it was slight.[15]

Somewhat jittery after their close encounter, another contact was soon made, this time the aircraft swooping low and surprising a fully surfaced U-boat with the blinding Leigh Light. With heavy flak buffeting the aircraft, the pilot, Sgt. Don Cornish RCAF, flew overhead and dropped six depth charges as his gunners returned fire. *U-431* and its entire crew went down in the spume of depth charge detonations. It was the final loss for the flotilla during October, though on the penultimate day of the month the submarine HMS *Ultimatum* narrowly missed torpedoing *U-73* as the latter approached Toulon harbour at the end of her patrol.

Once more Hitler ordered Dönitz to reinforce the 29th U-Flotilla. Five Atlantic Type VIICs were to enter the Mediterranean at the end of October after having been equipped with new 'Naxos' radar detectors. Only two – *U-450* and *U-642* – would make the perilous journey intact. On 24 October *U-566* was badly damaged by aerial depth charges from the same 179 Squadron Wellington that had destroyed *U-431*. The crippled boat was nursed into Spanish waters where Kaptlt. Hans Hornkohl and his men scuttled their boat and were rescued by the Spanish trawler *Fina* and interned. A week later Oblt.z.S. Claus-Peter Carlsen's *U-732* was sunk at the western end of the Straits by the ASW trawler HMT *Imperialist*. Only hours later Oblt.z.S. Hans-Joachim Klaus' *U-340* was also depth charged at the mouth of the Strait. Dönitz's new message transmitted to the Mediterranean-bound boats on 1 November arrived too late:

> According to reports from Tangier, the Straits of Gibraltar are very heavily guarded at this time.
>
> Boats *en route* for the Mediterranean which are still to the W. of the Straits, should abandon the breakthrough ordered, and should turn aside to the west.[16]

November saw a smattering of victories for the decimated flotilla. Egon-Reiner von Schlippenbach laid a minefield from *U-453* off Brindisi and Bari, ports used on Italy's east coast by the Allied forces inching along the Italian mainland against fierce and skilful German forces. The destroyer HMS *Quail* struck one that damaged her so badly that she sank while under tow, while the minesweeper HMS *Hebe* also hit one and sank with thirty-eight men killed after trying to sweep near Bari. A mine exploded abreast the bulkhead between the boiler rooms on the port side, soon followed by a second explosion near the same place. The small ship capsized within four minutes. The last casualty of the mines was the 335-ton Yugoslavian tramp MV *Jela*. Another warship, the cruiser HMS *Birmingham*, was hit by a torpedo from Brüller's *U-407* and seriously damaged, though she was towed to Alexandria and repaired.

Oberleutnant zur See Johann Otto Krieg's *U-81* sank the 2,887-ton British steamer SS *Empire Dunstan*, dispersed from Convoy KMS31 and carrying

1,550 tons of military stores, including 700 tons of land mines. *U-81* hit the British freighter southwest of Taranto, two crew members lost before the master, twenty-nine crew members, seven gunners and three passengers were picked up by the Norwegian SS *Lom* and landed at Taranto.

It is also possible that Henning's *U-565* operating in the Aegean accounted for British submarine HMS *Simoom* on 15 November. Henning launched a *Zaunkönig* torpedo at a surfaced enemy submarine southeast of Kos and heard a detonation after 3 minutes 42 seconds but could not visibly confirm success due to the necessity of diving after the firing of a T5 lest it circle back on them. The British submarine's last communication with her base had been ten days previously, instructions to respond to another on the 19th remaining unanswered.[17]

During December the flotilla sank a single steamer, the 8,009-ton SS *Cap Padaran* sailing from Taranto to Augusta. However, the single most effective attack was mounted by Kelbling's *U-593*. Operating alongside Wächter's *U-223* against Convoy KMS34 on 11/12 December, Kelbling hit and sank the destroyer HMS *Tynedale* while Wächter damaged the frigate HMS *Cuckmere* so badly she was later written off. Both had been hit by *Zaunkönig* torpedoes. The Royal Navy swiftly responded by sending a Hunter-Killer group out to battle the U-boats, Kelbling calmly torpedoing and sinking HMS *Holcombe* from this group. But Kelbling had sealed his own fate. The remaining four warships of the group hounded him for 32 hours with intemittent contact before USS *Wainwright* finally obtained firm sonar contact. She and HMS *Calpe* bombarded the boat with depth charges, causing a large leak in a sea inlet for the diesel cooling system onboard the U-boat which began taking on water at a rate of nearly 400 litres a minute. When the boat's LI reported this to Kelbling he misunderstood the message in the noise and confusion, registering that only a quarter of a litre of water per minute was entering his boat and so he elected to remain submerged.

U-593 quickly became stern-heavy and reports that the bilges were flooding and the main electric motors were in danger meant the captain grasped the full implications of their situation. Spare crewmen were rushed to the bow to try and keep *U-593* in trim and tanks were blown, but the supply of high-pressure was insufficient to lift the boat and she fell further within the water column. Finally, with electric motors nursed up to half-speed, *U-593* reached the surface where the enemy opened fire on her. Kelbling ordered scuttling charges set and the boat abandoned and after nearly half of the crew had leapt overboard and the boat obviously sinking the destroyers ceased fire. Kelbling, assisted by some engine-room men, wedged open the stern torpedo hatch to ensure quicker flooding, the L.I. and and a pair of the boat's senior ratings taking submachine guns to the bridge to ensure that no boarding party could reach the boat before she sank, a motorboat seen to be approaching from the destroyers. Kelbling managed to persuade his would-be captors that the scuttling charges were due to blow at any moment as the motor boat pulled alongside, and subsequently no attempt to board U-593 was made before she sank. The entire German crew, miraculously with no-one killed by the heavy surface fire, were rescued.

The final successful U-boat attack in the Mediterranean for 1943 was launched by Deckert's U-73 against Convoy GUS24 on 13 December. A single torpedo struck the Liberty ship ss *John S. Copley* on the starboard side forward of the mainmast, flooding the empty number 2 hold and causing an 8° list. The ship was carrying sand ballast and five landing craft as deck cargo and the blast ripped an enormous hold in the hull while throwing four of the five landing craft into the air. The master ordered the thirty-four crewmen and twelve armed guards to abandon ship and stand by in their lifeboats as the ship's steering failed. Meanwhile, a skeleton crew remained aboard and soon determined that the damage was not fatal, the engines restarted and many of the nearby men taken back aboard. Three harbour tugs later arrived to assist the ship into Oran while the navy tug USS *ATR47* successfully took her in tow. The damaged ship was later repaired and returned to service. But Deckert had given his position away and three American destroyers departed Mers-el-Kebir to track him down. After an hour of scouring the area in which the Liberty ship had been hit, USS *Woolsey* made firm sonar contact and began dropping depth charges. The U-boat's hull was fractured and serious flooding forced Deckert to surface where U-73 came under concentrated fire. As the Germans abandoned ship and scuttled their boat many were cut down by the hail of shells and bullets until U-73 slid beneath the waves and fire was halted. Deckert and twenty-two survivors were rescued and taken to North Africa.

The apparent success of the T5 *Zaunkönig* homing torpedo, designed to target the high-pitched propellers of Allied warships, was welcome news to Dönitz in Berlin. Because of the nature of the weapon and its short arming range U-boats were instructed to dive deep after firing which helped in no small measure to somewhat exaggerate its success rate, with the sound of detonation taken as proof of a hit. Supplies of the torpedo were scheduled to be increased during December, although heavy bombing of German construction facilities forced a postponement of this plan. Nontheless, in comparison to the Atlantic and what BdU described as 'home waters', the Mediterranean received the greater number allocated per boat, reflecting the peculiar and difficult conditions that the 29th U-Flotilla fought under. Each boat was to be equipped with four to six *Zaunkönig* torpedoes, the number to be increased as the supply improved.

By the year's end the 29th U-Flotilla had been whittled down to thirteen boats, Paul Siegmann's U-230 having arrived in the Mediterranean on 5 December from the Atlantic. Aboard the boat was IWO Oblt.z.S. Herbert Werner whose autobiographical book, *Iron Coffins*, recalls his boat's passage through the Straits and into Toulon.

Through the low-lying haze, I counted at least six British warships guarding the entrance to the Mediterranean. I trained the scope to starboard and spotted the North African coast rising almost perpendicularly out of the ocean. On top of the high cliffs near Spanish Ceuta, a Civil War memorial projected still higher, and the coast on either side of the monument melted away in the afternoon haze. I was so captivated by the view that I spotted the airplane almost too late to shout 'Dive, fast, dive to 60 metres, aircraft!'

I retracted the long scope shaft, then ducked my head and waited. But *U-230* arrived at the designated depth without interference from above . . .

Almost 24 hours later . . . we ventilated the boat and proudly transmitted our first radio message to Admiral U-boats: 'Special mission completed. Request new orders. *U-230*.'[18]

Eleven days later *U-230* entered Toulon harbour.

At daybreak we dived and Siegmann soon spotted our escort through the scope as she crawled over the horizon. One hour and 20 minutes later we surfaced 30 metres off port of the nervously cruising trawler. Her skipper requested us to follow her, and a signal by flags told us to be on our maximum alert, for British subs had sunk one of our vessels and one of our U-boats two weeks previously. We raced after the zigzagging escort with all hands on deck, wearing their life jackets. At the harbour entrance, a tugboat admitted us, then shut off the entrance by dragging the submerged anti-submarine net from one pier head to the other.

We sailed into full view of Toulon. The bright sun shone on green mountains, on the red and green tile roofs of whitewashed houses, on the rusty superstructures of several damaged and grounded French warships. *U-230* carefully manoeuvred through the harbour basin, past two sunken French destroyers, past three U-boats which lay unprotected alongside a quay. The Captain, spotting a small assembly of men in blues, steered his boat toward the empty place at the quay, and *U-230* came to rest parallel to the land.[19]

The lack of a suitable shelter for the new boats would become more critical as the months passed. The USAAF Fifteenth Air Force, comprising six heavy bomber groups, five medium bomber groups and four fighter groups became active in Tunisia at the beginning of November 1943, their initial B 17 raid made against La Spezia's town and harbour that day. On 24 November at 13.10 the first full-scale Allied aerial bombardment hammered the port of Toulon as a total of 100 B 17s, based in Tunisia and escorted by P 38 fighters, attacked during daylight. Damage was caused to three U-boats lying in harbour and the 9,591-ton passenger/cargo ship ss *Belle Isle*, seized by the *Kriegsmarine* in Marseilles in January 1943 was hit and sunk as she lay in a flooded drydock.[20] In the smoking rubble 500 people had been killed by that first major raid (including *Matrosenobergefreiter* Karl Meyer from *U-380*, Heinz Haberland and Harry Lüdecke of *U-450* and Kurt Hörseljau from *U-642*), the picturesque district of Mourillon and the port being particularly hard hit. The Boulevard Bazeilles (housing the barracks for *Kriegsmarine* guard detachments), the streets Castel, Castillon, Lamalgue and the district of Besagne were reduced to rubble.

The U-boat base immediately received reinforcements in the form of *Korvettenkapitän* (*Marine Artillerie*) Dr Karl Franz's *Marineflakabteilung* 819 and its extra anti-aircraft units and K.K. (MA) Georg Claussen's 3. *Marine-nebelabteilung* (naval smoke detachment) over the ensuing weeks. Nonetheless the pace of bombardment increased, *The Illustrated London News* screaming the headline on 11 December:

Blasting Germans From the Air – 'Toulon, German U-Boat Base in France Blasted by Flying Fortresses' – 'The Entire Target Area, Toulon Harbour is Aflame from Over 400 tons of High Explosive.'

Chapter 9

Between the Hammer and the Anvil
– Retreat from France

AT THE BEGINNING OF 1944 the 29th U-Flotilla stood at a strength of thirteen boats: *U-371, U-380, U-616, U-410, U-223, U-450, U-642* and *U-230* based at Toulon; *U-565* at Salamis; and *U-81, U-407, U-453* and *U-596* at Pola. The New Year was planned to bring some major changes to U-boat service in the Mediterranean, not least of all the planned introduction of brand new weaponry suited to the kind of clear water inshore campaign that was now being waged by the U-boats. As far back as July 1943 Dönitz had acquired Hitler's approval of the new 'electro-boat' design planned to revolutionise U-boat warfare. With a high submerged speed, the ability to remain submerged for extended periods of time and to fire homing torpedoes from depth the Type XXI and Type XXIII U-boats could counter the failings of the now obsolete Type VII. Though the large ocean-going Type XXI was patently unsuited to the Mediterranean, the smaller, more agile Type XXIII was perfect. Coupled with these electro-boats, the so-called 'Walter' boat under development powered by hydrogen peroxide promised a new age of submarine warfare. Dönitz also enthusiastically proposed to Hitler that the Rhône Canal would provide the means by which to send these small boats to the Mediterranean from Germany. No longer would they face the daunting gauntlet of Gibraltar.

The Type XXIII had been designed specifically for use in the Mediterranean or coastal waters. With a streamlined hull formed by two flattened cylinders and prefabricated into four separate sections that were then welded together, the Type XXIII boasted no external weaponry or deck casing. Its most significant flaw was a limited weapon load, being capable of carrying only two torpedoes. In fact the interior was so compact – or cramped depending on your point of view – that the two bow torpedo tubes had to be loaded from the outside, the stern lowered into the water and torpedoes allowed to slide tail-first into the tubes. Thus the boat could not reload at sea, itself not a problem in the Mediterranean as it would have been suicidal in any case.

While the 'Martha' bunker complex at Marseille and Toulon's

Castigneau dock conversion were never fully realised, an even more ambitious plan had also been hatched involving U-boat deployment in the Mediterranean and Aegean. Plans to convert the Rove Tunnel near Marseille into a shelter capable of dealing with the planned deployment of the Type XXIII within the region were also advanced by the time of the Allied invasion of southern France. The Rove Tunnel comprises the southern section of the 7,120-metre long, 22-metre wide Marseilles-Rhône Canal, an engineering achievement opened in 1927 cutting through the Chaîne de l'Estaque at sea level. Within a selected portion of the tunnel complex incorporating five dry-docks and eight wet pens were planned to be constructed. Also, five raised pontoons for U-boats would be provided, making a total space for sixteen Type XXIIIs at one time. Workshops were strategically positioned along the 680-metre area earmarked for the development. Needless to say, the project was shelved, the first Type XXIIIs not seeing action until February 1945 by which time France as an operational base was a distant memory for the U-boat service.

Likewise, plans for U-boat bunkers at Salamis and at a proposed new U-boat base on Lemnos were never advanced beyond the planning stages as the reality of German defeat loomed large. Plans in Salamis envisaged two bunkers, one capable of handling Type VIIC U-boats within nine wet and nine dry pens, the other designed for the Type XXIII again with nine wet and dry pens.

As events transpired the first example of the 234-ton U-boat design was not even laid down until 10 March 1944. Launched on 17 April the boat (*U-2321*) was finally commissioned on 12 June 1944 and never despatched to the Mediterranean. The Walter boat was never stable enough to pass beyond two prototypes. The war in the Mediterranean would continue to be waged by Type VII U-boats. Their only reinforcement would later in 1944 be the use of *Kleinkampfverbände* midget submarines and human torpedoes – themselves of relatively limited effectiveness.[1]

During January the combat veteran K.z.S. Werner Hartmann replaced K.z.S. Leo Kreisch as FdU Mediterranean, the new FdU ensconcing himself in the Château Costabelle overlooking Toulon from the east. Below the Château, dock facilities were being prepared for what German prisoners later called 'small U-boats', many Organisation Todt workers being transferred there for the job. Hartmann had recently finished a 200-day patrol as captain of the Type IXD-2 *U-198*, the third longest combat patrol carried out by a U-boat during the war and, like his predecessor, would try to be on hand to welcome every boat returning to port after combat.

January resulted in another rash of claimed sinkings by the flotilla. Among the possible successes Koitschka aboard *U-616* claimed two submarines sunk after hearing *Zaunkönig* explosions following an attack against a clustered group of six British submarines. He also later claimed a destroyer, as did Brandi aboard his new boat *U-380*. For Koitschka there was the reward of the Knight's Cross bestowed on 27 January. The young captain and crew were justifiably proud of what they believed they had achieved.

> Our captain, Siegfried Koitschka, drove us to a state of efficiency that must have been hard to match by another boat. He had previously served as Watch Officer with the famous Erich Topp, who commanded *U-552* – the Red Devil boat, so called because of the emblem painted on the conning tower. We adopted the crest of a red devil with a pistol in each hand.
>
> Fighting the French gendarmes in Toulon or fighting the British and Americans at sea was all the same to us, and made for great *esprit de corps*. With Koitschka a holder of the Knight's Cross, we were perhaps a little unbearable when ashore, full of our own importance, and if our 'chummy' boat was in – the *U-410* under her skipper Fenski, another Knight's Cross holder – we were even more boisterous in the bars of Toulon. But perhaps we could be excused our high spirits. Kipling, in one of his poems about British submarines in the first war, wrote, 'We arrive, we lie down, and we move in the belly of death'. We knew what he meant, and that our time would surely come.[2]

On 22 January new Allied landings at Anzio – Operation 'Shingle' – just south of Rome offered fresh opportunities to attack. Between 25 and 30 January Gerlach's *U-223* and Siegmann's *U-230* claimed to have attacked and sunk two destroyers, one patrol vessel, three LSTs and an LCF as well as damaging two other destroyers. In reality during the entire month there were no confirmed sinkings made by the 29th U-Flotilla. The disadvantage of the 'fire and forget' weaponry that allowed the U-boats a slim chance of success with the possibility of survival remained an inability to observe results. However, in turn, no U-boats were sunk at sea.

The sole loss for the flotilla was the veteran boat *U-81*, bombed and sunk by USAAF Fifteenth Air Force B 17 bombers as she lay in the naval harbour at Pola's Vergorola Bay on Sunday 9 January, *Maschinengefreiter* Heinz Klischies and *Maschinenobergefreiter* Heinz Schmickler from *U-81* were killed in the raid. Four men from *U-407* that also lay in harbour were killed by the bombing as well; *Oberleutnant* (*Ing*) Heinz Weser, L.z.S. Eberhard Baumgart, *Maschinenobergefreiter* Rudolf Güttge and *Maschinenobergefreiter* Heinz Bönisch.[3]

But January also saw the arrival of four new boats in the Mediterranean. Wolfgang Rahn's *U-343* passed Gibraltar on 3 January, narrowly avoiding destruction five nights later when a Wellington of 179 Squadron RAF detected the boat on radar and attacked. Six depth charges were dropped that narrowly missed the twisting boat below, which in return managed to shoot the bomber down, only the pilot, Flying Officer W F M Davidson, surviving to be later rescued by Allied forces. The brief but heavy fire had attracted nearby Catalina 'J' of 202 Squadron RAF who spotted the U-boat in the bright moonlight. Both Catalina and *U-343* opened fire at the same time, the aircraft narrowly missing *U-343* with six depth charges. Enough damage had been caused to both protagonists that they retreated, *U-343* docking in Toulon on 19 January. Other boats to arrive were *U-952* and *U-455*, both successfully reaching Toulon which came under attack again in early February.

On 4 February B 17s again unloaded bombs on Toulon, this time severely damaging *U-343*, *U-380* and *U-642*. The latter two U-boats would never sail again; *U-380* destroyed on 11 March in another USAAF raid, which also killed crewmember *Maschinenmaat* Jonny Christoph, while *U-642* was damaged again during a raid in July and decommissioned on 12 July, as she lay stricken in the Bassin 2 Missiessy dry-dock. The pace of the American bombing of Toulon increased between March and August 1944. B 17s and B 24s were the main aircraft used to attack the harbour installations, oil stores, a telegraph cable factory, *Kriegsmarine* barracks, repair shops, ships in harbour and, of course, U-boats. During March a huge fire devastated the department store '*Dames de France*', the main post office, the *Hotel de Ville*, and the *Palais Vauban*. Eyewitnesses amongst the French population remember burning paper from the gutted department stores circling lazily in the sky and coming down like 'black snow'. The district of Mourillon soon became uninhabitable and was closed off by the Germans who evacuated the civilians from the area. The bulk of the remaining population also began to depart the shattered town. Those that remained behind shared the privations of the largely *Kriegsmarine* personnel that inhabited Toulon. On 11 July the inhabitants of Seyne had taken refuge in a tunnel to escape the bombs, a panicked stampede for the exit as the tunnel shuddered under the blasts killing ninety-six people.

At sea the struggle continued as well. Desperate counter attacks against the forces of Operation 'Shingle', largely using T5 *Zaunkönig* torpedoes, at last yielded some results. Horst-Arno Fenski's *U-410* hit and sank the 7,154-ton freighter ss *Fort St Nicolas* east of the island of Capri on 15 February after following the ship as it left harbour at Salerno. Not long after the Liberty ship had been hit the 'pinging' of ASDIC was heard through the water and soon *U-410* was under attack. Depth charges caused a slight water entry in the control room, making it difficult to maintain trim. *U-410* went deep to 180 metres, but the flooding was making the boat stern heavy and it was necessary to blow some of the tanks. Though the German crew were concerned that the blowing of some tanks would give their position away they were relieved shortly thereafter to hear the destroyer give up the hunt and steam away, believing that their attacker, hearing the tanks being blown, probably believed that the U-boat had fired a *Zaunkönig* and therefore had got out of the way as quickly as possible. Fenski withdrew to repair the leak and also a tear in one trimming tank.

The next morning, near the island of Ischia off Naples, *U-410* sighted an LST escorted by a PC boat and destroyer. Bow tubes one and two were loaded with *Zaunkönigs*, but after firing tube two, it was discovered that the first torpedo had failed to leave the tube. Following some frantic effort by the torpedo crew it was finally ejected with the aid of a small explosive charge, but it had apparently been damaged, as it failed to run correctly and just fell out of the end of the tube. After a lapse of six to eight minutes a terrific explosion was heard and *U-410* departed as quickly as possible.

Two days later Fenski also sank the cruiser HMS *Penelope*, the unescorted cruiser being hit by a single T3 torpedo fired from tube No. 4 at a range of about 800 metres. Following the first hit the cruiser's speed reduced to two knots and tube one, loaded with a FAT, was fired to administer the *coup de grâce*. But this torpedo was another 'hot runner' – hung up inside the tube with propeller racing. It was finally expelled, however, and a T5 was fired from tube two. This struck HMS *Penelope* amidships, the cruiser sinking in less than a minute 35 miles west of Naples. The *Arethusa* class cruiser had been returning from bombarding German positions at Anzio as part of the Gunfire Support Group TG 81.8, and sank with 415 dead from a crew of 621 men. Fenski then scored a third victory when he sank *LST348* 40 miles south of Naples, the blaze caused by the exploding landing ship lighting up the nearby coastline as *U-410* escaped at high speed on the surface.

Kapitänleutnant Paul Siegmann's newly arrived *U-230* also destroyed two 1,625-ton British landing ships, *LST418* and *LST305* both sunk off Anzio. Away from Operation 'Shingle' Max Dobbert's also newly arrived *U-969* hit two American Liberty Ships near Bône in Algeria, both beached but declared total losses. In the east, Oblt.z.S. Dierk Lührs who had taken over the command of *U-453* from Kaptlt. Egon Reiner von Schlippenbach in December 1943 as the boat lay in Pola, attacked and destroyed four sailing vessels off Soueidie, Lebanon, by gunfire and ramming. Lührs then headed for Salamis where on 24 February during the test firing of one of the boat's machine guns, two men were killed onshore. The last sinkings were also in the east, Korndörfer's *U-407* destroying the 55-ton Egyptian sailing vessel *Rod el Farag* by gunfire and damaging the British tanker MT *Ensis* on the early evening of 29 February. Almost incredibly, despite the odds stacked against them, there were no U-boats sunk in action during February while *U-969*, *U-967* and *U-586* all arrived from the Atlantic, *U-421* in March. This survival trend would not continue during the following month.

As *U-616* continued its futile attacks near Anzio, Oskar Curio brought his *U-952*, which had arrived during January, to the southeast coast of Sicily where he torpedoed and sank Liberty Ship ss *William B. Woods*. The most successful boat was Kaptlt. Waldemar Mehl's *U-371* which encountered Convoy SNF17 and sank MV *Dempo* and ss *Maiden Creek*. The ensuing retaliation from escort forces was evaded by Mehl whose actions earned him the Knight's Cross, awarded on 28 March.

Two reinforcements arrived from the Atlantic, *U-466* slipping past Gibraltar on 22 March and *U-471* on 31 March, but the 29th U-Flotilla lost five U-boats to the enemy.[4] On 10 March Wolfgang Rahn's *U-343*, which had sailed from Toulon after repairs to the bomb damage sustained during February, was detected by the trawler HMT *Mull* north of Bizerte and sunk in a depth-charge attack. There were no survivors from the boat that had achieved no success during its short career.

That day Oblt.z.S. Kurt Böhme's *U-450* was found off Anzio by the destroyers HMS *Blankney*, *Blencathra*, *Brecon* and *Exmoor* that formed a hunter-killer group tasked with defending the beachhead. Despite their initial ASDIC contact being classed as 'doubtful', HMS *Exmoor* and *Brecon* mounted a depth charge attack that caused considerable flooding aboard *U-450* and forced Böhme to surface. Under intense surface fire, the crew abandoned ship and scuttled their boat, all of them except *Matrosengefreiter* Thomas Heneka being rescued by the British. Böhme, too, had sunk nothing in *U-450*.

More Allied bombing of Toulon destroyed the next two U-boats – *U-380* and *U-410* hit and damaged beyond repair on 11 March, the latter as it lay moored alongside Quai Noël. The French cruiser *Jean de Vienne*, which had recently been part salvaged by the *Kriegsmarine* was also hit, set on fire and severely damaged. Bombs fell in the U-boat repair yards and all over Toulon itself, twelve to fifteen large fires raging out of control in the city. A 3,000-ton freighter was sunk at anchor and a 14,000-ton Italian passenger ship burned out in dry-dock. At the harbour entrance a small freighter was also sunk.

The two veteran commanders of the damaged U-boats, Oak Leaves holder Albrecht Brandi and Knight's Cross holder Horst-Arno Fenski, both remained in Toulon and were assigned fresh boats with the majority of their crews coming with them while the boats' existing complements returned to Germany.[5] Brandi would take command of *U-967* that had freshly arrived while Fenski would take command of the veteran *U-371*, allowing recently decorated Waldemar Mehl to join Hartmann's FdU Mediterranean Staff.

A three-ship hunter-killer group operating off Palermo made the final sinking of March. During the early hours of 29 March they detected the ASDIC trace of submerged *U-223* as Peter Gerlach stalked the waters off Sicily. HMS *Laforey*, *Tumult* and *Ulster* then began a hunt, during which three more British and two American destroyers and three American PT-boats would reinforce them.

> We were depth charged for 25 hours by at least four destroyers. We went down to about 200 to 230 metres, very deep and the boat creaked and groaned ... well it was very hard with the sound through the water, it was so loud. It was really frightening – it was a hard thing being depth charged for so long. The air was thick and nearly unbreathable. We were all frightened and tried to will them to go away, we thought the hull was going to snap and that would be the end of us.[6]

Twenty-two separate depth charge attacks hounded *U-223* into the depths, the boat's air and battery power both rapidly dwindling. With many of the crew almost comatose, Gerlach realised they would have to surface and try to slip away in the darkness unseen. *U-223* rose cautiously out of the water, hatches thrown open to allow the stinking fetid atmosphere to escape and be replaced by fresh air, before starting the diesels and attempting to escape on the surface. However, the boat was detected on radar and HMS *Blencathra, Hambleton, Laforey* and *Tumult* opened fire as they gave chase. Desperately trying to escape, the IWO Oblt.z.S. Gerhard Buske ordered a single stern-loaded T5 *Zaunkönig* fired as a last-ditch attempt to dissuade pursuit. The torpedo arced immediately toward HMS *Laforey*, hitting the destroyer, which exploded killing 189 and leaving only sixty-nine survivors.[7]

However, despite this last success, Gerlach realised that his boat was doomed and ordered the crew to prepare to abandon ship. As the crew assembled on deck, making the most of the temporary confusion sown amongst their pursuers, the LI Ernst Scheid set scuttling charges, the last man to leave the boat. Gerlach ensured his men were out and then remained aboard, determined to go down with his ship. The crew began jumping over the side as *U-223* circled out of control back through the struggling Germans, all the while pursued by the British destroyers and their hammering gunfire.

> We were gathering around little rescue boats, many of which were hit as *U-223* came back towards us, the propellers chopping the water. So after she finally went down just over half the crew were rescued and nearly the same number died, most from gunfire. The commander was wounded during the first bombardment and I think maybe they thought another U-boat was there because the *Laforey* had been hit in this position and they dropped more depth charges so that many of those rescued died aboard the ship. We buried them at sea later. At about dawn, with sunrise, we were on and around a little one-man lifeboat, about eight or nine of us. We were near the destroyer that was trying

to get the lifeboats on deck. So I said 'we will never get this little boat over to them, so anybody who can swim now just swim, the launch will pick us up and take us to the ship'. So our *Obersteuermann*, Walter Fitz, and the IIWO, two others and me, we swam and I told an officer that there were still men out there in the water and he said 'oh yes, we won't leave them there', but I never heard that they were rescued. I know that I heard later on that some men managed to catch ropes from the ship but were pushed down ... but that's war you know.[8]

The dwindling 29th U-Flotilla achieved two confirmed sinkings in April; the torpedoing by *U-407* of the American ss *Thomas G. Masaryk* and *Meyer London* on 16 April north of Derna. A spread of three torpedoes fired at the overlapping steamers in Convoy UGS37 yielded two detonations. The *Thomas G. Masaryk*, sailing in station no.23, was hit on the port side at the no.3 hatch, tearing a huge hole in the side plating. Almost immediately acetone stored in the hold caught fire and ignited the magazine that carried ammunition for the 20mm AA guns. The ensuing blaze and exploding ammunition forced the bridge to be evacuated and the American ship circled slowly to starboard, missing the other torpedoed ship by not more than 20 feet. ss *Meyer London* had also been struck by a single torpedo on the port side, the blast hurling a large column of oil and water over the stern, demolishing the gun crew quarters, injuring the gun crew standing watch and blowing off the screw and rudder. Both ships were abandoned. The former was later towed to Maneloa Bay, Libya, where shellfire was used to extinguish the blaze before the remaining cargo was salvaged and the ship written off. The other rudderless ship sank slowly by the stern.

During April two U-boats were lost – *U-455* disappearing after 6 April with no trace after departing on a minelaying mission, and *U-421* destroyed by bombing in Toulon on 29 April as she lay in basin 2 of the Missiessy dry dock. Albrecht Brandi continued his almost habitual over-claiming on 26 April when he claimed a destroyer hit and sunk south of Sardinia from his new boat *U-967*. During the month that followed he was more successful, torpedoing and sinking uss *Fechteler* with a *Zaunkönig* as the American ship escorted Convoy GUS38. The ship exploded, broke in two and sank with twenty-nine dead. The huge 107-ship Convoy GUS38, travelling in ballast in sixteen columns and escorted by Task Force 66, had already come under attack by Fenski in his new boat *U-371* after the boat surfaced to recharge batteries and found itself almost in the middle of the convoy, crash-diving immediately to 100 metres in the early hours of 2 May. Fenski surfaced after an hour and gave chase, recharging his batteries while in the process. Soon the boat's radar detector warned that they been found and Fenski immediately changed course and attempted to run while his batteries slowly filled. With a pursuing destroyer closing to a range of about 3,000 metres, Fenski fired a single T5 *Zaunkönig* from *U-371*'s stern tube, and immediately dived to over 100 metres. After about five or six minutes an explosion and sinking noises were heard, and the German crew assumed the pursuing destroyer had been sunk. In fact they had hit and damaged the escort destroyer USS *Menges*. The destroyer, manned by a Coast Guard crew, had been patrolling 3,000 yards astern of the convoy when it had detected a radar contact six miles astern. The American captain ordered battle stations and 'Foxer' gear streamed behind the boat – designed to counter the *Zaunkönig*. Zigzagging at slow speed after the radar contact had disappeared and preparing to begin a sonar hunt, the destroyer was hit by the sudden blast of a torpedo in the stern. Both propellers were shorn off as well as the rudders, as the ship juddered to a halt, the stern compartments wrecked and thirty-one crewmen killed, another twenty-five being injured. All weapons, bar the ship's forward batteries and four 20mm AA guns amidships, had been put out of commission.

Two destroyer escorts were ordered to assist *Menges* and hunt for the attackers and USS *Pride* and *Joseph E. Campbell* were soon alongside their damaged compatriot. In the meantime Fenski had given the order to surface until his hydrophone operator reported faint screw noises and distant depth-charge explosions audible when they reached 60 metres. With the screws becoming more clearly audible Fenski took his boat down again to 160 metres and headed toward the coast at slow speed, thinking that this was just the opposite of what would be expected of him.

But USS *Pride* had made sonar contact and began a depth-charge attack, exploding around the boat, putting out all lights, damaging the hydroplanes, and rupturing the trim tanks. Finally Fenski was forced to blow the No.3 diving tank to level the boat off at about 200–215 metres. The glands leaked badly at this depth and the water entry increased as the attacks continued at about 30-minute intervals, each one being more accurate than the one before.

As the attack developed further the starboard propeller shaft was thrown out of line, the armature of the starboard motor ran excessively hot while the motor/generator supplying the current to the gyrocompass became noisy, necessitating turning off the gyros.

The final series of depth-charges during this first onslaught was delivered at about 06.00 on 3 May and, with those explosions the closest so far, Fenski decided to bottom *U-371* on the muddy seabed to make ASDIC detection more difficult and to conserve what power remained in his batteries which were becoming dangerously low after his curtailed charging. Fenski first touched the seabed at 170 metres, the boat lying at a steep angle – too steep for Fenski and he lifted it off and lowered it to the bottom again, this time at a depth of 240 metres where a more level trim was possible. Leaks under such pressure were getting worse as the crew frantically tried to plug them, but their attackers appeared to have lost them.

At 06.27, before Fenski bottomed his boat, one pattern of depth charges had brought a swarm of bubbles to the surface, but the Americans above were still not convinced of a kill. That morning, the destroyer HMS *Blankney*, the minesweeper USS *Sustain* and the French destroyers *Sénégalais* and *L'Alcyon* also joined the sonar hunt, which dragged into the afternoon. With very little breathable air remaining aboard *U-371*, no functioning lighting, nearly exhausted batteries and nearly 15 tons of water inside the boat, Fenski had had enough and had ordered the boat brought to the surface where he would attempt an escape on full diesel power. The crew tried to blow their tanks but the boat was so heavy with flooding by this time that the 40kg of high-pressure air that remained was insufficient to do the job, and the resultant bubbles that reached the surface only attracted the destroyers who increased the tempo of their depth charging once more. *U-371*'s situation was now becoming desperate with the control room knee-deep in oil and water. The whole crew was ordered aft, and the last dregs of battery power were used to run the electric motors full speed ahead. The boat failed to budge, so the crew was sent running forward and the engines set to astern full. After repeating this procedure several times *U-371* finally lurched free of the mud's suction and began rising to the surface at a steep angle. All tubes were loaded and made ready for firing, and when the boat finally reached the surface all guns were manned and *U-371*, with her batteries practically exhausted, ran for open water.

After over 24 hours of dogged cat-and-mouse the *Sénégalais* made radar contact on the fleeing *U-371*. The French ship opened fire while the others moved to block *U-371*'s escape route. As intermittent fire was returned by the boat's two 20mm and one 37mm flak weapons, Fenski ordered his men to prepare to abandon ship, apart from the engine room and torpedo crews, a desperate attempt at thwarting pursuit still in Fenski's mind. Five minutes after the surface chase had begun a torpedo fired as a final defiance from the U-boat hit *Sénégalais* aft and smashed the ship's stern though she remained afloat. But unable to escape his pursuers who were closing from several directions on his boat, Fenski ordered *U-371* scuttled and abandoned after a briefly transmitted signal to headquarters telling them they were going down was sent. The LI, Oblt. (Ing.) Ferdnand Ritschel and MaschMt Kurt Kühne went below to open vents and ensure the boat began to sink. They were never seen again, unable to escape as *U-371* rapidly sank. One other man, ObMt Richard Ritter, was killed; Fenski and forty-five survivors were rescued.

For Brandi's incorrectly claimed previous successes and the torpedoing of USS *Fechteler* he was awarded the Swords to his Knight's Cross and Oak Leaves after *U-967*'s return to Toulon. His accumulated claims were impressive: two light cruisers, eight destroyers and sixteen other ships. The reality was not so dazzling: two escort destroyers, a minelayer, an ocean tug and eight other vessels.

In May 1944 Dönitz decided that only one more U-boat would be despatched to the Mediterranean, *U-960* passing Gibraltar on the night of the 14th. With mounting concern in Berlin on the possibility of an Allied cross channel attack on France or an assault on the Norwegian flank, Hitler was determined to concentrate his available U-boat strength in those areas, the Atlantic war long ago having come to a head and transformed from the offensive against Britain's supply lines, to a desperate defensive battle to prevent Allied troops once more reaching occupied Europe. The nature of the battle had changed irrevocably and the Mediterranean was no longer of prime concern to an embattled Germany. Forces in Italy were holding the Allied advance largely in check, giving up ground as it was pried from them. The required strength that Generals Clarke and Alexander pleaded for to allow a breakthrough in Italy would never be granted as it was distributed elsewhere, including a fresh assault against southern France that had been planned under the code-name 'Anvil' for later in 1944. The 29th U-Flotilla stood no chance of breaking through the cordon of forces at Gibraltar to effect a return to the Atlantic, the physical properties of the narrow waterway making it impossible to do within a single night while surfaced. They were destined to wither and die on the Mediterranean vine.

Kapitänleutnant. Paul Siegmann's *U-230* torpedoed 335-ton USS *PC558* during the early morning of 9 May as the patrol boat was escorting a coastal convoy north of Sicily. The previous night *PC558* had sunk a Marder human torpedo near Anzio, rescuing its pilot *Oberfähnrich* Walter Schulz. Siegmann hit *PC558* with a single torpedo and sinking her with many lives lost, three other torpedoes narrowly missing USS *PC1235*, which later returned to rescue thirty survivors. Five days later it was Kaptlt. Siegfried Koitschka's *U-616* that attacked, sighting the westbound Convoy GUS39 between Algiers and Oran and hitting and damaging two merchants travelling in ballast with *Zaunkönigs*. Immediately, four American destroyers escorting the convoy commenced a hunt for *U-616* that yielded sporadic sonar contact and depth charge attacks. That afternoon the local Royal Navy authorities launched Operation 'Swamp' targeted on the destruction of *U-616*.[9] One of the destroyers, USS *Hilary P. Jones*, remained at the scene in order to guide two American hunter-killer groups, totalling seven destroyers, to *U-616*'s general area. They were joined by Leigh Light equipped Wellingtons of 36 Squadron RAF. Below them the German crew was not yet aware of their dire predicament.

We attacked a convoy and torpedoed two ships, which managed to make port safely. All we received in exchange were several depth charges from an American escort, but we just went deep and carried on reloading torpedoes, then playing cards. When we surfaced to charge our batteries that night, an aircraft attacked and bombed us, and down we went. Any attempt to surface found an unwelcome visitor in the shape of a Wellington aircraft ... We stayed down and later surfaced to find an aircraft coming at us through the darkness. An exchange of gunfire took place and down we went again. Unknown to us we were the star of an 'Operation Swamp' which was an operation designed to swamp the area where a U-boat was hiding with ships and aircraft, waiting for him to surface with exhausted batteries.

Koitschka was not unduly concerned and ordered all unecessary electrical gear to be switched off to conserve power and conferred with the navigator on which was the best way of eluding pursuit.

Probably early on 15 May, USS *Ellyson* opened the ball with a pattern of depth charges and, as the hours passed, it seemed that the whole of the US Navy was above us intent on our destruction. At first Koitschka offered bursts of high speed and alterations of course, but with the battery getting lower, we went deep and prayed. I cannot be sure how deep we were, but I would think possibly deeper than 800 feet, which made the old *U-616* creak a bit.

Everything but the kitchen sink was being dropped on us and all sorts of tactics were being tried, including creeping attacks, in which the ship did not appear to alter speed to deliver its attack, and our listener had no way of knowing that it was an attack developing. Fortunately for us, a new engineer had joined the boat, his own being sunk by a bombing raid on Toulon harbour, and to Lt.(Ing.) Karl Friedrich Kieke we owed our lives. At 800 feet, possibly deeper, the submarine is subjected to considerable pressure and any mistake in handling would cause the boat to cave in ...

Eventually the battery power, without which we could not operate, began to fail, and Koitschka ordered everyone to don life jackets and to be ready to jump overboard the moment we surfaced. With the last dregs of the battery power and with high pressure air screaming into her ballast tanks, *U-616* made her last dramatic surface. The longest hunt of the war was over, lasting over three days.

The crew got out of the boat in record time and jumped over the side, not even pausing to look at the ships that surrounded us. Shellfire and machine gun fire were whistling over our heads and it was surprising that only one man was slightly wounded. The *U-616* careered on her way, pursued by gunfire, the last two people diving off the bandstand into the water accompanied by a muffled explosion as our U-boat headed for the bottom of the Mediterranean.[10]

The crew of *U-616* were dragged from the sea and the ships of Operation 'Swamp' made their way toward Oran. As the destroyers prepared to enter the port on 17 May, USS *Ellyson* – carrying most of *U-616*'s crew – reported three torpedoes passing astern of them. It was the newly arrived *U-960*, her commander Oblt.z.S. Günther Heinrich taking his boat deep after the attempted attack and turned back for Toulon. However, a repeat of Operation 'Swamp' ensued, *U-960* being spotted by a Wellington of 36 Squadron RAF the following day while running on the surface. The destroyer forces raced to the area, but *U-960* slipped away beginning another hunt that would drag into the early hours of 19 May when *U-960* was again spotted by a Wellington as Heinrich surfaced to charge batteries. This time guided to the spot of the crash-diving boat by flares, USS *Ludlow* and *Niblack* pounded the U-boat with depth charges as they followed its movements of sonar. The attack was sustained and accurate, all electrics save one motor knocked out of commission, steerage lost and flooding throughout *U-960* creating deadly chlorine gas. As the sun rose so did *U-960* and when the crippled boat broached the surface she came under sustained destroyer and aircraft attack while the crew attempted to abandon ship. *U-960* was doomed, a final depth-charge pattern sending her under bow first, twenty-two survivors, including Heinrich, rescued out of fifty-three men aboard.

On 19 May Lührs sank the last ship destroyed by the 29th U-Flotilla when *U-453* torpedoed the British SS *Fort Missanabie* travelling in ballast from Taranto to Augusta as part of Convoy HA43. During the late afternoon the ship staggered under the impact of a three-torpedo salvo. The ship's master, ten crew members and one gunner were lost while thirty-five crew members and thirteen gunners were picked up by the Norwegian merchant ship SS *Spero* and Italian corvette *Urania*. In response three British destroyers, HMS *Liddesdale*, *Tenacious* and *Termagant*, located and hammered Lührs with depth charges. *U-453* went deep and silent, resting throughout the night on the seabed. At dawn the following day Lührs attempted to escape the area but was located and subjected to 12 hours of depth-charge attacks that forced the boat to the surface. Under fire the crew abandoned her, only *Gefreiter* Albert Wange killed during their escape, the remainder rescued and taken to Italy. It was an inglorious end to the combat record of the 29th U-Flotilla.

Of the twelve remaining U-boats of 29th U-Flotilla, on 1 June 1944 only three were at sea: *U-471*, returned to Toulon on 15 June and was subsequently badly damaged by bombing on 5 July and finally sunk by bombs on 6 August;[11] *U-952* returned to Toulon on 21 June and was also damaged in the bombing raid on 5 July, and the hulk decommissioned one week later, finally sunk in another bombing raid on 6 August; *U-586* also returned to Toulon on 21 June and was badly damaged by bombing on 5 July, decommissioned on the same day as *U-952*.

In port on the first day of June, *U-230* was in La Spezia and *U-407* and *U-565* were being equipped with snorkels in Salamis and would not be ready before August. Within the heavily bombed yards of Toulon *U-421*, which had been damaged by bombing on 29 April, would finally be decommissioned on 27 June while *U-466* was undergoing repairs but was damaged by bombing on 5 July. Never able to sail again, the boat was scuttled on 19 August. *U-642* had been damaged in an air raid in February and again on 5 July, on which day the boat was decommissioned as beyond repair. Bombs damaged *U-969* on both 5 July and 6 August, the wreck finally blown up on 19 August. *U-967* was undergoing repairs and was damaged slightly by bombing on 5 July and again on 6 August. The cumulative effect of the bombs put the boat beyond repair and she was eventually scuttled on 19 August.

Within Toulon, and in the subsidiary ports of Salamis and Pola, groups of German specialist technicians had arrived in order to begin equipping the boats with the newly developed snorkel that would allow batteries to be charged as the boat ran submerged, its extended mast discharging diesel exhaust fumes while drawing in fresh air. It was, however, not to have any effect on the fate of the 29th U-Flotilla boats, few of them so equipped ever taking to the sea again. The extra time required to undertake the work held the boats in their yards and at the mercy of Allied bombs. At the naval dockyard of Pola *U-596* was undergoing repair, not ready for combat once more until the end of July. The port of Pola was also beginning to receive attention by the USAAF, fifty-two B 17s with P 47 fighter escort bombing the naval yard and dry-docks on 8 June, causing delay to the repair work on *U-596*.

So only *U-230*, *U-407*, *U-565* and *U-596* would leave port on combat patrols during the second half of 1944. On the Allied side, plans were advanced for yet another controversial invasion in the Mediterranean. Where once the proposed landings on France's Normandy and Côte d'Azur coastlines had been named 'Hammer' and 'Anvil' respectively, the Normandy operation had since assumed greater strategic importance than its poorer relation to the south. Churchill vehemently argued against a landing on the southern coast of France, claiming that that this would divert vital resources that could be put to better use either in Italy with a concerted attempt to break German resistance or in an invasion of the oil-producing regions of the Balkans, possibly from there into eastern Europe. In addition to denying German access to these supplies, it would also forestall Soviet occupation of the region and put the Western Allies in a stronger position to dominate the peacetime European continent.

The American military, on the other hand, were dismissive of the Balkans and felt that the capture of a major port such as Marseille would aid supply of a western offensive into Germany from central France. The need to keep pressure on the main German lines of resistance were paramount in the reasoning of the US military hierachy. The original plan for 'Anvil' envisaged a mixture of Free French and American troops taking Toulon and later Marseilles, with subsequent revisions encompassing Saint Tropez, thereby also diverting crucial German strength away from Allied forces in Normandy, spliiting the defensive power of the *Wehrmacht*. America prevailed in what had become a larger strategic debate between the two nations, Churchill renaming the invasion of southern France Operation 'Dragoon' as he felt 'dragooned' into it against his will.

On 6 June, Operation 'Overlord' landed on the coast of Normandy and the battle for France began. In Italy the Anzio beachhead had finally been breached by the Operation 'Shingle' forces and Rome fell to the Allies in early June. By the end of the month American forces had broken out of their Normandy pocket and the final decision was made to launch Operation 'Dragoon' – the D-day set for 15 August 1944. The day dawned clear and bright as Allied troops surged ashore between Cape Bénat and Mandelieu-la-Napoule. The sole U-boat that sailed to meet the challenge was Oblt.z.S. Heinz-Eugen Eberbach's as the young captain sailed his first war patrol as captain of *U-230*. [12] However, their attempts to engage the enemy were constantly frustrated by shallow water and the lack of a snorkel, forcing the boat to withdraw well to sea and recharge batteries. It was a near suicidal task at any rate and the captain and crew were ultimately fortunate when the boat ran aground on the shores of the Saint Mandrier peninsula near Hyères east of Toulon and beneath the guns of the Saint Elme coastal artillery battery. The crew abandoned ship and *U-230* was blown up with scuttling charges. Eberbach and his crew were captured by Allied forces later that day.

The success of the Allied landings during Operation 'Dragoon' was absolute and the final battle for the prize of the French naval base at Toulon began on 21 August, the U-boats lying in harbour having been blown up by the remaining troops of the 29th U-Flotilla. Within one week of often fierce defensive fighting by the embattled German garrison, including the virtual destruction of the *Wehrmacht*'s 242nd Infantry Division, *Konteradmiral* Heinrich Ruhfus, the *Kampfkommandant* Toulon, and his last 1,000 soldiers surrendered on the Saint-Mandrier peninsula. That same day the last defenders of Marseille also surrendered and the Allies had their deep-water port. Amongst the confusion of captured troops were K.K. Gunter Jahn, Chief of the 29th U-Flotilla and Kaptlt. Josef Röther from his staff, both veterans of the long battles in the Mediterranean.

Interestingly, several T5 *Zaunkönig* torpedoes and four dissembled sections of a Type XXIII U-boat were found by the French troops that took Toulon. The pieces were discovered in the sheltered *Tunnel de Cepet* that ran beneath Saint Pierre Hill. In the port itself lay the battered remains of *U-952*, *U-421*, *U-642* and *U-471* in the *Bassins Missiessy*, *U-969* in the *Bassin Castigneau*, *U-410* alongside the Quai Noël and across the harbour *U-466* and *U-967* at Saint Mandrier. It was a shabby end for the Type VII boats.

In August 1944 the post of FdU Mediterranean was formally abolished, K.K. Werner Hartmann returning to Germany. Instead of the FdU structure the dregs of units that still remained would be overseen by a staff officer attached to V.A. Werner Lange's Aegean Naval Command, Kaptlt. Mehl attached as U-*Bootsadmiralstaboffizier*, a post he held between August and October when the abandonment of Salamis heralded the end of the flotilla.

Chapter 10

Retreat from Greece

WARTIME GREECE HAD BECOME A QUAGMIRE of political factions apart from the occupation forces. With the evacuaton of King Georgios II from Crete to London in 1941, the head of state was established as a government in exile, recognised by Britain and her allies. However, Georgios' government, headed from April 1944 by M. Papandreou, came in for strong criticism from a significant proportion of the Greek population after endorsing General Metaxas' military dictatorship which was subsequently defeated by the Germans.

Occupied Greece was divided into three zones of occupation: Bulgarian, Italian and German. By far the largest area was that occupied by the Italians, though in May 1943 Germany abolished the distinction between their own and the Italian area, though still relying on Italian garrisons until the latter's surrender in September 1943. Ioannis Rallis held the nominal post of Prime Minister of occupied Greece from April 1943, General Carlo Geloso being appointed Military Governor of the Italian zone.

In the political vacuum left by the departure of the Royalist government, small bands of resistance fighters began operating against *Wehrmacht* forces whilst also aligning themselves with different political ideologies. The most significant were the National Liberation Front (EAM) and its military branch the People's Liberation Army (ELAS) and those remnants of the Greek Army that gathered in the hills of the northwest under the leadership of Colonel Napoleon Zervas eventually being labelled the National Democratic Greek League (EDES). The ELAS, under the command of Stephanos Seraphis, was dominated by a hardcore of Communists, which gradually pervaded their entire stance. General Nikolaos Plastiras headed the political branch of the EDES, with Colonel Napoleon Zervas, originally a Republican, heading its military branch, becoming more and more anti-Communist as time passed and often collaborating with German forces to secure supply lines from Communist intervention.

With the Italian surrender the ELAS benefitted from the capture of much Italian equipment, their operations against German forces virtually ceasing as they mounted an offensive against Zervas' troops in a bid to be in a position to assume political control of the country after the inevitable German withdrawal. This debacle was later reflected by a mutiny in the Greek brigade based in Italy and aboard ships of the Hellenic Navy. The stated intention of the King to return and re-establish the monarchy appeared to be the catalyst for the short lived mutiny, quelled by Greek loyalists and British troops.

Winston Churchill persuaded representatives of the three main factions to meet in the Lebanon during May 1944 where they agreed to form a united military front against the German occupiers – thus hopefully postponing the political struggle between the factions. However, by July the Greek monarch was complaining directly to Churchill about EAM extremists violating the fragile agreement. Rumours of a German evacuation from Greece raised the temperature between the different factions, Churchill asking his Chief of Staff to plan a British expedition to Greece in such an event, the plan code-named Operation 'Manna' and demanded to be ready for instigation by 11 September. The essence of the British plan was to occupy Athens and its airfield, clear Piraeus harbour to enable reinforcement by sea from Egypt, and to facilitate the early return of Greek government ministers.

During the upheaval in Greece, *U-596* made the last complete operational U-boat patrol in the Mediterranean, departing Pola on 29 July and sailing the Ionian Sea, off Malta and off Cyrenaica. With no success Oblt.z.S. Hans Kolbus took his boat into Salamis on 1 September. In the meantime the snorkel-equipped *U-565* had also put to sea from Salamis on 26 August to patrol north of Crete. The boat remained on station until relieved by *U-407* on 10 September whereupon Kaptlt. Fritz Henning took *U-565* back to its Greek base, arriving on 13 September.

U-407 had put to sea with Oblt.z.S. Hans Kolbus, late of *U-596*, at the helm. After relieving *U-565* Kolbus patrolled near Crete until 18 September when exhaust from the boat's snorkel was spotted by the Polish destroyer *Garland*. The destroyer raced to intercept and fired a Hedgehog (ASW mortar) salvo to no discernible effcect. Two British destroyers, HMS *Troubridge* and *Terpischore*, arrived to assist in the hunt. A firm ASDIC contact on *U-407* was made as the boat crept northward and for the next ten hours the destroyers subjected her to depth charge attacks until Kolbus was forced to the surface in the morning of 19 September. The boat was immediately fired upon as the crew abandoned ship, six men being killed while Kolbus and forty-eight others were rescued. It was the final U-boat kill in the Mediterranean.

By this stage the *Wehrmacht*'s end in Greece was rapidly approaching. It had been previously proposed to Hitler that following the Italian surrender German forces should abandon the southern portion of the Balkan Peninsula in order to withdraw to a more defensible line in northern Greece. Hitler, however, would not allow such a move. Aside from his perpetual desire to never yield territory he was also acutely aware that by abandoning southern Greece he risked opening up the supply routes for many strategic raw materials to Allied attack from Greek bases. An estimated 50 per cent of Germany's oil, all of its chrome, 60 per cent of its bauxite, 24 per cent of its antimony and 21 per cent of its copper were obtained from Balkan sources. Thus despite the capture of southern Italy by Allied forces and the complete superiority of Allied air forces over southern Greece and the Greek islands, the German defenders were ordered to remain in place.

Amidst this climate of impending disaster, the weekend beginning Friday 25 August 1944 was one of unmitigated misery for the *Wehrmacht*, the latest in a long chain of reversals. French troops entered Paris which surrendered despite explicit orders to the German commander General von Choltitz from Hitler for the destruction of the city. In the days that followed, Allied forces continued their rapid drive across France, the final 1,800 troops holding Toulon finally surrendering while Soviet troops took Galatz in eastern Romania. Faced with the inevitability of turmoil in Greece, Hitler finally relented and ordered his valuable troops stationed there to withdraw. However, the actual retreat did not begin until September during which Allied forces launched Operation 'Ratweek' to hinder the German withdrawal from the Balkan region. On 2 September German forces began departing islands in the Aegean, while the mainland entered a curious state of limbo.

On 8 September, under increasing pressure from the Soviet Union as the troops of the 3rd Ukrainian Front entered the country from Romanian soil, Bulgaria declared war on Germany and immediately dispatched strong forces from Sofia towards their frontier with Yugoslavia. With fierce clashes taking place in the north of Greece between German mountain units and Bulgarian troops and partisans, it became obvious that German units below the Corfu-Yannina-Kalabaka-Olympus line would be forced to fight their way northwards towards Germany. The ELAS and EDES both attempted to block major roads and railways to prevent the *Wehrmacht*'s escape.

On Friday 15 September the US Fifteenth Air Force mounted the first of its new raids against the U-boat base at Salamis. Two hundred and seventy-six B 17 and B 24 bombers attacked the base and other targets in Greece such as the Tatoi, Eleusis, and Kalamaki airfields and Salamis submarine base. Administrative (*Verwaltungs*) *Maat* Otto Wagner, Head of the Kitchen (*Kuchenchef*) for the Salamis U-boat base, was near Salamis when the raid came over.

On [that day] I found myself with a truck driver from the 5. Flak Battery [*Marineflakabteilung* 720] in Ambelakia, about 5 kilometres from our base, picking up food supplies for the battery. It was between midday and 13.00 when the flak started firing. Over the island cruised two enemy fighter planes. About an hour later 100 to 150 American bombers followed. They flew over our island, returned and unloaded their bombs on us. During the attack I saw enormous smoke clouds and heard massive explosions and thought immediately about the base and the shipyard. The bombers then flew on, but after about 15 minutes a second squadron appeared and dropped their bombs in the same place. I had to supply the U-boat base with food and wondered how I was going to do that if the kitchen and food supplies were all destroyed.

As I returned I saw the damage. We couldn't take the truck to the main gate any more because in the street there was a bomb crater. By the canteen was where a bomb had landed and the door was smashed in with the air pressure. The door to the cool cellar was also blown in, and the one from the kitchen was also half taken off and the food for the U-boats had taken a direct hit. The houses for the troops were also virtually destroyed.

The dock plant had been very heavily damaged, our V-boat couldn't be found anymore and the F-boat lay in the street; briefly said, it was a heap of rubble.

The troops and Greek civilians had taken shelter in the air raid bunker (a bomb-proof cave in the mountain). Unfortunately though, one sailor lost his life during the raid, hit by a bomb splinter, another 10 to 15 wounded by splinters, but that was all.

The supply depot and the shipyard were very heavily hit and virtually destroyed. At the pier a small freighter and a torpedo boat had been hit and both lay on the seabed. To our great regret we also determined that *U-565* and *U-596*, which lay next to the torpedo boat, were both heavily damaged. With a large part of the shipyard destroyed and repairs not possible, we were ordered by BdU that unserviceable boats in Piraeus were to be scuttled.

Over the next eight days we made what small repairs we could. On 29 September [author's note: USAAF records put this on 25 September] at 10 o'clock in the morning, I was sat in my office when the air-raid siren went signifying more enemy bombers headed our way. We all ran to the bunker and then came our second blessing. The air-raid shelter shook with the explosions and the Greek women screamed in fear. The attack lasted about 30 minutes and after the all clear we left the bunker to find the kitchen and provisions store untouched. This time the enemy had had less luck and the bombs fell for the most part in the water. But we were not to be completely spared. Our last U-boat from the base – *U-596*, already damaged – lay in *Neu-Pirama*, tied up to the pier. A bomb had landed in the water not 20 metres from the boat. The water pressure ruptured the outer [fuel] bunker of the boat. The boat's Chief Engineer Lt.(Ing.) Friedrich Schreiber, who had been on the U-boat bridge, was blown ashore and severely wounded. He died on the way to the hospital. On the orders of the FdU *Mittelmeer*, Kapt Mehl, we had to leave our last U-boat in Athens on the seabed. Finally, the enemy had achieved their target and in September 1944 our U-boats in the Mediterranean were eliminated.

As the U-boat presence was eliminated from the Mediterranean, the Germans vacillated over beginning their withdrawal from Athens. Meanwhile the British engineered a meeting at Caserta, Italy, between Papandreou, the communist ELAS and nationalist EDES. They agreed on 26 September to unite all Greek guerilla forces under the orders of the legitimate Greek government, who in turn deferred to the British commander General Scobie.

While the Allies prepared for the retaking of Greece, the men of the 29th U-Flotilla in Salamis found themselves irrelevant to naval operations. The distant sound of Ju 52 transport aircraft could be heard day and night as the *Wehrmacht* airlifted combat troops from Crete and Rhodes to Athens, 11,500 troops from Crete alone, most of them from the 22nd *Fallschirmjäger* Division. In time, however, Allied carrier-borne aircraft were able to interfere with the airlift, leaving up to 26,500 troops still stranded on Crete, Rhodes and other German island garrisons by 12 October. The flak batteries that had protected Salamis were removed from the island and the remaining U-boat crews from *U-565* and *U-596* transported by *Vorpostenboot* to Salonika, from there to entrain for Germany.

We – the rest of the U-boat base personnel – waited for the order also to begin the retreat to Germany. We had been issued with a new grey navy uniform. The rest of the clothes that we had worn on the Greek island were burnt. We were ready to march – all we needed was the order. An Admiral gave us a speech which he ended with saying 'Goodye until home'. For him his time in the south-east was over, but for us we had to deal with the mess first. We waited four or five days on the island of Salamis. In Athens Greek saboteurs had become active. They blew up the gas works, quite a lot of military targets and by night they shot at our troops.

On 1 October 1944 Dönitz finally broadcast instructions for his beleaguered men in Salamis: 'Soldiers of the U-boat base Salamis are to begin the return journey to Germany.' With Soviet troops rapidly moving west through Hungary and Bulgaria, Hitler ordered the retreat of all German forces from Greece, Southern Albania and Southern Macedonia on 3 October. On Salamis the final evacuation had already begun. Almost immediately after Dönitz's order to depart, the staff of the Salamis base had departed by tugboat to Piraeus. They boarded one of the last trains to Athens where they joined the general retreat.

178

The train station's platforms were full of soldiers, all wanting to return to the homeland as quickly as possible. That evening, about 22.00, we were embarked, about 650 people: officers, about 100 Greek civilians, paratroopers from Crete, crew from the R-boat Flotilla at Piraeus [12th R-Flotilla], and us from the Salamis base. Covering the transport were three *Vierlinge* flak cannons on flat freight cars.

We travelled from Athens through Lamia, Larisa, Kozani, Skopje, Kos, Mitrorica, Kragwjerac in the direction of Belgrade. We had five days journey behind us when I was asked by the supply officer in the ration car, if I and my two assistants Obergef. Mayer and Künzel could help. So with two men we had to feed over 600 people, which was a lot of work. My two sailors and I handled distribution and the two other comrades the cooking.

However, the chaos of the retreat soon overtook Wagner and his men. On Wednesday 4 October Operation 'Manna', the planned British intervention in Greece, began. The 2nd Airborne Brigade landed near Patras and occupied the city with the aid of commando units. They then headed along the southern shores of the Gulf of Corinth while other units began landing on Crete and other Aegean islands. The following day, Tuesday 10 October, *General der Flieger* Alexander Löhr's Army Group E began its final withdrawal from Greece and within four days the British had secured Athens on the heels of the retreating Germans. By 16 October the Greek government was in its capital. However, Greece was in a state of some ruin as the retreating *Wehrmacht* destroyed transport infrastructure. The fragile alliance formed between the various Greek factions rapidly disintegrated and on Sunday 3 December communist demonstrators clashed with police and the Greek civil war began.

In the meantime, to facilitate his evacuation, Löhr had ordered all available German troops thrown into the fighting against the Soviets and Bulgarians along a line running roughly parallel to the southeastern Yugoslav border Accordingly, Army Group E directed the complete evacuation of Greece and the establishment of a new defence along the line Scutari-Skoplje-Negotin. On 14 October the headquarters of Army Group E moved to Macedonia, where it estimated it had the equivalent of four German divisions holding a line of 375 miles against thirteen and a half Soviet and Bulgarian divisions. While the rugged country allowed them to confine their efforts to holding the mountain passes and other avenues of approach, this advantage was more than offset by the German inferiority in numbers and lack of air support and by the activities of the guerrillas. The use of Ju 87 Stuka aircraft by the Bulgarians, who had obtained them under the Axis equivalent of lend-lease during the period of the alliance with Germany, was particularly exasperating to the troops of Army Group E. By 2 November the last German troops had departed Greek soil. The inevitable power struggle that resulted in civil war within the liberated nation ironically helping Löhr's hard-pressed troops as it prevented Greek and British forces from pursuit.

As these events had overtaken Greece, Wagner and his men had found themselves virtually trapped in Montenegro as part of the Alpine unit the 104th *Jäger* Division (XXXIV *Korps*). The enemy had severed the rail line in the north and soon Wagner and the rest of the Salamis base men were offloaded and formed into an ad-hoc infantry unit. They were named '*Kampfgruppe* Scheuerlein' and Wagner's battalion, numbering 315 men in total, comprised 1. *Kompanie* of men from the 12th R-boat Flotilla, 2. *Kompanie* of *Luftwaffe* men from Crete and 3. *Kompanie* from 'U-*Stützpunkt* Salamis', under the command of an infantry *Hauptmann* Gardewein. Wagner's company commander was Oblt. (VO) Wachholz. They had six trucks with trailers, two Italian 2cm flak cannon, one car for the company commander, two motorcycles and one motorcycle with sidecar. *Oberinspektor* Weselin acted as Purser, while Wagner and his staff Meyer and Künzel were charged with the ration truck and mobile kitchen.

The retreating columns of German forces that Wagner was a part of painted a sorry picture, their numbers soon swelled with a regiment of White Russians, a company of Italians and Yugoslav Chetnik troops all attempting to escape the Balkan bottleneck.

It was the beginning of November 1944, the rain had come and so had the winter. Along the path of our retreat were houses, for the most part destroyed and plundered. Our Battalion mostly had to camp in tents, there was no straw available, only one or two blankets, it was a hard time. We had about 200 kilometres behind us already and were all dead tired, but it wasn't until we reached the barracks at Bijelo Polje that we had a rest for two days. There we had decent food and a rest. But then the snowfall began, 30 to 50 centimetres of new snow and very cold with it.[1]

In Bijelo Polje Wagner's battalion commander, *Hauptmann* Gardewin, departed to join the General Staff, replaced by *Hauptmann* Metze, a man remembered by Wagner as a 'quiet, businesslike man who brought no humour to the battalion'. Shortly thereafter Wagner's unit was ordered into action against partisan units on the 1,827-metre peak Zlatar to the east, leaving its barracks with pack mules and horses carrying the unit's ammunition and mortars. Leaving the valley that carried the meandering Lim River, '*Bataillon* Metze' struggled through thick snow and woods, terrain that their Yugoslavian opponents were accustomed to. They finally encountered Tito's men at midnight, 1,520 metres up their target peak, coming under accurate mortar and sniper fire. Wagner and his comrades dug themselves into the snow, shivering miserably, unable to light fires for fear of attracting the enemy's attention.

Our battalion, for the most part airmen and sailors, had of course had infantry training but with no practical experience. It was about 02.00 when we heard rifle fire and then mortar fire. We were taken by surprise and scrambled for cover. Our machine-guns and 2cm flak began defensive fire and after about 30 minutes the enemy stopped shooting. We also ceased fire and prepared a counter attack. We also had communication with a 10cm flak battery who were now ready to fire. At about 04.00 the 10cm flak cannon began firing about 50 shots into the Partisans' lines. We also opened fire again with our machine guns and 2cm flak. In the meantime the '*Battaillon* Herbert' from the right flank of the had begun to attack the enemy. After 20 minutes we stopped firing again and everything went quiet. The *Battaillon* Herbert had managed to set foot on the top of Zlatav mountain and begun to fight. Under cover from them we began to slowly move forwards.[2]

So the remnants of U-*Bootstützpunkt* Salamis took part in the bloody battle of attrition that characterised the partisan war in Yugoslavia. In conditions they were completely unfamiliar with they moved and counter moved through the densely forested moutains. By the end of their first battle Wagner's battalion had lost ten dead and twenty-three wounded, on 17 November Wagner's company commander Oblt. Wachholz and his deputy Btmt. Hein were both severely injured by shrapnel, later dying in the field hospital at Prijeplolie as the town came under attack from American aircraft harassing the German forces.

Finally, on 25 November, Batallion Metze was ordered to continue its retreat from the Balkans, headed first for Sarajevo.

We suffered yet another casualty on 8 December. An *Unteroffizier* from the *Marine-Artillerie* fell under the rear wheels of an Italian Sparta truck. We dug him a grave and left him to rest in peace 90 kilometres from Sarajevo.

They spent Christmas huddled in the church and fifteen houses that comprised the village of Sjetlina. Once more they were called to fight local partisan attacks, this time reinforced with a single panzer, though the latter overturned while negotiating a sharp bend in the mountain road, killing one crewman and injuring the four others. Retreating dispirited to Sarajevo in the final days of 1944, the 162 naval personnel that had departed *U-Stützpunkt* Salamis had been whittled down to seventy-four through death and injury. Finally, on 3 January, the shattered remains were loaded into freight cars at Sarajevo's marshalling yards or aboard trucks and began a torturous and interrupted journey to Germany, travelling through Austria into Germany distributing men to their homes for a brief leave before recalled to Plön. Wagner arrived in his hometown of Heilbronn near Stuttgart on 19 January. Within days he had moved on to Plön where the men from Salamis were placed into the 1UAA training school to be returned to action in the dying days of Hitler's *Wehrmacht*.

So the tenure of *Kriegsmarine* U-boat forces in the Mediterranean was finally ended with the retreat from Salamis of the last personnel of the 29th U-Flotilla. While *Kleinkampfverbände* operations and various scattered surface forces would continue until the war's end, conventional U-boats had been decisively beaten. The initial foray by *U-26* during 1939 marked the only time that a U-boat successfully entered and escaped the Mediterranean Sea during the Second World War – albeit with no success. Over the years that followed, the increasing number of U-boats that were despatched to the Mediterranean ultimately failed in their assigned tasks. At no stage did they significantly interdict Allied convoy traffic as it passed from the Middle East to Gibraltar and the gateway to Europe. Short-lived attempts to attack Soviet traffic in the Dardenelles also amounted to nothing, though in truth the merchant traffic was not a significant factor in Soviet military strategy anyway. The difficult conditions the U-boats endured in the Mediterranean Sea – clear water, high temperatures, inefficient dockyards, Allied air and sea power that grew exponentially between 1941 and 1944 – meant that offensive operations were not only extremely hazardous but largely ineffective. Coupled with that, the U-boat was a completely unsuitable weapon with which to oppose a large enemy seaborne invasion force, particularly when that force is persistently alerted to the U-boats' presence and actively seeking them out. The invasion of Norway had already demonstrated the inability to both screen an invading force and intercept enemy counter offensives, Operation 'Torch' confirmed it and by the time of the landings on Sicily, Italy and southern France, the idea of a successful U-boat defence against them was ludicrous. Whatever support was hoped would be provided by boats of the 23rd and 29th U-Flotilla for Rommel's *Afrika Korps* was also largely fleeting. Occasional depredation of Allied supply shipping was all that could be managed. In truth the land war in North Africa was lost in Rommel's own tangled logistics train and in the diversion of crucial *Luftwaffe* air power to the Eastern Front when it could have tipped the balance in the Mediterranean. North Africa, despite its array of glittering prizes that lay beyond El Alamein, was always a 'sideshow' to Adolf Hitler who, as head of the Armed Forces, could decide military life or death.

However, that is not to say that the Mediterranean U-boats achieved nothing. Indeed their star rose as the fortunes of the Italian submarine force largely began to wane. In total the U-boats sank an impressive array of naval vessels, totalling thirty-eight warships: one battleship, two aircraft carriers, four cruisers, one large fast minelayer, sixteen destroyers or destroyer escorts, one frigate, one sloop, one submarine depot ship, one corvette, three minesweepers, five LSTs and two ASW trawlers. They also destroyed several troopships from a total of 116 merchant vessels and twenty-four sailing vessels that came to a tonnage figure that exceeded half a million tons. In the early months of the U-boats' deployment in the region they certainly added to the general air of despondency that gripped the Royal Navy who appeared to be losing major units at every turn and in several far-flung geographical areas.

There have been arguments that the allocation of major British warship strength for convoy runs to Malta sapped offensive and defensive capabilities elsewhere. While this may well be so, the threat of U-boats actually achieved more than the boats themselves. The main enemy to the now-famous Malta relief convoys were surface units of the German and Italian navies and, above all, aircraft.

The later introduction of more advanced weaponry may have eased the burden on U-boat commanders. Virtual 'fire and forget' T5 *Zaunkönig* homing torpedoes allowed U-boats to retreat from the scene immediately after firing – but in turn they led to some stunning exaggeration of successes. While it must be accepted that in the heat of battle and reliant totally on sound most such overclaims were accidental, several commanders built reputations on the number of phantom warships they had destroyed. However, sixty years after the battle, armchair generalship is an easy thing to succumb to.

The men who fought at sea during the Second World War, and other wars, faced hardships, privations, fear, an enemy intent on their destruction and, often, the implacable foe that is the sea itself. Without lapsing into too much emotive hyperbole, I have met many of the veterans of this last great conflict and several that fought in the Mediterranean during the war. Their experiences deserve to be remembered, as do the thousands of men who are still there, in graveyards that span Europe and beyond, and still lying in their silent battlegrounds, buried at sea.

Appendices

FdU Italian / Mediterranean

From September 1941 to November 1941 operational U-boats within the western Mediterranean up to the Straits of Messina were controlled directly by BdU Ops in Lorient. Eastward of the Straits of Messina, U-boats were under the control of the 23rd U-Flotilla based in Salamis, who in turn was subordinate to Admiral Aegean.

Formed in November 1941 as the *FdU Italien* (FdU Italian) this office took control of all Mediterranean U-boats (although localised command of eastern boats by 23rd U-Flotilla continued until February 1942) and was immediately subordinate to *Marinekommando Italien*. Renamed *FdU Mittelmeer* (Mediterranean) in August 1943 when the headquarters was relocated from Rome, Italy, to Toulon/Aix en Provence in the south of France. This command eventually disbanded in September 1944 after the successful Allied Operation 'Dragoon' landings in southern France, the remaining three U-boats still in operation in the eastern Mediterranean grouped under the command of *Kommandierender Admiral* Aegean (Admiral Commanding the Aegean).

FdU: K.K. Victor Oehrn (November 1941 to February 1942)
Kapt.z.S. Leo-Karl Kreisch (February 1942 to January 1944)
Kapt.z.S. Werner Hartmann (January 1944 to August 1944)

1st Admiralty Staff Officer:
K.K. Victor Oehrn (November 1941 to May 1942)
K.K. Georg Schewe (May 1942 to September 1944)

2nd Admiralty Staff Officer:
Kaptlt. Georg Wallas (December 1942 to September 1944)

Chief Engineering Officer:
K.K.(Ing.) Johannes Gottwald (February 1943 to February 1944)
Kaptlt.(Ing.) Otto Zschetzschig (February 1944 to July 1944)

Administrative and Judicial Matters:
Oblt.z.S. Becker.

With the disbanding of FdU Mediterranean in August 1944, the three remaining U-boats were subordinated directly to Admiral commanding the Aegean, Kaptlt. Mehl serving on staff as U-Asto (*Unterseebootsadmiralstaboffizier*) until October 1944 and the loss of all operational Mediterranean boats.

23rd U-Flotilla

Formed in September 1941 at Salamis, Greece. Held operational control over eastern Mediterranean U-boats until February 1942, subordinate to Admiral Aegean.
Main port: Salamis
Flotilla Chief: Kaptlt. Fritz Frauenheim (September 1941 to May 1942)

29th U-Flotilla

Formed December 1941 at La Spezia. Moved in August 1943 to Toulon which remained the flotilla headquarters until September 1944.
Main ports: La Spezia, Toulon
Subsidiary ports: Pola, Marseille, Salamis (the latter while subordinated to Admiral Aegean)
Flotilla Chief: K.K. Franz Becker (December 1941 to May 1942)
K.K. Fritz Frauenheim (May 1942 to July 1943)
K.K. Gunter Jahn (July 1943 to September 1944)

Ports

Primary ports used by the 23rd and 29th U-Flotilla:
La Spezia, Italy.
Salamis, Greece.
Pola, Croatia.
Toulon, France.

Secondary or auxiliary ports:
Palermo, Italy.
Maddalena, Italy.

Augusta, Italy.
Cagliari, Italy.
Livorno, Italy.
Messina, Sicily.
Naples, Italy.
Patras, Greece.
Taranto, Italy.

U-boats assigned to the Mediterranean

Boat	Date entered Mediterranean	Date Sunk	Group
1941			
U-371	21 September	3 May 1944	'Goeben'
U-559	26 September	3 October 1942	'Goeben'
U-97	27 September	16 June 1943	'Goeben
U-331	30 September	17 November 1942	'Goeben'
U-75	3 October	28 December 1941	'Goeben'
U-79	5 October	23 December 1941	'Goeben'
U-205	11 November	17 February 1943	'Arnauld'
U-81	12 November	9 January 1944	'Arnauld'
U-433	15 November	16 November 1941	'Arnauld'
U-565	16 November	29 September 1944	'Arnauld'
U-431	24 November	21 October 1943	
U-95	26 November	28 November 1941	
U-557	26 November	16 December 1941	
U-562	27 November	19 February 1943	
U-652	29 November	2 June 1942	
U-372	8 December	4 August 1942	
U-453	9 December	21 May 1944	
U-375	9 December	30 July 1943	
U-374	10 December	12 January 1942	
U-568	10 December	29 May 1942	
U-77	16 December	28 March 1943	
U-74	16 December	2 May 1942	
U-83	18 December	4 March 1943	
U-573	19 December	9 August 1942 Sold to Spain	
U-133	22 December	14 March 1942	
U-577	23 December	9 January 1942	
U-374	30 December	12 January 1942	

Boat	Date entered Mediterranean	Date Sunk	Group
1942			
U-73	14 January	16 December 1943	
U-561	15 January	12 July 1943	
U-605	10 October	14 November 1942	'Tümmler'
U-458	11 October	22 August 1943	'Tümmler'
U-593	11 October	12 December 1943	'Tümmler'
U-660	11 October	12 November 1942	'Tümmler'
U-617	8 November	12 September 1943	'Delphin'
U-407	9 November	19 September 1944	'Delphin'
U-595	9 November	14 November 1942	'Delphin'
U-259	9 November	15 November 1942	'Delphin'
U-596	9 November	24 September 1944	'Delphin'
U-755	9 November	28 May 1943	'Delphin'
U-380	11 November	4 February 1944	'Delphin'
U-443	4 December	23 February 1943	'Taucher'
U-602	8 December	23 April 1943	'Taucher'
U-301	9 December	21 January 1943	'Taucher'
1943			
U-224	12 January	13 January 1943	
U-414	9 April	25 May 1943	
U-303	9 April	21 May 1943	
U-616	6 May	17 May 1944	
U-410	6 May	22 March 1944 Decommissioned	
U-409	5 June	12 July 1943	
U-223	26 September	30 March 1944	
U-450	1 November	10 March 1944	
U-642	3 November	12 July 1944 Decommissioned	
U-230	5 December	21 August 1944	
1944			
U-343	5 January	10 March 1944	
U-952	3 January	6 August 1944	
U-455	22 January	6 April 1944	
U-969	3 February	19 August 1944	
U-967	13 February	19 August 1944	
U-586	13 February	12 July 1944 Decommissioned	
U-421	20 March	27 June 1944 Decommissioned	
U-466	22 March	19 August 1944	
U-471	31 March	6 August 1944	
U-960	15 May	19 May 1944	

Known failed attempts to pass into the Mediterranean

Boat	Date Attempt Failed	Reason	Group
1941			
U-204	19 October	Sunk	
U-206	November	Sunk by unknown causes	
U-433	17 November	Sunk	
U-96	30 November	Badly damaged by aircraft.	'Bennecke'
U-552	December	Attempt called off by BdU	'Bennecke'
U-402	December	Attempt called off by BdU	'Bennecke'
U-332	December	Attempt called off by BdU	'Bennecke'
U-558	1 December	Damaged by aircraft	
U-208	11 December	Sunk	
U-432	17 December	Damaged by aircraft	
U-434	18 December	Sunk	
U-451	21 December	Sunk	
U-575	December	Damaged by aircraft	
U-202	December	Damaged by aircraft	
U-71	December	Damaged by aircraft	
U-563	December	Damaged by aircraft	
1942			
U-572	19–21 January	Driven off by enemy forces	
U-440	November	Technical problems	'Delphin'
U-662	November	Technical problems	'Delphin'
U-258	8 December	Aborted through illness	'Taucher'
U-257	December	Aborted through illness	'Taucher
1943			
U-447	7 May	Sunk	
U-659	3 May	Sunk in collision	
U-594	4 June	Sunk	
U-614	29 July	Sunk	
U-454	1 August	Sunk	
U-706	2 August	Sunk	
U-667	24 September	Damaged by aircraft	
U-455	September	Attempt called off by BdU	
U-264	September	Attempt called off by BdU	
U-450	September	Attempt called off by BdU	
U-466	September	Attempt called off by BdU	
U-455	September	Attempt called off by BdU	
U-420	September	Attempt called off by BdU	

Boat	Date Attempt Failed	Reason	Group
U-732	1 November	Sunk	
U-340	1 November	Sunk	
U-732	2 November	Sunk	
1944			
U-761	February	Sunk	
U-392	16 March	Sunk	
U-731	May	Sunk	

Knight's Cross Winners of the 23rd and 29th U-Flotillas

Kaptlt. Friedrich Guggenberger – 10 December 1941
Kaptlt. Eitel-Friedrich Kentrat – 31 December 1941
Kaptlt. Hans-Dietrich Freiherr von Tiesenhausen – 27 January 1942
Kaptlt. Hans-Werner Kraus – 19 June 1942
Kaptlt. Helmut Rosenbaum – 13 August 1942
Kaptlt. Heinrich Schonder – 19 August 1942
Kaptlt. Wilhelm Dommes – 2 December 1942
K.K. Albrecht Brandi – 21 January 1943
                     – 11 April 1943 (Oak Leaves)
Kaptlt. Hans Heidtmann – 12 April 1943
Kaptlt. Wilhelm Franken – 30 April 1943
K.K. Gunter Jahn – 30 April 1943
Kaptlt. Gerd Kelbling – 19 August 1943
Oblt.z.S. Dietrich Schöneboom – 20 October 1943
Kaptlt. Egon Freiherr von Schlippenbach – 19 November 1943
Oblt.z.S. Horst-Arno Fenski – 26 November 1943
Oblt.z.S. Siegfried Koitschka – 27 January 1944
Kaptlt. Waldemar Mehl – 28 March 1944
K.K. Albrecht Brandi – 13 May 1944 (Swords)

Notes

Introduction

1. Hugh Trevor-Roper, *Hitler's Table Talk* (Weidenfeld & Nicolson: 1953), p 68.
2. Correlli Barnett, *Engage the Enemy More Closely* (W W Norton & Co: 1991), p 32.
3. Winston Churchill, *The Second World War* (Cassell Publishing: 1954), Vol 1, p 335.

Chapter 2: U-Boats into the Mediterranean

1. BdU *Kriegstagbuch* (KTB), 9 October 1939.
2. Torpedo failure caused by inadequate research and testing dogged the U-boat service throughout the early years of the war. To add a final tragedy to Schütze's abortive patrol, *Bootsmaat* Wilhelm Lützeler was washed overboard and drowned during their return voyage.
3. BdU KTB, 5 December 1939.
4. See Ian Kershaw, *Hitler: Nemesis 1936–1945* (Penguin Books: 2000), pp 291–2.
5. John Winton (ed), *The War At Sea* (Book Club Associates: 1974), p 147.
6. Ibid.
7. Indeed the British attack and its use of torpedoes modified to run in shallow water was closely studied by the Japanese Admiral Isoroku Yamamoto, soon to attempt his own copycat attack on Pearl Harbor in December 1941.
8. Only a single He 111 of *Gruppe Junck* was able to escape from Iraq, arriving in Rhodes on 31 May.
9. See Jak Mallmann Showell (ed), *Führer Conferences on Naval Affairs* (Greenhill Books: 2004), p 226.
10. Ibid, p 224.
11. BdU KTB, 7 September 1941.
12. Knight's Cross holder Oblt.(Ing.) Erich Zürn, late of the illustrious *U-48*, was named as Flotilla Engineering Officer, a post he later held in the 29th U-Flotilla until January 1944.
13. *Vizeadmiral* Erich Förste had replaced V.A. von Stosch in September 1941 and served in this post until February 1943.
14. Otto Wagner, '*U-Stützpunkt Salamis in Greece. The last days and the retreat*', unpublished memoir, author's collection.

Chapter 3: Success!

1. BdU KTB, 4 November 1941.
2. This incredible story was first told to me by Georg Högel, the artist who had been a radioman aboard *U-30* and *U-110*. Indeed he had even drawn a pencil sketch of Oskar that occupied pride of place in his collection. Oskar has become almost legendary, being aboard the destroyer HMS *Cossack* at some point as well. After the sinking of HMS *Ark Royal*, he lived for some years on Gibraltar, his wartime adventures at an end.
3. 'Gata' was in fact MV *Thalia* and 'Bernardo' SS *Bessel*.
4. BdU KTB, 16 November 1941.
5. BdU KTB, 20 November 1941.
6. Winton (ed), *The War At Sea*, pp 159–60, recollection of Lieutenant-Commander Hugh Hodgkinson, First Lieutenant on HMS *Hotspur*.
7. Churchill, *The Second World War*, Vol 3, p 451.
8. *The News of the World*, January 1942. Reproduced on Mike Strange's website www.yourtotalevent.com/events/galatea.htm.
9. FdU Italian KTB, 8 December 1941.
10. BdU KTB, 18 December 1941.
11. 1st U-Flotilla KTB, 16 December 1941.
12. BdU KTB, 30 December 1941.
13. Related by Ton Biesemaat, son of the submariner Jan Biesemaat and featured on www.dutchsubmarines.com.
14. Kentrat was awarded the Knight's Cross on 31 December 1941.

Chapter 4: From West to East

1. BdU KTB, 2 January 1942.
2. David Isby, *The Luftwaffe and the War at Sea* (Chatham Publishing: 2005), p 254.
3. FdU Italian KTB, 31 March 1942. Driver was replaced as captain after his return by Kaptlt. Waldemar Mehl. Driver, awarded the German Cross in Gold on 6 August 1942, spent the remainder of the war as a staff officer for the 26th U-Flotilla that dealt with training new U-boat crews to shoot.
4. Hesse, a former *Luftwaffe* man before his transfer to the U-boat service in 1940, would return to active service as commander of *U-194* in January 1943, being killed in action on 24 June 1943 when his boat was sunk in the North Atlantic.
5. FdU Italian KTB, 14 March 1942.
6. FdU Italian KTB, 7 April 1942.
7. On 11 March Kreisch was absent from his headquarters, otherwise engaged on a trip to Lorient, from which he did not return until 28 March. In his absence Oehrn deputised.
8. Three of the mines were successfully swept on 28 April.
9. The British crew were later reprimanded for this course of action. Coastal Command directives stated that offensive actions were to be continued in such a case to prevent scuttling before surface forces could arrive.
10. *Kapitänleutnant* Heinsohn and his crew were later repatriated in March 1943. Heinsohn then took command of *U-438*, aboard which he perished with all his crew on 6 May 1943.
11. The 23rd U-Flotilla did indeed come into being again, this time though it was

a purely training establishment formed in Danzig during August 1943 and in existence until March 1945 when the region was overrun by Soviet troops. Frauenheim went on to command units of the *Kleinkampfverbände* (Small Battle Units). See Lawrence Paterson, *Weapons of Desperation: German Frogmen and Midget Submarines of the Second World War* (Chatham Publishing: 2006).

12. '*Engagement Between British Destroyers and U-568*', Written by Lieutenant Commander W F N Gregory-Smith, DSO, DSC, RN, Commanding Officer, HMS *Eridge*. Reproduced on www.erols.com/sepulcher/568details.html.

13. FdU Italian KTB, 27 May 1942.

14. Oehrn was subsequently severely wounded and captured after the vehicle that he was riding in was intercepted by Australian troops. At the time he was travelling to offer Rommel the use of a *Schnellboot* unit. Hit by five bullets, he was later repatriated by the Red Cross to Germany in November 1943, returning to BdU Staff and marrying his patient fiancée. This remarkable man's career is covered fully in Theodore Savas (ed), *Silent Hunters* (Savas Publishing: 1997).

15. Churchill, *The Second World War*, Volume 4, p 320, taken from a letter to General Auchinleck.

Chapter 5: Attrition

1. FdU Italian KTB, 2 July 1942.

2. There were many agents supplying German forces with intelligence on British convoy movements, both in the United Kingdom and without. Among those apprehended were Gibraltar resident Jose Estella Key, who had been caught reporting shipping movements from Gibraltar and taken to Britain for interrogation and trial. He was executed on 7 July 1942. Another was 21-year-old merchant seaman Duncan Alexander Scott-Ford, who was convicted of treason on 16 October 1942 after admitting to having been in German pay whilst working on ships travelling between Britain and Portugal. He was hanged on 3 November 1942.

3. Winton (ed), *The War At Sea*, pp 233–4.

4. This was the end of Rosenbaum's operational career. He docked *U-73* at La Spezia on 5 September where the ribbon of the Knight's Cross was draped around his neck, awarded by radio the day after sinking HMS *Eagle*. He was then transferred to command the six Type II U-boats of the 30th U-Flotilla in the Black Sea. His place was taken aboard *U-73* by his IWO, Oblt.z.S. Horst Deckert. Rosenbaum was killed on 10 May 1944 in an air crash in Romania.

5. The use of ULTRA information to target enemy convoys was tricky. In order not to give away their penetration of the code, RAF and Royal Navy units were alerted to the potential target only when it could be sensibly shown to have been found by a secondary source, generally aerial reconnaissance.

6. Showell (ed), *Führer Conferences on Naval Affairs*, p 292.

7. FdU Italian KTB, 1 September 1942.

8. The Navy Army and Air Force Institute (NAAFI) was an official canteen organisation whose purpose was to provide serving men and women with a homelike atmosphere during leisure hours. NAAFI personnel wore uniform but were not subject to military discipline and the rules governing men

serving in the NAAFI on board HM ships were slightly different. NAAFI Canteen Assistant Brown's George Cross was presented to his mother at Buckingham Palace at a later date.

Chapter 6: Operation 'Torch'

1. *U-259* and *U-380* were replacements for the original 'Delphin' boats *U-440* and *U-662*, which had been forced to abort due to engine problems.
2. BdU KTB, 15 November 1942.
3. BdU KTB, 4 November 1942.
4. The supply of torpedoes to the Mediterranean and Aegean was handled generally by *Torpedarsenal Mitte* at Rudolstadt/Thüringen.
5. The expected conversion dates were *U-375* in Pola 17 November, *U-562* in Spezia 22 November, *U-453* in Spezia 28 November and *U-83* in Spezia 29 November.
6. Trevor-Roper, *Hitler's Table Talk*, p 407.
7. Churchill, *The Second World War*, Vol 4, p 509.
8. The position that Pétain and many of the Vichy government and military found themselves in was difficult in the extreme. It was fair to say that Pétain and many of his commanders were more anti-German than anti-Allied, despite actions such as the British bombardment of Mers el Kebir and other such clashes. However, Pétain's hands were largely tied by his obligations towards the 1,500,000 French POWs that remained in German hands and were used as powerful leverage, making concessions to the Axis powers in order to attempt to secure their release. The Vichy situation was extremely complex and requires its own study to be fully comprehended.
9. Churchill, *The Second World War*, Vol 4, p 498.
10. It was to be Dommes' final patrol as commander of *U-431*. His nerves stretched to breaking point by war in the Mediterranean, he was awarded the Knight's Cross upon his return and was rotated out of Italy and back to Germany to take command of *U-178* scheduled for transit to the Far East where he commanded the U-boats based in Malaya and Singapore. See Lawrence Paterson, *Hitler's Grey Wolves* (Greenhill Books: 2004).
11. Norman Franks, *Search, Find And Kill* (Grub Street: 1995), p 218.
12. Crewmen were later at a loss as to explain why they were running surfaced in such a dangerous area, many blaming it on the 'rashness' of their captain.
13. *Interrogation report of the crew of U-595*.
14. Franks, *Search, Find and Kill*, p 217.
15. All the aircraft returned safely to their airfield despite their extensive damage. One of them, Hudson 'K', was forced to land on only one engine.
16. The other man, who had become separated from the rest during the swim for shore, was later picked up by HMS *Wivern*.
17. Statement made by Jürgen Quaet-Faslem, taken aboard the USAT *Brazil* as the *U-595* crew was transported from North Africa to the United States.
18. *Interrogation report of the crew of U-595*.
19. Franks, *Search, Find and Kill*, p 219.

Chapter 7: France

1. Karl Dönitz, *Memoirs: Ten Years and Twenty Days* (Greenhill Books: 1990), pp 283–5.

2. *U-81, U-83, U-375, U-380, U-443, U-453, U-561, U-562, U-565, U-593* and *U-602* were all active while *U-73, U-77* and *U-371* were headed to base.
3. Barbara Tomblin, *With Utmost Spirit: Allied Naval Operations in the Mediterranean, 1942-1945* (The University of Kentucky Press: 2004), p 92.
4. She was later cut in two parts and towed to Portsmouth where they became the base ships HMS *Pork* and *Pine* until scrapped at Plymouth in May 1946.
5. Courtesy of www.lifestories.ca/excerpts.shtml, which is an excerpt from a 'LifeStories' project: 'Of the Sea' by journalist Bernadette Hardaker.
6. She was in fact the fifth largest ship sunk by U-boats during the Second World War.
7. www.thestrathallan.com/survivor_reports.htm
8. During the previous war, another SS *Cameronia*, sister-ship to the *Lusitania*, had been torpedoed and sunk in the Mediterranean by *U-33* while also acting as a troopship.
9. Statement made by Seaman First Class Quinten S Lederman; www.armed-guard.com/middle.html
10. Sönke Neitzel, *Die deutschen Ubootbunker und Bunkerwerften* (Bernard & Graefe: 1991), p 88.
11. Karl Alman, *Graue Wölfe in blauer See, Der Einsatz der Deutschen U-Boote im Mittelmeer* (Erich Pabel Verlag: 1967), p 200, quote from Kreisch.
12. 'Report on Interrogation of the sole survivor from *U-301*', author's collection.
13. HMS *Welshman* continued to claim enemy ships after her sinking, the Italian destroyer *Saetta* and the destroyer escort *Uragano* sinking northeast of Bizerte on the field that *Welshman* had just laid.
14. Vice Admiral Sir Henry Harwood was moved sideways to become Commander-in-Chief, Levant.
15. It has never been fully established how important to the cracking of Enigma codes these captured books were, or whether the Royal Navy chose to explore the reachable wreck of *U-205* though there is strong speculation that divers recovered some material from the boat. See Clay Blair, *Hitler's U-Boat War* Volume 2 (Cassell & Company: 2000), pp 211–12.
16. *Kapitänleutant* Freidrich Bürgel had been transferred from command of *U-97* during October 1942 when the boat underwent extensive repair work in La Spezia. He transferred to command *U-205*, which was sunk on 17 February 1943.
17. Recollection of 'German' Joe Eckert. Author's collection.
18. BdU KTB, 19 May 1943.
19. See Lawrence Paterson, *Second U-Boat Flotilla* (Pen & Sword: 2003).

Chapter 8: Operation 'Husky' to Anzio

1. *U-617* would move to Toulon before its next patrol, while *U-596* transferred to Pola before it sailed for active duty.
2. Frauenheim moved on to command elements of the *Kleinkampfverbände*.
3. These sinkings, and his calculated total to date, earned Kelbling a Knight's Cross awarded on 19 August.
4. Basil Liddell-Hart, *The Second World War* (Cassell and Company: 1970), p 443.
5. Franken was killed in an accident in Germany on 13 January 1945.
6. Showell (ed), *Führer Conferences on Naval Affairs*, pp 344–5.
7. *Monthly Anti-Submarine Warfare Report*, Sept 1943.

8. Showell (ed), *Führer Conferences on Naval Affairs*, p 347.
9. Basil Liddell-Hart, *The Other Side Of The Hill* (Cassell & Company: 1951), p 359.
10. Hans Joachim Brennecke, *The Hunters and The Hunted* (Burke Publishing: 1958), p 230.
11. Ibid, p 231.
12. Ibid, p 235.
13. BdU KTB, 26 September 1943.
14. Interview conducted by author with Gerhard Buske, Munich, 20 October 2002.
15. Franks, *Search Find and Kill*, p 238.
16. BdU KTB, 1 November 1943.
17. The largest Allied ship lost during November 1943 was the *Luftwaffe* sinking of the troopship SS *Rohna* off Bougie on 26 November after hitting it with Hs 293 guided bombs, in which 1,149 men were killed, nearly 1,000 of them American, making it the worst loss of US soldiers at sea during the war.
18. Herbert Werner, *Iron Coffins* (Henry Holt & Company: 1969), pp 182–3.
19. Ibid, pp 183–4.
20. The ship was later hit in another air raid on 11 March 1944 and set on fire, the flames completely gutting the ship.

Chapter 9: Between the Hammer and the Anvil – Retreat from France

1. See Paterson, *Weapons of Desperation*.
2. Joe Eckert, *Images of War*, Vol 58 (1988).
3. To augment existing dockyard facilities at Pola a *Kriegsmarinewerft* had been officially established in December 1943 under the command of K.z.S. (Ing) Hartlef.
4. *U-466* narrowly avoided being torpedoed by the British submarine HMS *Uproar* lying in wait off Toulon as Gerd Thäther's boat approached the port on 30 March.
5. Amongst Fenski's crew was IWO L.z.S. Walter Müller, chiefly remarkable for the fact that he had spent some years in California and had attended Los Angeles Junior High School.
6. Gerhard Buske interview.
7. Among those killed was the commander of the 14th Destroyer Flotilla, Captain H T Armstrong.
8. Gerhard Buske interview.
9. Codenamed Operation 'Monstrous' by the Americans.
10. Joe Eckert, *Images of War*, Vol 58 (1988), pp 1623–4.
11. Later raised and recommissioned into the French Navy as the submarine *Mille*.
12. Paul Siegmann had rotated back to Germany, in time to take command of the Type XXI *U-2507*.

Chapter 10: Retreat from Greece

1. Otto Wagner, '*U-Stützpunkt Salamis in Greece. The last days and the retreat*', unpublished memoir.
2. Ibid.

Bibliography

Primary Sources

Des Sous-Marins Allemand à Toulon, Report from the *Groupe de Récupération Des S/M Allemands, Toulon.* Unpublished. Author's Collection.

Engagement Between British Destroyers and U-568, Written by Lieutenant Commander W F N Gregory-Smith, DSO, DSC, RN, Commanding Officer, HMS *Eridge*. (Reproduced on www.erols.com/sepulcher/568details.html).

German Torpedoes and Development of German Torpedo Control, (Technical Staff Monographs) Underwater Weapons Department, Admiralty, U.W.O.5314/50. 1951.

Interrogation report of the crew of U-595.

Monthly Anti-Submarine Warfare Report, Sept 1943. Copy held in Royal Navy Submarine Museum.

Report on Interrogation of the sole survivor from U-301, Author's collection.

Typewritten account by 'German' Joe Eckart, *U-616*, copy held in Royal Navy Submarine Museum, Gosport.

U-Stützpunkt Salamis in Greece. The last days and the retreat, Otto Wagner, unpublished memoir. Author's collection.

War Diary (*Kriegstagebuch*, or KTB) 1. Ubootsflottille, Nara Microfilm, T1022, Roll 3403.

War Diary (KTB) *Befehlshabers der Unterseeboote* (BdU, Commander in Chief Submarines). Nara Microfilm, T1022.

War Diary (KTB) FdU Italy/Mediterranean. Translated copies held in Admiralty Library, Portsmouth.

War Diary Naval War Staff (*Seekriegsleitung Kriegstagebuch*), Part A, Naval HQ Berlin 1939 to 1945. Nara Microfilm T1022.

Periodicals

Images Of War, Marshall Cavendish (1988) Volumes 1 to 60.

Selected Books

Alman, Karl, *Graue Wölfe in blauer See, Der Einsatz der Deutschen U-Boote im Mittelmeer* (Erich Pabel Verlag: 1967).

Barnett, Correlli, *Engage The Enemy More Closely* (W W Norton & Co: 1991).

Blair, Clay, *Hitler's U-Boat War* Vols 1 & 2 (Cassell & Company: 2000).

Brendon, Piers, *The Dark Valley* (Jonathan Cape: 2000).

Brennecke, Hans Jochim, *The Hunters And The Hunted* (Burke Publishing: 1958).

Churchill, Winston, *The Second World War* (Cassell Publishing: 1954).

Dinklage, Ludwig and Hans-Jürgen Witthöft, *Die Deutsche Handelsflotte* (Nikol Verlagsgesellchaft: 2001).

Dönitz, Karl, *Memoirs: Ten Years And Twenty Days* (Greenhill Books: 1990).

Franks, Norman, *Search, Find And Kill* (Grub Street: 1995).

Greene, Jack and Alessandro Massignani, *The Naval War in the Mediterranean, 1940–1943* (Chatham Publishing: 1998).

Hague, Arnold, *The Allied Convoy System* (Chatham Publishing: 2000).

Isby, David, *The Luftwaffe And The War At Sea* (Chatham Publishing: 2005).

Kershaw, Ian, *Hitler: Nemesis 1936-1945* (Penguin Books: 2000).

Köhl, Fritz & Niestlé, *Vom Original zum Modell: Uboottyp VIIC* (Bernard & Graefe: 1994).

Kurowski, Franz, *Kampffeld Mittelmeer* (Ullstein Buchverlage: 1999).

Liddell-Hart, Basil, *History Of The Second World War* (Cassell & Company: 1970).

_____, *The Other Side Of The Hill* (Cassell & Company: 1951).

Lucas, James, *Das Reich* (Cassell Publishing: 1991).

Martienssen, Anthony, *Hitler And His Admirals* (E P Dutton & Co: 1949).

Neitzel, Sönke, *Die deutschen Ubootbunker* (Bernard & Graefe: 1991).

Padfield, Peter, *War Beneath The Sea* (Pimlico: 1995).

Paterson, Lawrence, *The First U-Boat Flotilla* (Pen & Sword: 2002).

Rohwer, Jürgen, *Axis Submarine Successes of World War Two* (Greenhill Books: 1999).

Rossler, Eberhard, *The U-Boat* (Arms & Armour Press: 1981).

Santoni, Alberto, *Ultra siegt im Mittelmeer* (Bernard & Graefe: 1985).

Schramm, Percy E (e), *Kriegstagebuch des OKW* (Bernard & Graefe: 2002).

Sebag-Montefiore, Hugh, *Enigma* (Weidenfield & Nicholson: 2000).

Showell, Jak Mallmann (ed), *Führer Conferences On Naval Affairs* (Greenhill Books: 2004).

Tomblin, Barbara, *With Utmost Spirit: Allied Naval Operations in the Mediterranean, 1942-1945* (The University Press of Kentucky: 2004).

Trevor-Roper, Hugh, *Hitler's Table Talk* (Weidenfield & Nicholson: 1953).

Werner, Herbert, *Iron Coffins* (Henry Holt & Company: 1969).

Wilmot, Chester, *The Struggle For Europe* (W M Collins: 1952).

Winton, John (ed), *The War At Sea* (Book Club Associates: 1974).

Internet Sources

The Blue Star Line (www.bluestarline.org)
Norwegian Merchant Fleet 1939 to 1945 (www.warsailors.com)
Life Stories (www.lifestories.ca/excerpts.shtml)
The Story of the Strathallan
      (www.thestrathallan.com/survivor_reports.htm)
The Armed Guard (www.armed-guard.com)
U-568 (www.erols.com/sepulcher/568details.html)

Suggested Websites
The U-Boat War (www.uboatwar.net)
U-Boat History (www.ubootwaffe.net)
U-Boat Operations (www.uboat.net)
Submarine Art Gallery (www.subart.net)
German Armed Forces History (www.feldgrau.com)

Index